D1611910

THE FRENCH NEW NOVEL

Claude Simon, Michel Butor, Alain Robbe-Grillet

JOHN STURROCK

THE
FRENCH NEW NOVEL

Claude Simon, Michel Butor
Alain Robbe-Grillet

LONDON
OXFORD UNIVERSITY PRESS
NEW YORK   TORONTO
1969

Oxford University Press, Ely House, London W.1

GLASGOW NEW YORK TORONTO MELBOURNE WELLINGTON
CAPE TOWN SALISBURY IBADAN NAIROBI LUSAKA ADDIS ABABA
BOMBAY CALCUTTA MADRAS KARACHI LAHORE DACCA
KUALA LUMPUR SINGAPORE HONG KONG TOKYO

Printed in Great Britain

For
Jenny and Oliver

CONTENTS

Introduction   1

1. Claude Simon   43

2. Michel Butor   104

3. Alain Robbe-Grillet   170

   Select Bibliography   236

   Index   241

INTRODUCTION

*'However, many of the most learned and wise adhere to the
new scheme of expressing themselves by things . . .'*

S W I F T. A Voyage to Laputa.

D o e s the term *nouveau roman* actually define a homogeneous literary
movement or not? A number of critics both inside and outside
France have accepted that it does, that there is a sufficient co-
herency of principle among the writers so labelled to justify their
being herded together into a new orthodoxy. More recently,
however, there has been considerable dissent from this view, a
dissent often most forcefully expressed by the writers of the New
Novel themselves. They have protested that their so-called
'movement', like all such literary groupings, was an invention
partly of harrassed critics, seeking to impose order in the chaos of
contemporary writing or to dismiss the divergent trends of *avant-
garde* writing conveniently as a single entity, and partly of their
less scrupulous followers, the literary publicists: reviewers, jour-
nalists, and other commentators, who certainly enjoy more outlets
in France for their ideological or hierarchical assessments of the
current artistic scene than they do in any other country. The
position of those who protest in the name of a critical nominalism
that they should not be grouped together is to some extent justified by the fact that most of those who used the collective appella-
tion, *nouveau roman*, were hostile to what they took to be the intentions of these writers. The protests have been an attempt to
get a fair hearing. It is noticeable, however, that responsible
critics who show a keen and sympathetic understanding of the
practices of the New Novelists, have not abandoned the term.
It is naturally hard to be quite sure when this term was first
used, or by whom. What really matters is when it first imposed
itself and became a useful term of reference for a certain type of

writing. This was certainly some years after the first published novels of the writers now thought of as the high priests of the movement (if it proves to be one). Nathalie Sarraute, for instance, published her first novel shortly before the war, in 1939; Claude Simon wrote his, *Le Tricheur*, in 1941, even though it was not published until after the war; Robbe-Grillet published *Les Gommes* in 1953; and Michel Butor *Passage de Milan* in 1954. Yet the first recorded public appearance of the words *nouveau roman* seems to have been delayed until July 1958, when the *personnaliste* review, *Esprit*, produced a special number devoted to the 'nouveau roman'; these quotation marks were no doubt intended as the badge of an infant and contestable categorization, but the more cautious commentators are still prone to use them. *Esprit*'s special number was produced, as is explained in an editorial preface, in answer to a number of requests from participants to a congress of intellectuals held the previous year. The review seemed anxious to show that it, at least, was not creating a literary movement out of nothing, but attempting to contribute to a debate that was already under way.

To my mind it is not a very sensible argument to claim that, because the term *nouveau roman* post-dates the appearance of the first novels supposed to have inaugurated the new genre by four or five years, the idea of a movement is a sham. I see no reason at all why the birth and the christening should have been simultaneous. The New Novelists have never, unlike some previous groups of writers in France, issued joint proclamations of intent. Their collectivity must be defined by a convergence of interest and of aesthetic conviction.

In their time they have had to endure other group-names, as well as New Novelists. They were once held to constitute an *école du regard*, for example, because of what many people took to be an excessive preoccupation in their novels with brute objectivity. This was a much more flattering and accurate title than those who coined it can have appreciated, as I shall hope to prove in this book. Another even more desperate name found for them was *école de Minuit*, so attributed because the *avant-garde* publisher, Jérôme Lindon of the Éditions de Minuit, seemed to have become the impresario of all progressive novelists. Already the publisher of Samuel Beckett, Nathalie Sarraute, and Robert Pinget, he added to his list Robbe-Grillet, Butor, Claude Simon, and, for the space of a single novel, Marguerite Duras. This title was eccentric enough for a special number of *Yale French Studies* devoted to the New Novel in France to appear under its English translation 'Midnight Novelists'.

But these were the heady days of a nascent revolution, since when it has become more fashionable to concentrate on what divides the novelists who had previously been grouped together. Some of the more acute and structurally-minded French critics, notably Roland Barthes (often accused of promoting over-portentously ideas too intricate and austere to have entered the head of the iconoclastic Robbe-Grillet whom he was supposedly elucidating) had been doing this almost from the start, by showing certain radical divergences in purpose and seriousness between two of the writers studied in this book, Michel Butor and Alain Robbe-Grillet. This no doubt makes it seem as if my own purpose is reactionary, since, somewhat against the current fashion, I insist on looking for fundamental similarities in the concerns of the *nouveau roman*. But any tendency to declare these writers free from all contagion from each other's practices is as inaccurate as the opposite tendency, and I am not siding blindly with those who have been using the term *nouveau roman* eagerly all along. Indeed, it is doubtful whether many of them troubled to uncover or to define the elements in the novels in question which did in fact indicate an identity of purpose or technique.

It is perfectly understandable that the New Novelists themselves should have been outraged by the glib way in which their differences had been obscured. Some critics and reviewers used, and still do use, the term *nouveau romancier* as a conclusive value-judgement on a writer's work, implying that it does not need further particularization. It is, for example, only necessary for a novelist to spend too long (as it is thought) on the description of an apparently trivial object to be dismissed as a sterile follower of Robbe-Grillet. Such hasty judgements are generally both unfair and superficial.

In what I have myself written about three New Novelists, Claude Simon, Michel Butor, and Alain Robbe-Grillet, I do not feel that I have neglected or diminished the divergent tendencies or convictions which individuate their novels. On the other hand, I have tried to uncover in their methods of composition sufficient evidence that they share a certain conception of the novel, and that they can be studied together in a single book without incongruity.

These three novelists were chosen because, first, they exemplify with a greater or lesser degree of clarity a central proposition about the *nouveau roman*: that these novels must *never* be read as exercises in naïve realism or naturalism, but as studied dramatizations of the creative process itself. The second reason for choosing them was that, together with Nathalie Sarraute, they have emerged by common consent as the most prestigious figures of the New Novel. Some of the lesser writers who might have been included here, and whose novels are certainly very rigorous exercises in the creative discipline I shall hope to define—such as Claude Ollier or Jean Ricardou—have been left out because they are not well known outside France and have not been widely translated. The omission of Nathalie Sarraute is harder to justify, but her novels are, in their concern with the infra-structures of consciousness and with the pre-verbal gyrations of the psychic life, structurally less apt for the sort of textual demonstrations I shall rely on. Moreover, the inclusion of another study of an individual writer, of the same length as those already included, would add an unwelcome weight. The aim of these studies is to prove convergence as well as divergence; the more convergence that is proved the greater the danger of sterile iteration.

It would be absurd to claim that the New Novel was launched on the day on which Robbe-Grillet published *Les Gommes* in 1953. Literary revolutions do not explode with such drama, they are more in the nature of reorientations, exploiting certain aspects of the literary past that may not have attracted much attention hitherto, but which the new movement tries to show to have been the true indicators of the future. As I have said, the property common to all *nouveaux romans* is that they embody the creative activity of the novelist—they display the novelist at work. This in itself is nothing new; *A la recherche du temps perdu* draws attention to its own methods of composition, so does Gide's *Les Faux-*

Monnayeurs. The New Novel, indeed, belongs to that twentieth-century tradition to which so many of the more significant novelists can be closely or loosely related—the tradition which insists that the novelist explain or reveal his principle of organization in the text itself.

The brashest and least compromising polemicist of the New Novel has been Robbe-Grillet, though his literary proclamations seem to have ended with his entry into the cinema as the director of his own screen-plays. But Robbe-Grillet has always claimed that he was not overturning the past, but extending it in the only possible direction. His tradition of the novel extends back through Samuel Beckett, Faulkner, Kafka, Joyce, Proust, Roussel, and Flaubert, whom he values for their successive technical contributions to the form. Yet there is every justification for this aesthetic historicism, even if it is a mode of synoptic literary criticism not greatly favoured in this country. Anyone who has read Erich Auerbach's remarkable series of *explications de texte* in *Mimesis* will be reluctant to admit that aesthetic forms do not evolve consciously, or that their true history cannot be written. Auerbach's subtitle for that book, 'The Representation of reality in Western Literature', indicates how closely aesthetic forms are connected with new ideas in philosophy, cosmology, psychology, and so on. In the same way, Marxist critics, and notably Georg Lukács, have never ceased to explore the links between forms of representation and the economic substructures of the societies that favour them. The New Novel belongs with that way of thinking which sees the notion that there exist absolute forms of representation as an absurdity, and insists that the novelist should question all attempts to pretend that it is not.

One of the most frequent and helpful of all the terms that have been used to classify the sort of novels we are concerned with, therefore, is that of 'anti-novel'. The known history of this term goes back a very long way. In France, for instance, it was in 1633 that Charles Sorel published a book called *L'Anti-roman*, which was in fact a re-edition of a book he had published six years before under the title *Le Berger extravagant*. Sorel's intentions were to mock the conventional pastoral modes of contemporary fiction by grossly exaggerating them—to write a novel as an act of literary criticism. This significant publication has not escaped the notice of one particularly acute and archaeologically-minded modern French critic, Jean-Pierre Faye.[1] Quite properly, Faye relates the critical and didactic intentions of Sorel to a novel published earlier in his century which still remains the greatest of all anti-novels, *Don Quixote*. Cervantes's novel mocks the conventions of the romances of chivalry not by exaggeration but by deformation; they are made to seem ridiculous by being overlaid on the events and characters of contemporary reality. They are not the conventions appropriate to a contemporary citizen of Spain; indeed the man who accepts them, Don Quixote, is a victim of alienation or madness: his environment has become a fatality which he finds himself powerless to change in accordance with his wishes. The attitude of Cervantes to the novelistic conventions he was assaulting is precisely that of the New Novelists to the conventions that they would abolish: these conventions are unwholesome because they perpetuate outmoded philosophical and thus, Marxists would add, economic systems.

To some extent all considerable novelists of the past have been anti-novelists, since they must all have found something unsatisfactory about the formal conventions which they inherited or which they saw being seriously misapplied by their contemporaries, and have been determined to give new life to the novel as a tradition by restoring its vital ties with reality. Their intentions may have been largely burlesque, as in the case of Fielding's *Joseph Andrews*, conceived as a parody of Richardson; more severely moral, as with Jane Austen and her notorious distaste for the more preposterous fictions of her time; or altogether ambivalent, as with Flaubert, whose Emma Bovary is destroyed by the insidious myths imprinted in her mind by a diet of reading which might have been that of any young French Romantic of the nineteenth century.

If the term 'anti-novel' had been used more generously since it appeared in the seventeenth century, then it might have lost the aggressive implications which it has today and the aesthetic philosophy to which it alludes might have appeared less wither-

[1] See his essay, 'Surprise pour l'anti-room' in *Le Récit hunique* (Paris: Le Seuil, 1967).

ingly negative. But the explicit category of 'anti-novel' seems not to have been resurrected until soon after the Second World War by Jean-Paul Sartre, in the Preface which he wrote for Nathalie Sarraute's *Portrait d'un inconnu* in 1947. In this Preface, Sartre, after what now seems the mild eccentricity of classing Evelyn Waugh among the anti-novelists (and the startling prescience of adding to Waugh's the name of Nabokov), defines the anti-novel as an attempt, just like that of Sorel, to undermine the accepted forms of the novel from within:

Il s'agit de contester le roman par lui-même, de le détruire sous nos yeux dans le temps qu'on semble l'édifier, d'écrire le roman d'un roman qui ne se fait pas, de créer une fiction qui soit aux grandes œuvres composées de Dostoëvsky ou de Meredith ce qu'était aux tableaux de Rembrandt et de Rubens cette toile de Miró, intitulée 'Assassinat de la peinture'. Ces œuvres étranges et difficilement classifiables ne témoignent pas de la faiblesse du genre romanesque, elles marquent seulement que nous vivons à une époque de réflexion et que le roman est en train de réfléchir sur lui-même.[2]

The final words of this quotation are a particularly valuable definition of that much more widespread movement in the western arts of which the New Novel is demonstrably a part. This movement, in music and painting especially, is one that has shown a gathering obsession with technique, which is why it has always been accused of aridity, sterility, and obscurity, of producing work that can only be appreciated by other artists. Quite so: it also follows that if the non-artist feels the urge to appreciate such work then he must struggle to learn the trade of the artist and turn himself into something more than a passive and opinionated consumer. It seems to me that with the New Novel writing has begun to measure itself against music and the plastic arts, where it has

---

2 It is a question of challenging the novel through itself, of destroying it in front of us at the same time as seeming to be building it, of writing the novel of a novel which cannot be written, of creating a fiction which is to the great composed works of Dostoevsky or Meredith what Miró's canvas entitled 'The murder of painting' was to the pictures of Rembrandt and Rubens. These strange, difficult to classify works are not evidence of the weakness of the novel form, they simply indicate that we are living in an age of reflection and that the novel is engaged in reflecting on itself.

been understood for many years that a work of art may be shown to be a process as well as a product. Hegel can be quoted in support of the view that this represents a gain in vitality: 'The work [of art] is, therefore, not by itself really an animated thing; it is a whole only when its process of coming to be is taken along with it'.

It is unfortunate that the concept of an 'anti-novel' should appear to be such a negative and destructive one, for this has led to a quite misleading emphasis being put on certain antithetical aspects of writers like Robbe-Grillet, and a consequent neglect of more positive aspects. All revolutions or revaluations *can* be interpreted, though not objectively, as negative, for the good reason that the form which revolt takes is determined by the form of what it sets out to replace. But the negative, as all faithful students of Hegel will remember, is not less than the positive but more, it is a transcendence of the determinate content and tends towards a new and richer synthesis.

The writers of the New Novel know very well, therefore, that the old certainties and contentions which they have set out to challenge will be present in the minds of those who read them. It is against these conventions, certain reflections of which are preserved in the text of the *nouveaux romans* themselves, that they expect their books to be read. Robbe-Grillet has announced that he *wants* his readers to feel disappointed, and that if they do feel disappointed then he knows he has succeeded. But a feeling of deprivation, which is an essential part of the purpose of the New Novel, certainly does not exhaust this purpose.

A negative definition of the New Novel, the one which has been so often made, is justified only as a moment in a wider and more positive definition. Every refusal to pursue a certain course is also a proposal to follow another course. The considerable hostility and ill-informed derision which the New Novel has sometimes aroused in France and elsewhere is a predictable response to its negative ambitions. The loudest opposition has been expressed in terms which we, in England, should be able to understand more readily than most, since they are robust and sceptical, rather than analytical. Hostile critics have been furious at being deprived of 'plot' and 'characters'. Sometimes it has seemed that the novels they are complaining of contain nothing at all, no events and no human beings. Of course they contain both, all that has changed is their presentation; Robbe-Grillet has declared that if he finds it impossible to 'tell a story' he is stressing the word tell and not story. The 'plot' is no longer so confident or coherent; things happen, but the relation between them is seen to be problematical, a fiction. 'Characters' appear but they too are problematical, they are exposed for what characters in novels have always been, projections of the novelist's own intimate concerns. What the New Novel is depriving its readers of are the consolations of a mechanistic sequence of events, with its confident marriage of causes with effects, and of an essentialist psychology which lends a spurious coherence to the activity of unknowable other minds.

It is important to realize that the New Novel is not (or need not be) in the least bit negative in its attitudes towards life or reality — no-one could be more glowingly optimistic at times than Michel Butor—but only in its attitudes towards certain literary conventions. Critics have before now implied that Robbe-Grillet's admittedly aggressive modernism is seeking to destroy the literary monuments of the past. This is not the case at all. In its dealings with this past it seems to me that the New Novel is activated by a much more refined and profitable ambition, which is to deny the timelessness of these monuments, to prevent them, that is, from being uprooted from the age that produced them in the interests of a pious and misguided belief that art is eternal even if man is not.

Robbe-Grillet has never once said that the conventions of the traditional novel were not valid for their own time, only that they are no longer valid for ours. Indeed, it is just because they *were* valid for their own time that it has become imperative to replace them. Many of the more significant novelists of the twentieth century have already done so, of course, yet their lessons have not been generally absorbed. One of the aims of the New Novel might therefore be said to be the vulgarization of the innovations of certain mandarin and lonely predecessors.

The novels of Balzac or Stendhal were, according to Robbe-Grillet, the entirely logical products of an age when 'tout visait à

B

imposer l'image d'un univers stable, cohérent, continu, univoque, entièrement déchiffrable'.[3] But to those people who demand that today's novelists should model themselves formally on the nineteenth-century masters, he says: 'Pour écrire comme Stendhal il faudrait d'abord écrire en 1830.'[4] Robbe-Grillet does not claim or show himself to be a great reader of other men's work, and it is perhaps a pity that he should have selected for his demonstration Stendhal, a novelist so little of his own age as to be led to declare 'Je serai lu vers 1925'; yet this supports rather than invalidates Robbe-Grillet's argument, since Stendhal was looking forward to an age that would appreciate the conventions of his own fiction even if the present one did not. Moreover, the most famous of all passages in Stendhal's novels, the description of Fabrice's experiences at the Battle of Waterloo in *La Chartreuse de Parme*, is surely a brief anti-novel in its own right, directed at contrasting prevalent literary conventions of military glory and heroism with the reality.

The *nouveau roman* is thus in revolt only against literary habit, against the formal stereotypes which we accept because we suppose them wrongly to be absolute or essential in the philosophical sense, rather than relative or existential. The novel is in need of redefinition, and the responsibility of the novelist is now to show what a fiction consists in, and, by extension, what the role of the imagination is in our daily lives.

Yet it is inevitable that such an attack on the conventions of the novel should be interpreted as an attack on reality itself. An earlier writer of this century who did much to modify the hitherto stable forms of fiction and also suffered for it in misunderstanding and outright hostility, was Proust, who predicted the reception his own great novel would get in the text itself: 'D'ailleurs toute nouveauté ayant pour condition l'élimination préalable du poncif auquel nous étions habitués et qui nous semblait la réalité même, toute conversation neuve, aussi bien que toute peinture,

---

[3] everything aimed at imposing the image of a stable, coherent, continuous, unequivocal, wholly decipherable universe (*Pour un nouveau roman*, p. 31).

[4] In order to write like Stendhal you would first of all have to have written in 1830 (ibid., p. 9).

toute musique originale, paraîtra toujours alambiquée et fati-
gante.[5]

Critical complaints of excessive formalism, such as were made
against *A la recherche du temps perdu*, and such as have been made
since against many other lesser books, including those of the
New Novel, are thus exposed as the defence mechanism of minds
that are determined for one reason or another to cling to their
stereotypes, either from the sheer inertia that seeks comfort and
repose for the brain in changelessness, or deliberately and per-
versely as an attempt at ideological repression in a monolithic
state, such as Russia in the time of Zhdanov.

Yet those who, like the Stalinists, set out to curb or suppress
formal experiment in the arts, are showing a clearer understanding
of what is at stake than those in democratic societies who decry
formalism simply as a vexation or as a deprivation for the artist's
public, which has been used to something different and apparently
more substantial. Because to change aesthetic stereotypes *is*,
ultimately, to help in changing reality. When Robbe-Grillet uses
as the title of an essay 'Nouveau roman, homme nouveau' he may
seem unduly optimistic about the effects of the *cordon sanitaire* he
has tried to throw around the traditional narrative forms, in view
of the very restricted public there is for the novel. But he is aware
that the artist does have this responsibility, that he is, in however
small a way, one guardian of a society's myths and that it is these
myths which are reality, to a greater or a lesser degree, for all of
us.

The *nouveau roman*, therefore, asks to be interpreted in terms of a
contemporary *Zeitgeist*, if its technical or structural methods are to
be seen as a conscious and necessary response to the age. Any talk
of a *Zeitgeist* tends to arouse strong feelings of animosity in those
of a more positivist turn of mind, for whom all such outbreaks of
Hegelianism call for an immediate antidote. But to characterize
aesthetic manifestations by reference to the corpus of philosophical ideas prevalent in the society within which they arise is not

---

[5] Moreover, the condition of any novelty being the previous elimination of
the stereotype to which we had become accustomed and which had seemed
to us to be reality itself, any new conversation, just like any original painting
or music, will always appear over-subtle and wearisome.

in any way deterministic. Something like the New Novel is not the *inevitable* product of the age, even though it may be, in many aspects, a conscious reflection of it.

In order to fix a starting-point for an investigation into which fundamental notions of the time can be used to elucidate the structures of the New Novel I shall return to Sartre's Preface to *Portrait d'un inconnu.* There he characterizes the present age as one of reflection. In this he has been echoed, much more recently, by Michel Butor, a most elegant and persuasive apologist for modernism in the arts. In an essay called 'Critique et invention' Butor compares the new forms of the novel with those that have become apparent in the theatre and cinema (elsewhere he has made the same comparison with music and painting as well): 'Cette réflexion est une des caractéristiques fondamentales de l'art contemporain: roman du roman, théâtre du théâtre, cinéma du cinéma . . .; elle l'apparente étroitement à celui de certaines époques antérieures, l'art baroque en particulier; dans les deux cas ce repli interrogatif sur soi est une réponse à un changement de l'image du monde.'[6]

Reflective, interrogative: these are certainly the moods that characterize the *nouveau roman*, which has tried to systematize the questionings and self-consciousness already apparent in novelists like Joyce, Kafka, Gide, or Proust. But what are the ways in which our image of the world has changed, to the point where traditional narrative forms are seen to be invalid? To reply to so vast a question with a hurried encapsulation may well seem tendentious or one-sided, but it is a question that cannot be suppressed altogether.

Why reflective, therefore; why does the novelist now have to be self-conscious, and expose the process of composition? No one, presumably, would deny that interest has grown exaggeratedly in recent years in the techniques of production of every sort, mechanical and, more generally, cultural. This new interest may be a function of increased leisure, of an increased social mobility

---

[6] This reflection is one of the basic characteristics of contemporary art: the novel of the novel, the theatre of the theatre, the cinema of the cinema . . .; it links it closely to the art of certain earlier epochs, baroque art in particular; in both cases this interrogative falling back on oneself is a response to a change in the image of the world (*Répertoire 3*, p. 18).

(which can often be a reward for technical skill), or of an increased scepticism towards all imaginable forms of imposition, whether they be technological or ideological. The result, in any case, is a widespread phenomenon: answers no longer have the authority they once did unless they show the working. A comparison between the arts and cooking is especially apt for my purposes in this book, as I hope the chapters on Robbe-Grillet will prove, and by no means intended facetiously; a trend in restaurants has been towards exposing the chefs as they work to the scrutiny of their customers.

The novelist (or the chef) who denies himself the ancient prerogative of invisibility, is certainly one who identifies himself more sympathetically with his audience. He can find no justification for maintaining the pretence that he possesses supernatural powers; for one reason or another his whole philosophy has changed. Forced to rationalize what might well be an intuitive stance towards his work, as easily adopted in order to be modish as to be scrupulous, he could do so most embracingly by reference to the death of the confident metaphysical beliefs which subtended the great fictions of the nineteenth century and most of the lesser fictions of this one: the modes of realism and naturalism. The philosophy and psychology that sustained positivistic conventions in the novel have not been tenable for many years. Mechanistic philosophies with their simple chains of cause and effect are outmoded, so are mechanistic psychologies; they have been replaced by systems that are dynamic and allow for uncertainty or unpredictability—that is, where they have been replaced by systems at all. Moreover, the status of the mind has changed in respect of its epistemological links with the external world. Realism and naturalism were 'objective' modes, by means of which the novelist gave the impression that what he was describing, people, places, and events, were objectively 'there', that anyone else who happened to be passing at that moment might have witnessed what he witnessed. The need for selection and for invention on the part of the novelist is concealed, with the ultimate result that his own presence on the scene is made to seem fortuitous.

Such objectivity could be justified by invoking the scientific ideas of the nineteenth century; it can no longer be justified by those of the twentieth. The old simplified models of the physical world have vanished; it is no longer supposed that we can ever know or legislate for the thing *an sich*, physical and other theories being now acknowledged as constructs of human intelligence and in need of constant revision. It was long ago discovered that the behaviour of particles was affected by the presence of the observer, or at least by the light, which was the condition necessary for his observations. It was discovered, too, that precise prediction in physics was impossible, that it was only possible to determine the limits between which particles moved. And with Einstein it became the common belief that there were no longer models in the physical universe, in terms of motion or position, for the absolute viewpoint which might set the observer free from the predilections or prejudices of his own time and place.

Such a brisk summary of a few major scientific revaluations is, no doubt, naïve, yet these are ideas that have spread outside science into the minds of intelligent non-scientists, and it is such ideas, absorbed, it may be, most often in an incomplete or even inaccurate form, which will condition the approach to his work of any novelist who is not content to inherit without question the formulae of his profession from his predecessors. Confronted with the movement towards relativism and incoherence of scientific speculation in this century, the response of a novelist alert to the metaphysical implications of his chosen techniques must surely be to question or to abandon the traditional role of God or Absolute Mind. The cloud of unknowing that now floats between the hypotheses of the human intellect and the natural world makes us suspicious of definitive attempts to impose order on things. All absolutisms are now seen as dishonest, and a writer who proposes one must feel guilt, or so the argument would run. And the French writer, traditionally more influenced by current ideologies of one sort or another, has more reason to feel guilt than any other, having read Sartre's furious pre-war attack on François Mauriac for his divine pretentions.

The divergence and fragmentation of human knowledge are usually interpreted as a cause for alarm and confusion, but they can also converge into a single conviction—that when knowledge is so compartmentalized then there are no gods among us, but only men. The physicist speaks for physicists, the philosopher for philosophers, and so on. The age is one that favours the redefinition of spheres of influence and authority. The New Novelist, then, is intent on showing in his novels that he is simply a man, equipped with the universal human power of imagination. He does not ask any more that his readers should identify themselves with the creatures of his fancy, but that they should understand the act of creation itself. There are obvious parallels here with what has been happening in the theatre and the cinema since the last war. Dramatists, having learned from Brecht, Artaud, and others, as well as from the theatrical conventions of countries (particularly Eastern countries) where realism has never been countenanced, now know how to alienate the spectacle by the use of intermediary presences beside the stage, by extreme formalization of the once naturalistic décor, by putting the actors into masks so as to divorce them visibly from their role, and so on; while film directors achieve the same sort of effects by using hand-held cameras that do not keep still or level, sequences speeded up or slowed down, interpolations of flash-backs so brief as to be almost subliminal. In both the theatre and the cinema, as well as the extreme *avant-garde* of modern music, a great belief in improvisation has grown up, which exposes the procedures of creation or composition to public view. The effect of these manoeuvres is to distinguish representation from reality and to define the true syntax of the particular art-form.

Other stimuli, too, have prompted the self-questioning that the New Novel displays, ones again that can be linked with the prodigious growth of science in this century, science in both its meanings: as a discipline and as a body of knowledge. This enormous and continually accelerating advance, in terms both of capacity and prestige, has brought with it a promotion in the epistemological virtues of the public or scientific fact. Nor is it only the status of the fact that has improved: so has its availability; there was once a time, perhaps, when there were hardly enough facts about the world to go round: now there are too many. Those who crave the unknown rather than the known, and respect the urge to supplement facts with fancies, have been forced to retreat from stronghold after stronghold in the face of scientific investigation. Through use of film it is now possible to have incontrovertible visual evidence of what is going on anywhere in the world and even the nearby atmosphere.

This expansion of the field of empirical inquiry and of science's provision of verifiable data, poses a sinister threat to the continued existence of a form of writing, fiction, which is by definition non-fact. The death of the novel has indeed been vigorously proclaimed many times over the years, sometimes mournfully and sometimes almost with satisfaction. More books are being read, but the increase is in manuals of instruction, in travel books, in biographies, in the sciences. But these weighty proclamations go disregarded because there are always other commentators who can point to some ancient precedent for them. This defence is surely too optimistic; every patient, however resilient, eventually dies, and repeated bulletins about his condition are hardly an indication of robust health. The pious horror often expressed at the thought of a society in which no new novels were being written is not always convincing. Do we have to have new novels? There are a great number of excellent old ones in a great number of languages and if, as some people suppose, the functions of the novel are now usurped, it would be far healthier to accept the demise of this particular form of writing, rather than allow it to become thoroughly degraded. If the novel dies a dismal death it may take its past down with it.

It is a contention, and a very important one, of the *nouveau roman*, that many of the purposes which the traditional novel once served can now be more satisfactorily and persuasively served by different types of book or different media altogether. Why should we any longer go to novels for information about certain sectors of society, or about certain 'types' of character? The behavioural sciences, sociology or psychology, can provide this information perfectly well, with the guarantee that it is 'true', that it has resulted from statistical or experimental techniques which remove from it almost all taint of subjectivity.

The New Novel, then, refuses to be a vehicle of documentary facts about the real world, to abrogate the function of other types of writing, or of other media. The argument is that there is no

longer any point in inventing 'real' people, when we are surrounded by opportunities for reading about or watching real
people who have not been invented. What is at stake is the
authority of a liar in a society swarming with people accepted and
even revered for telling the truth. There is a further extension of
this same argument; that there is no point either in inventing
'real' stories in books when we are surrounded by newspapers
and television channels quite capable of telling real stories that
'actually happened'.

Nathalie Sarraute has expressed not only the self-doubt that
may attack the novelist but even more the guilt. By choosing her
examples carefully she is able to suggest something dishonourable
or even inhuman about the novelist who invents stories in a world
full of terrible events:

> Quelle histoire inventée pourrait rivaliser avec celle de la séquestrée de
> Poitiers ou avec les récits des camps de concentration ou de la bataille de
> Stalingrad? Et combien faudrait-il, de romans, de personnages, de
> situations et d'intrigues pour fournir au lecteur une matière qui
> égalerait en richesse et en subtilité celle qu'offre à sa curiosité et à sa
> réflexion une monographie bien faite?[7]

At the moment most monographs are not 'well-made', because
those who write them lack the literary skill and incentive to turn
them into works that will appeal outside the boundaries of their
own specialization. But what would happen if practised novelists
did abandon fiction as such and attempt a monograph? One
writer who has done this with a perverse success is the American
novelist, Truman Capote. His cunning piece of reportage, *In Cold
Blood*, was signalled by his British publishers as a 'non-fiction
novel'. This description gains an unexpected accuracy from the
macabre nature of what Capote was attempting. *In Cold Blood* is
the patient record of a multiple murder in the American mid-
West, written as the result of lengthy interviews with all those

[7] What invented story could compete with that of the woman prisoner of
Poitiers or with the accounts of the concentration camps or the Battle of
Stalingrad? And how many novels, characters, situations, and plots would
it take to provide the reader with a subject equal in richness and subtlety
to that which a well-made monograph offers to his curiosity and his reflection? (*L'Ère du soupçon*, p. 82).

connected with the crime and in particular with the two murderers themselves. Capote's book was not published until after the two men had been executed, and since much of what it contained had been communicated to him, and only to him, by the murderers, their deaths altered the status of *In Cold Blood*, at any rate in theory. The question is: is it possible to write a documentary book about the dead? If the difference between fact and fiction is that one can be verified and the other cannot, then the death of the murderers turned *In Cold Blood* from fact to fiction, in so far as their own evidence was concerned.

Of course I am not suggesting that these apparently hair-splitting questions of definition influenced Messrs. Hamish Hamilton's qualification of Capote's book. What they presumably meant to convey was that here was a 'true' story that was the equal if not the peer of any invented ones, a banal enough proposition among publishing houses and book reviewers, and one which adds its own measure of prestige to the real world at the expense of imagined ones. It is a proposition, on the other hand, which contradicts the memorable and shrewd dictum of the film actor, Humphrey Bogart, that 'life writes lousy plots'. The writers of the New Novel are on the side of Bogart, they are anxious to expose a plot for what it is, a conspiracy; the conspirator is the novelist and the victim is reality.

The readers of a book like *In Cold Blood*, and it has attracted millions of them, do not worry, I imagine, about *actually* verifying the facts it purports to contain, it is enough that the book should offer them the *possibility* of verification. Truman Capote is accepted as having told the truth, irrespective of his technical problems in the selection and arrangement of facts, and irrespective too of the impact of his own personality and philosophy on those of the murderers with whom he communicated over a period of years. The possibility of verification is all that matters.

A novel, on the other hand, can be defined on an exactly contrary principle, that it is *impossible* to verify it in any way at all. The characters it presents have never existed, the events it records have never taken place. A novel deploys or projects a private world, it is a full record of successive states of consciousness of the person who writes it. It is, as Michel Butor has written, 'le domaine phénoménologique par excellence'. By this he means that it is a domain of pure consciousness, containing both subject and object; but this subject and object are not independent entities, they are twin poles of a single relationship.

*   *   *

The *nouveau roman* has thus tried to redefine the proper territory of a fiction, in response to the challenge of scientific knowledge and ideological fragmentation. As yet science is not able to record (or to verify) the activities of the human consciousness in such a way as to communicate them in full to another consciousness. These activities can, of course, be submitted to certain forms of scrutiny—by electro-encephalographs, for example, which measure the regularity and intensity of electric currents in the brain. But the graph which these machines inscribe are of little interest to anyone except a neuro-surgeon or other scientific investigators. It is not, in human terms, a meaningful record of another person's thoughts; successive peaks of activity on the graph may relate to totally disparate images in the patient's mind and, until these are differentiated, their significance is minimal. The only forms of transcription which make thoughts communicable in an ordinary sense are ideographic or linguistic ones. Some time in the future no doubt far more sophisticated machines will be developed, able to transcribe the neural patterns in a brain into pictures on a screen. Society's more distinguished creative minds—if such terms still have any meaning—may then be forcibly conscripted into the provision of public entertainment, simply by being suitably wired up.

For the time being, however, the contents of the individual consciousness remain private unless that individual feels the urge to express them. There is no great difficulty, then, in situating the action of the New Novels which I shall later analyse: it takes place in the reflective consciousness of the novelist. The New Novel subscribes to the old Platonic belief that imagination is memory, and what it does is to dramatize the processes of imagination. This involves a partial or, in some cases, a total disconnection of the mind from the events of the external world. The writer no longer pretends (or if he does so pretend then he makes it clear that he *is* pretending) to be able to be in more places than one, sitting writing at his desk as well as roaming the world outside. The withdrawal into the reflective consciousness is itself modelled on the withdrawal into the place of work; once he has started to write, the novelist's praxis on the material world is dramatically restricted to a few objects that are within reach, a factor which has inspired, in the case of one of the subtler and more gifted of the post-New Novel writers in France, J. M. G. le Clézio, a fascination with ash-trays.

The narrative tradition to which the *nouveau roman* belongs is therefore that of the interior monologue, generally agreed to have been systematized for the first time by the Symbolist writer Edouard Dujardin, in *Les Lauriers sont coupés*, which appeared in 1887. This novel of exasperated sensuality might have remained submerged for ever in the past if James Joyce had not later acknowledged his own debt to it for the use he made of Dujardin's technique in *Ulysses*. Although the narration remains strictly within the narrator's mind in *Les Lauriers sont coupés*, Dujardin does not exploit the freedom which this allows him very forcefully. He is much more concerned with the psychological implications of the technique than its ontological ones. His hero is an incompetent young man whose retreat into the refuge of the imagination can only be interpreted as a defence mechanism —it is a stage in the Decadents' fastidious dismissal of reality as being unequal to the demands of their minds.

The same sort of charges have naturally been freely made against the writers of the New Novel, and I will examine these later. But it does not seem to me that they are justified as they are in the case of Dujardin, for the good reason that these writers are simply drawing attention to the fact that *any* novel is the creation of a mind temporarily disconnected from reality; the psychological or social pressures that might be construed as having led to this disconnection are irrelevant. Directly or indirectly, the New Novelists have been influenced profoundly by the phenomenologist philosophers—I will also examine this question in more detail—and one of the brightest achievements of the phenomenological movement has surely been to rescue epistemology from psychology. The difficulty it has had in persuading people of this is dismally illustrated by the readiness with which Sartre, whose philosophical works are furiously opposed to all psychologism, has been criticized in psychological or sociological terms, particularly outside France.

One especially interesting detail of *Les Lauriers sont coupés*, which links this novel directly with the preoccupations of the New Novel, is the name of the hero: Daniel Prince. This name suggests, though it does not of course prove, that Dujardin wanted to express by it his concept of the sovereignty of consciousness over its own microcosmic domain. If this was his intention then it is ironic, since Prince's position in Parisian society is a peculiarly futile and unprincely one—he is the unseeing slave of a mercenary and vicious *cocotte*. But it is striking that both Michel Butor and Robbe-Grillet should have repeated, or re-invented, Dujardin's device, by bestowing names which likewise indicate the degree of authority of the consciousness that has been set free from the mechanical necessity of its involvement in the natural world.

The novelist as a king of creation? The idea sounds a somewhat rhapsodic one, and it needs to be defined more precisely. The sovereignty of the reflective consciousness is the measure of our freedom as human beings: 'all that separates us from objects', says Sartre in *L'Être et le néant*, 'is our freedom'. This freedom stands dialectically opposed to the necessity of physical involvement with the external world, our praxis. It is the interval of time during which the mind can be made up, its contents that is to say reassembled in such a way as to enable the body subsequently to act in a purposeful manner. To use a metaphor that has been exploited in different ways by both Michel Butor and Robbe-Grillet, the reflective consciousness, of whose operations the novel contains a record, represents the 'play' in the machine of necessity. But if the New Novel wants to dramatize the creation or attempted creation of a fiction it also needs to make clear to its readers within what limits this creation takes place, or what the obstacles are that stand in its way. The intrusion of necessity must also be represented, in ways which I will demonstrate in the chapters that follow.

All play takes place within certain limits and also in accordance with certain rules. The play of the mind as it is embodied in the *nouveau roman* is constituted by our freedom to rearrange the images or memories of the past without reference to a perceived reality. The images are irreducible facts, the patterns that are made with them are fictions. The relationship between facts and fiction is also paralleled on the linguistic plane. Here the rules of the game which the sovereign consciousness must recognize are the rules of language, those governing the meaningful combination of words. In respect of language as in respect of reality the powers of the mind are truly combinatory and not inventive; we cannot add to the stock of language (except by neologisms based on existing formations) any more than we can add to the stock of matter. The freedom of the individual speaker is perfectly defined in the terms first introduced by Saussure; the necessity that he must accept as the guarantee of his being able to communicate at all is the *langue*, what he is free to invent is his *parole*. More simply, the speaker, or the writer, invents a message by selection from a pre-existent code.

This particular relationship between freedom and necessity is crucial in any assessment of the aims and achievements of the New Novel. At the same time, the freedom of the individual speaker, or writer, to invent his own *parole* can easily be exaggerated; indeed the relationship of a human subject to an enclosed system such as language is a lively source of contention in the evolving debates about structuralism's underlying ideology. But without adopting extreme attitudes, of the apotheosis or the annihilation of the individual, it is still proper to admit that the influence of phonetic association on the individual's *parole* is immense. Many people find it reprehensible that in prose the sound of a word should take precedence over the concept it denotes, as it is sometimes encouraged to do in poetry. The autonomy of language, as it is displayed for example in Freud's *The Interpretation of Dreams*, seems to pose a further threat to the integrity of consciousness. Yet no one who was honest about his own utterances would deny that the sequence of concepts is determined for him sometimes by the sequence of sounds. Certainly, both Claude Simon and Robbe-Grillet, who write in a continuous mode as compared to the discontinuous mode of

Michel Butor, accord the homophone an important role in determining the sequence of their *parole*.

*   *   *

The methods of the New Novel will remain mysterious and apparently perverse unless this crucial distinction is kept in view: that the mind is free but the eye is not. The imagination comes into play only once the eye is closed—'the man who looks through an open window never sees as many things as one who looks at a closed window', wrote Baudelaire. The New Novel, indeed, has distinguished literary antecedents in Romanticism. Of course, the eye does not have literally to be closed for the imagination to be operative, since it is possible to look at one thing and see another. Moreover, two people looking at a single object do not see the same object, since the significance of that object for each of them remains invisible until such time as they betray it by expressing it in words or by some other form of physical action.

What the imagination has to work with are public facts that have been absorbed into the private consciousness and retained in the memory. It is the discontinuity of these facts—a discontinuity which is also reflected in our direct perceptions of the external world—which enables us, indeed solicits us, to assemble them into a fiction. A true total recall, one which brought back the past in its entirety, would need to be co-extensive in time with the original experience and would deny the possibility of a fiction; it would be an actual re-living of the past.

An important element of the sovereignty of the reflective consciousness is thus its capacity for denying the chronology of the past. We can, and invariably do, examine our past in a different order to that in which it was actually given to us. This new order will, inevitably, be a more personal and revealing one, it is the order which the psychoanalyst must try to extract from his patient by techniques of verbal association. The contiguities of chronology may well be peculiarly trivial compared with those of apparently heterogeneous images evoked successively in the mind. Chronology is mechanism and necessity; there can be no final escape from its harsh sequence, so we must cherish the play

we are allowed in relation to the clock by withdrawing into the
time-scale of consciousness itself.

In order to relate these two time-scales, that of the public
world and that of the private, to each other in a comprehensible
way it might be useful to borrow the terms applied to them by the
founding father of the phenomenological movement, Edmund
Husserl, and to go on to determine briefly the close connection
that exists between the ambitions of the New Novel and this
particular form of philosophy. One of the reasons why the New
Novel has been lamentably misunderstood in many quarters is
the Anglo-Saxon ignorance of a philosophical tradition which is
now apparently taken for granted in France and other European
countries. I am not proposing that the three New Novelists I am
concerned with here, or others of the same persuasion, have a
profound grasp of the technicalities of this difficult philosophy—
though Michel Butor very likely does—but simply that the ideas
of Husserl, Heidegger, and other less charismatic figures have
penetrated in simplified forms into the minds of intelligent
laymen, especially through the writings of Sartre and Merleau-
Ponty. One does not need to be a practising philosopher to share
the epistemological standpoint of phenomenology, and one
recent French commentator, R.-M. Albérès, has gone so far as to
say that we are all phenomenologists these days even if we don't
know it. Robbe-Guillet himself, moreover is in no doubt
about the significance of the movement having written: 'la
phénoménologie occupait progressivement tout le champ des
recherches philosophiques',[8] an insular statement, but an indicative one.

Husserl, then, distinguishes between the two time series we are
concerned with as 'cosmic' time and 'phenomenological' time, the
first being that of science and of public reference, the second that
of the individual experience of the world. That these two series
can be wildly at variance is an acknowledgement embodied in
many popular locutions, for example, 'the last hour has gone
terribly slowly'.

The writers of the New Novel are concerned with pheno-

---

[8] phenomenology progressively occupied the entire field of philosophical
research (*Pour un nouveau roman*, p. 120).

menological time as a reality and, in the case of Butor at least, with cosmic time only as a convention. The relationship between the two is one which Husserl himself seems to have struggled to define, and his own adumbrations of it are frequently too complex or technical for a non-philosopher to follow. But there are moments when Husserl seems to be excluding cosmic time altogether from his purview since, like the substantial world *an sich*, it is transcendent to our consciousness of time: 'Just as a real thing or the real world is not a phenomenological datum, so also world-time, real time, the time of nature in the sense of natural science including psychology as the natural science of the physical, is not such a datum.'[9]

Phenomenological time is constituted by the celebrated Husserlian disconnection from the natural world, the phenomenological reduction or 'epochè'. That is to say, instead of being wholly absorbed within the punctual 'now' the consciousness becomes aware that this point *is* the 'now', and that it is related to other past 'nows', that time in fact is an indivisible flux, and a duration. Duration is itself constituted by modifications of the contents of consciousness, so that it is simple to see how a novel can be written without reference to the objective measurement of time at all, it creates its own temporal series as it goes along. Traditionally, the novelist unfurled the events of his story in cosmic time, introducing gaps to account for the fact that a story narrated, say, in four hours (if read at a sitting) had taken five years to happen. But Claude Simon and Robbe-Grillet rely on the coincidence of the time-scale of the narration with the time-scale of what is narrated; Michel Butor extends the narrative of his novels in cosmic time, but only in order to display the final inadequacy of any such public scale to reveal the profound structures of the individual consciousness.

The epistemological importance of the Husserlian *epochè* is clearly considerable, and thoroughly relevant to the schema of the New Novelists. By it the consciousness is withdrawn from its object, which is a mental image, sufficiently for its relation to that object to be made apparent to it. The aim is to furnish philosophy with 'a pure descriptive theory of the essential nature of the

[9] *The Phenomenology of Internal Time-Consciousness*, p. 23.

C

immanent forms of consciousness'.[10] Keeping this aim in mind it becomes simpler to resolve the troublesome question of whether the New Novel, which has exploited this reflective strategy of consciousness to the full, is an exercise in the subjective or the objective modes.

Used to describe a work of fiction the word subjective has a pejorative ring, since it generally hints at a wilful obscurity on the part of the writer, or at an indulgence in the fantastic at the expense of the plausible. But the *nouveau roman* is completely subjective, if the word is used in its descriptive, epistemological sense, just as all novels must be unless written by a committee, when it might be argued that they were at least intersubjective. But this 'subjective' needs to be distinguished from 'ideal' in the traditional philosophic sense of that word. Phenomenology sets out to eliminate the old and damaging dichotomy between realism and idealism, first by reducing the world transcendental to consciousness to its appearances in consciousness (speculation as to the unknowable essence of things being wholly vain) and then by denying the self any separate existence from the succession of mental experiences that constitute it. Perception, retention, and memory are portrayed as relations; no longer is there me, on the one hand, and that tree, on the other, there is only me seeing, retaining, or remembering that tree.

The *nouveau roman* is therefore neither subjective nor objective, but both. The objects which each novel contains are the successive contents of a consciousness, that of the narrator, who can be identified more or less closely with the novelist himself. We do not have him (the narrator) and them (the objects) but him-seeing-them. This has been a great source of misunderstanding among critics of the New Novel, particularly in the case of Robbe-Grillet. Without objects there would be no self, without a self no objects. Charges that the New Novel is *chosiste*, too concerned with trivial and inanimate things, are pointless for two reasons: firstly because the presence of a thing is the evidence that a consciousness is there to sustain it, and secondly because things that have become the property of a consciousness are significant for that consciousness, not trivial. Robbe-Grillet was ultimately led

[10] E. Husserl, *Ideas*, p. 178.

to defend himself against attacks that he was anti-humanistic: 'Les objets de nos romans n'ont jamais de présence en dehors des perceptions humaines, réelles ou imaginaires; ce sont des objets comparables à ceux de notre vie quotidienne, tels qu'ils occupent notre esprit à tout moment.'[11]

Husserl's axiom, developed from a notion of Brentano and later taken up by Sartre, that consciousness must be consciousness *of* something is simple enough, yet often misunderstood to judge by the sort of criticisms I have outlined. The habits of transcendental realism, which posits a radical separation between the self and its experience, persist. This is the illusion which Husserl accused Descartes of fostering, with his introduction of a *substantia cogitans*, an illusion which Husserl implies perverted the course of Western philosophy. But some people no doubt find the phenomenological view, especially in its most prestigious though hardly most accessible formulation, in Sartre's *L'Être et le néant*, an unwholesomely negative or passive one, without human dignity. All that this view actually does is to acknowledge the fact that the substantial world as a whole pre-exists our individual acts of attention to it, and that it is out of the world-stuff that our selves will be constituted on their passage through time. The consciousness of the individual is a mirror held up to nature but a mirror endowed with the capacity to retain what it reflects, or some of it, and reproduce it in patterns of its own invention.

The objects contained in a New Novel, then, are significant for the consciousness in which they appear; they are *intended*, that is to say they are evidence of the mind's intentionality. None of these objects is a gratuitous presence in the novel, but a necessary one, demanded by the intentionality of the narrator who, as I have said, is a (or the) novelist. Thus an object is no longer important *per se*, it is important in its relationship to the consciousness in which it has appeared. From the novelist's point of view, this or that object is a pretext, since it is at the form of consciousness that he wishes to direct our attention and not exclusively at its content. Or, as Husserl himself defines it: 'I, the transcendental pheno-

[11] The objects of our novels have no presence outside human perceptions, real or imaginary; they are objects comparable with those of our everyday lives, such as fill our minds at every moment (*Pour un nouveau roman*, p. 116).

28 THE FRENCH NEW NOVEL

menologist have *objects* . . . as a theme for my universal descriptions: *solely as* the intentional correlates of modes of consciousness of them.'[12] Here one can again see the determination to escape from the subjective stance of psychologism in order to achieve a truly scientific description of consciousness. The universal element of the New Novel needs to be underlined, since it is a useful defence against those who accuse it of privacy and Parnassianism.

Sartre had recognized the tremendous importance for the novelist of the phenomenological concept of intentionality some years before the New Novel as such started to emerge as a corporate phenomenon. He, too, stresses the way in which it removes the taint of subjectivism from those who would explore a particular emotion: 'Voilà que, tout d'un coup, ces fameuses réactions "subjectives", haine, amour, crainte, sympathie, qui flottaient dans la saumure malodorante de l'Esprit, s'en arrachent, elles ne sont que des manières de découvrir le monde.'[13]

Once a novelist has grasped the way in which an emotion of the sort Sartre lists can be presented objectively, that is to say by a certain arrangement of mental images themselves retained from the mind's experience of the outside world, then the way is open for a profound shift in the manner of a novel's narration. A passion like fear could previously be presented as an abstract noun; a novelist pursuing a traditional course might write 'X was afraid'. A novelist who has been to school with Husserl could not be satisfied with this, since he must try to show what the successive contents of a frightened person's consciousness are. The abstract noun, or the emotion that has been abstracted, is only a superstructure erected above the material evidence. I use this Marxian term deliberately because it can be argued that with the narrative technique of the New Novel the novel has entered a materialist phase: Claude Simon, indeed, was quick to claim that Robbe-Grillet's *La Jalousie*, a book that exemplifies Sartre's

[12] *Cartesian Meditations*, p. 37.
[13] So, suddenly, these famous 'subjective' reactions, hatred, love, fear, sympathy, which had been floating in the malodorous brine of the Mind, are uprooted from it, they are simply ways of discovering the world (*Situations I*, p. 34).

doctrine quoted above admirably, was 'the first truly materialist novel'.

What has really happened is not that the process of abstraction has been made impossible, it has been delayed, since it is shown to be a later moment in the consciousness's process of reflection on itself. The scheme of the New Novel is such that the narrator, the proprietor of the consciousness whose contents are being deployed, does not withdraw from the sequence of mental images in order to perform acts of abstraction from them. The mode of narration is an implicit one, the narrator remains silent on the explicit significance of the images of which the novel is an inventory. The responsibility for abstraction is surrendered to the reader, who can at least be confident that each one of these images *is* significant, that each one of them is asking to be interpreted as an 'intentional correlate'.

A novel in which the narrator has thus been stripped of his traditional powers of conceptualization is one which relies on mental pictures. By the exclusion of the intermediate presence the New Novel is attempting an immediate mode of fiction, in which the reader is confronted by the contents of another consciousness, but contents assembled with a hidden purpose and not gratuitously. The contents of this consciousness are made explicit, therefore, but their mode of apprehension or form is not; 'a picture', writes Wittgenstein in the *Tractatus*, 'cannot, however, depict its pictorial form: it displays it'. The picture demands the presence of the Other in order for its form to become explicit.

The injunction of the Interflora service to 'say it with flowers' is one with perplexing implications for linguistics, but the type of message conveyed in this way is bound to remain rather primitive, since the language of flowers in our own society is extremely restricted. The writers of the *nouveau roman* are in the position of 'saying it with things', which is both a more ambitious and more complex form of language. It is as a result of this that they have had to put up with a good deal of hearty misrepresentation.

Yet ever since there was first discussion of the techniques of story-telling there have been those who advised their fellow-novelists to show and not to tell what they had to say, to embody their message in the actions, words, dispositions, and décor of their books and not to pass it on explicitly. Those novelists who, like Balzac or Henry James, not only understood the various possibilities open to them more clearly than most, but also fancied their chances (misguidedly as it turned out) as playwrights, were great advocates of the scene, the dramatic incarnation of the novelist's own discrete virtualities. The New Novel is proposing, simply enough, that a fiction should be all scene, or representation.

It is surprising that more New Novelists have not been associated with the theatre and the cinema, in view of their common concern with representation. Of the three novelists discussed here, Claude Simon has written one unsuccessful play, Michel Butor has adapted one radio play for theatrical performance, and Robbe-Grillet alone has pursued a career as a film-maker as well as a writer. But two of the New Novel's most rigorous practicians, Claude Ollier and Claude Mauriac, are excellent film critics, and have clearly appreciated the community of interest between themselves as writers and the more alert film directors. The screen of consciousness is a very common figure in the technical philosophical works of certain phenomenologists, notably Merleau-Ponty, who in a remarkable essay called 'Le Cinéma et la nouvelle psychologie' stressed the suitability of a film to embody the beliefs of *gestalt* psychologists and the phenomenologists: 'Une bonne part de la philosophie phénoménologique . . . consiste à faire *voir* le lien du sujet et du monde, du sujet et des autres, au lieu de les *expliquer*, comme le faisaient les classiques, par quelques recours à l'esprit absolu.'[14]

This crucial Husserlian concept of intentionality, which has determined a profound shift in narrative technique, also has obvious ethical implications. By withdrawing the mind sufficiently far from its involvement in the present moment, the 'here and now', to reveal its intentional stance towards the world, we are in a position to assume our full responsibility as human beings, as rational agents. The phenomenological *epochè* re-

---

[14] A good part of the phenomenological philosophy . . . consists in *showing* the link between the subject and the world, and the subject and other people, instead of *explaining* them, as classical thinkers used to do, by some recourse to absolute mind (*Sens et non-sens*, p. 105).

presents a gain in self-awareness; it may set us free from the accumulated cultural, social, or personal influences that we have absorbed but never acknowledged, and turn us from creatures largely of instinct into creatures largely of reason. Such a programme obviously is very close to that of psycho-analysis, whose methods of rationalizing our praxis also rely on the release of repressed material through the play of language.

* * *

The New Novel pursues the existential tasks already adumbrated in novels of a previous generation, and notably by Sartre in *La Nausée*. The man who writes a novel is revealing the activity of the free mind in its phase of disconnection from blind necessity. None of the writers of the New Novel deny the mind's freedom, even if they differ on the use that is made of it. What this free mind is shown as doing is bestowing significance. The world no longer has an absolute or essential meaning and the mind of the novelist sets to work to transform its contingency into a personal necessity, by creating from it a realm of meaning. The old relationship between Man and Nature has been overturned: 'L'existence humaine nous obligera à réviser notre notion usuelle de la nécessité et de la contingence, parce qu'elle est le changement de la contingence en nécessité par l'acte de reprise.'[15]

Where writing is concerned, the concept is the familiar one of the Alchemy of the Word, which transmutes leaden contingency into golden necessity though not, alas, permanently. After the novelist's 'acte de reprise' is finished the mind must be returned to the external world, to the bombardment of sense-impressions. Such order as has been achieved in its period of comparative respite is a personal and temporary one which cannot survive to be enthroned as a new metaphysic.

Writing a book and reading a book are symmetrical acts of withdrawal; the writer retreats from the flux in order to elaborate his small realm of meaning, the reader in order to seek the relief of the order which he knows the writer will have imposed on his

---

[15] Human existence will oblige us to revise our normal notion of necessity and contingency, because it is the turning of contingency into necessity through the act of repetition (*Phénoménologie de la perception*, p. 199).

experiences. It seems to me, therefore, that any novel which embodies the actual withdrawal of the writer, and gives up the pretence that the novelist can remain involved in the real world outside at the same time as he is writing, is promoting a new and stimulating form of realism. Of course, all literary revolutions or revaluations are made in the sacred name of realism, as Robbe-Grillet himself proposes: 'Le réalisme est l'idéologie que chacun brandit contre son voisin, la qualité que chacun estime posséder pour soi seul. Et il en a toujours été de même: c'est par souci de réalisme que chaque nouvelle école littéraire voulait abattre celle qui la précédait . . .'[16]

But realism is a confusing term; when a book is described as being 'realistic' what is it being related to? Lay readers of novels would no doubt answer to real life, whereas it would be more accurate to say that it was being related to other novels in the first place, and only through them, through a fictional tradition, to real life. For those people who read novels, see films, or even read newspapers, interpret real life around them in terms of their fictive stereotypes—unless, that is to say, they are ruthless be-haviourists, denying their minds any opportunity for invention to compensate for the gaps in their observations.

The New Novel sets out to reveal to its readers that literary realism is a convention, or a set of conventions; by exposing its patent artifice the New Novelists move closer at the same time to the common facts of human perception and retention. They are acknowledging the authority and consequently the dangers of literary conventions once these are uprooted from books and put to illicit use in our everyday lives. What suffers is reality, since we fail to distinguish between fact and fiction in the world around us, fail to draw a frontier between observation and imagination. A novel is exposed for what it actually *is*, a fabrication, the work of one man who has not been endowed by a sympathetic divinity with the traditional novelist's gifts of omniscience and ubiquity.

---

[16] Realism is the ideology which everyone brandishes against his neighbour, the quality which everyone reckons that he alone possesses. And it has always been so: it is out of a concern for realism that every new literary school has sought to overthrow the one preceding it . . . (*Pour un nouveau roman*, p. 135).

But this sort of realism is not always interpreted as a sign of health; a narcissistic preoccupation with the act of literary creation is thought to be the prelude to falling silent altogether. Paradoxically, it seems to me to be one of the virtues of the New Novel that it has exploited narcissism the way it has, and dramatized the assembly of a novel, because this does indeed reveal the opposition or tension that exists between language and silence. Writing is established as an exemplary activity, because it is the objectification of the only freedom we possess.

Of course there have been many critics reluctant to see the novelist expose himself as nothing more than a man, with a single viewpoint on the world from which he cannot escape. The abdication of the novelist from his old privileges is held to be a fresh *trahison des clercs*, to be the result of the lack of a dominant ideology in France, to reflect the decline of the individual in a society swamped by a mass culture, and so on. But it would seem fairer to say that if the novelists have climbed down from their previous Olympian position it is in order that their readers may climb up to meet them half-way, by co-operating in the construction of a work of art—the novel cannot be held to be complete until it has been read and, more important, understood.

The novels we are discussing are as much ante-novels as antinovels; without the attentive reader they are stunted creations. The technical devices that once erected a barrier between the novel-reader and the text he was reading have been removed for the most part. The narration is almost always in the first person, and a problematical first person at that, who is deprived of any full existence as an object for himself, since his narration *is* his own objectification of himself. To argue from this that the New Novel aims to abolish man is a mildly hysterical reaction, since it is in fact supplying the evidence of man as subject, proposing that the proof of a noumenal presence lies in a sequence of phenomenal presences. The other device which sets the reader at a distance from the events he is reading about is of course the narrative tense, in French the *passé simple*, which lends (according to taste) a spurious or convincing reality to the narrative. The present tense that very largely replaces it—the present participle in the novels of Claude Simon—is the tense of 'phenomenological' time, the tense of an experience we want to make immediate for somebody. It has traditionally been the tense, in novels as well as psychoanalytical works, in which dreams are recounted, and Freud himself, in *The Interpretation of Dreams*, remarks that it is also the tense of wish fulfilment. It is the tense, moreover, as Roland Barthes points out in *Le Degré zéro de la littérature* (a book written in 1953 which makes the *nouveau roman* seem to be the logical culmination of a historical evolution of the novel as a 'guilty' form of writing that had begun with Flaubert), which embodies the lesson that a complex reality must always overflow the narrow banks of language.

As a dramatization of the creative process the *nouveau roman* is clearly following a path towards generalization or universalization. A certain stage of that process can find different embodiments in the novels of different writers, but the intention in each case is much the same. To take a single example, and to limit myself to the three writers I have selected: they have each found different objective correlates for the reflective consciousness itself, the scene of the novel's composition. For Claude Simon, for example, this is a study or other room shuttered, not entirely successfully, against the sunlight—the artificial light is a clue to the equation he wants to establish with consciousness; for Michel Butor, in *La Modification*, the same scene becomes a railway compartment in a train—the train being a reminder that we are still carried along in time even when we reflect; for Robbe-Grillet, in *Dans le labyrinthe*, consciousness is figured as a bedroom at the top of a house, a traditional trope as well as a hint at the erotic nature of literary creation which this novelist stresses. Such parallels hardly constitute a sameness, but they do indicate a danger, that once readers learn to interpret the puzzles they are confronted with correctly then they can carry this knowledge with them from one novel to the next and from one novelist to the next. I think it is possible that the New Novel is an exhaustible form, in the sense that puzzles lose their attraction once they become too easily solved.

Certainly an individual novel by Butor or Robbe-Grillet is exhaustible, at least in theory, by which I mean that a total explanation of every detail in it is possible, once its significance for the narrator is established. But this is an exegetical task that no one could hope to achieve in a single reading or even two readings. An unusual problem is therefore raised as to how many times a novelist should expect his readers to re-read the same book. Many people will be content to accept the overall principle and neglect the details that escape them after one or two readings. In the same way a novel reviewer, or even a more serious critic, can take certain aspects of the puzzle on trust without feeling any absolute need to solve them. But faced by a structure as dauntingly secretive as that used by Michel Butor in, for example, *L'Emploi du temps*, it is understandable that readers, reviewers, and critics should take refuge in half-measures. Some writers of the *nouveau roman* could certainly be said to have over-estimated the powers of penetration of their probable readers, and some at least of those who have promoted these writers give the impression of having promoted something they do not fully understand, presumably *because* they do not fully understand it and so assume it to be impenetrable.

But it would be a lasting pity if the writers of the New Novel were classed with the devious and deliberate *mystificateurs* of surrealism, for instance, many of whose puzzles are surely insoluble. There is no cheating in the novels of Robbe-Grillet, Butor, and others; sufficient evidence is communicated for the puzzles to be satisfactorily solved, and those who refuse the challenge should be gracious enough to state the valid reason for doing so, which is that such obliqueness is not a moral virtue, and imposes demands on the reader which it is hardly worth his time or trouble to meet. It would be hard to deny that the satisfaction of the reader who *does* rise in whole or part to the challenge and does manage to elucidate the structure of a particular novel is an emotion far removed from what the same reader might feel after reading an ordinary exercise in naturalism. If the old virtues of the novel depended on the reader's powers of emotional identification with what he is reading about then the new virtues are restricted to ones of comprehension and this being so there is a danger that those who comprehend will feel superior to those who do not.

But supposing the phenomenological mode of narration which I have tried to define were to become the dominant one in the novel? Readers would gradually become perfectly accustomed to the tasks of interpretation set them by the novelist and would find them increasingly easy to solve. They would have achieved a new and far from negligible identification with the act of writing itself and that act, as I have said, is modelled closely on a certain philosophy's conception of the process of living. The ambitions of the New Novel in this respect are very dignified.

Yet, is there any sign that the *nouveau roman* is having its effect on reading (and writing) habits, or beginning to educate a new class of readers in a new sort of reading? It is premature and also presumptuous to offer anything better than a hesitant set of answers to this question. Some critics have quickly used the apparent failure of the New Novel to persuade novelists outside France to adapt their techniques as a sign of the fallibility of the whole enterprise. Moreover, this failure to export a French product is a boon to those literary observers who like to interpret all aesthetic movements in terms of a nationalistic sociology, and explain them away by reference to the political and economic conditions of a particular country at a particular time. Such explanations are only plausible until it is remembered that they are always made after the event, after the movement in question is in existence; they would be much more plausible if they could be offered as predictions subsequently fulfilled.

There are plenty of indications that many of the younger French novelists have appreciated the lesson of the New Novel, and have applied some of its rules with a greater or lesser degree of rigour. In general, one can say that many French novelists now go so far as to draw attention in their novels to the necessary conventions of the novel-form, while a smaller group display a remarkable obsession with the act of writing itself. Early in the 1960s the alert publicists struck again and founded the school of the *nouveau nouveau roman*, a movement associated closely at first, and rather more loosely since, with the literary quarterly *Tel Quel*. The creative writers of this group, Philippe Sollers, Jean Ricardou, Jean-Pierre Faye, Jean Thibaudeau, have proved their extremely acute understanding of the theory of the New Novel by the various critical essays they have devoted to it, and to the individual novelists who practise it. In their own practice of the novel they have shown themselves to be very much more extreme than the previous generation, having moved to what really seems, at present anyway, to be an ultimate position with regard to the business of reflecting, in a novel, on the process of writing one. Books like Sollers's *Drame* or Thibaudeau's *Ouverture* enact, with an austerity which even readers trained on Butor may find rather chilling, the creative process almost before it has taken place. If the *nouveau roman* offers *pré-textes* then these are *pré-pré-textes*, a voice duelling as it were with silence, externalizing itself with only intermittent enthusiasm for the task. Where in Robbe-Grillet or Butor the creative process is embodied quite robustly in terms of physical environment or 'characters', with Sollers and others it is reduced to little more than the adventure of a language or *parole* itself. The narrator of a Robbe-Grillet fiction may be anonymous, but even that is a status of some substance compared to the narrator of *Drame*, barely able to objectify himself as 'il'; the grammatical plane is the limit of his ambition, since it is sufficient evidence of a necessity having been established by the 'je', the active element of the novel. As Philippe Sollers says in his cover-note for *Drame*, 'Nous sommes donc, au présent, sur la scène de la parole'.[17]

This is a stage on which many readers will be reluctant to follow him, since they are not yet fully conditioned to abandoning the substantial satisfactions of more traditional modes of fiction. It seems rash to extend the generalization of the New Novel to its limit (if this really is its limit) before this generalization has been properly appreciated by more than a few sympathetic critics. The penetration of the literary world, even in France, of the *nouveau nouveau roman*, has been slight to date, and if its methods continue to convey the idea of a limit to a particular line of development in the novel then it may well be that its penetration will continue to be slight.

Outside France, the mode of the *nouveau roman* has not produced very many imitations as yet, except perhaps in Italy, where *avant-garde* writers are traditionally attuned to the experiments of the French and where criticism of the New Novel has been quite incisive, largely because the debt or the affinity of its techniques

[17] We are therefore, in the present, on the stage of speech.

with Husserlian phenomenology was quickly accepted. It is certainly in those countries or cultures that have generally taken their lead from Paris that one would expect to see signs of the New Novel making ground, rather than in this country or the United States, where literary groupings are comparatively rare and commonly treated with suspicion. Thus it would be a safe prediction that the South Americans will exploit the innovations of Robbe-Grillet and others most whole-heartedly; some of them are already doing so. On a visit to Europe the admirable Mexican writer, Carlos Fuentes, stated that the responsibility of the new writers of Latin America was to combine the insights of both Balzac and Butor, a statement which, whatever its merits as a persuasive synthesis for his fellow writers, at least indicates to which country they will be looking for advice.

Fuentes's compromise between the nineteenth and twentieth centuries is a very revealing one, since it points up the major issue concerning the direction which the French novel would take were the *nouveau roman* to become its dominant trend. By preserving Balzac in his pantheon Fuentes is preserving a writer cherished by the Marxist critics for his portrayal of a society sick with all the diseases of capitalism, a society in which the process of reification had gathered a terrible momentum. It is obvious why Fuentes is reluctant to abandon Balzacian naturalism, since he is a writer of the Left in a part of the world ripe for revolution.

But he is not prepared to join up with the many critics of the New Novel (not of all them Marxists or neo-Marxists by any means), who have accused these writers of turning their backs on real life, of withdrawing into Parnassian exclusivity. These critics are those who expect to find the more significant social, economic, or political issues treated or at least reflected in novels. Yet of the three writers discussed in this book, Claude Simon is the only one who makes any reference at all to recognizable public events, all of them, as it happens, in the past: the Spanish Civil War, the defeat of the French Army in 1940, the *épuration* of 1944–5, and so on. Not a word about Algeria, the rise of De Gaulle in 1958, or any other significant event in the post-war history of France.

This is something which those who hold to the tenets of social realism cannot understand. In Leningrad, in 1963, at one of those

periodic confrontations between writers and intellectuals from
East and West—the French delegation included both Robbe-
Grillet and Nathalie Sarraute—the misunderstanding seems to
have been absolute, to judge by the contributions made from both
sides which were later printed in the review *Esprit*. Bernard
Pingaud summed up the situation as follows: 'L'incompréhension
soviétique à l'égard de notre littérature veut dire simplement que
pour lui nos hantises n'ont pas de réalité. Et réciproquement, nous
ne voyons pas, ou nous voyons mal, ce qui le hante, lui . . .'[18]

But it is surely naïve or even contradictory to suppose that a
revolutionary poem or novel can only be constituted by its
explicit propaganda content. The writers of the New Novel would
say that writing a poem or a novel is no longer an appropriate
way of taking direct political or social action, though it certainly
may have been so once, before the invention of contemporary
mass media. Thus nothing is revealed explicitly of Robbe-Grillet's
or Michel Butor's political views in any of their fictions. Yet they,
like Claude Simon, were both signatories of the famous Declaration of the 121 on Algeria, which represented the view of all left-
wing French intellectuals at the time on the vicious dishonesty of
official French policy towards that country. To sign such a declaration clearly *was* an appropriate action taken in a manner that might
well have provoked an actual, even a measurable effect on govern-
ment policy. To have written a novel on the French iniquities in
Algeria would have been useless and possibly worse, since even
unsophisticated minds are capable of dismissing fiction as un-
truth.

The *nouveau roman* seems to me to be revolutionary in the very
best sense, being committed to producing a change in the structures of consciousness rather than any direct change in this or that
institution or practice. The New Novel challenges the tradition to
which it belongs itself, that of the novel, and challenges it from a
position of doubt and uncertainty. Its philosophy, if we exclude
the perhaps over-assertive scientism of Robbe-Grillet, is one that

[18] Soviet incomprehension with regard to our literature simply means that
for them our obsessions have no reality. And conversely, we cannot see,
or can see only dimly, what is obsessing them . . . (*Esprit*, July 1964,
p. 20).

must appeal to everyone who finds in his own doubts a source of tolerance and sympathy towards the world in general, and who accepts relativism as more of a pleasure than a frustration, as long as it guarantees him a certain freedom from moral or physical constraint.

Far from underestimating the power of books to alter the attitudes of those who read them, the New Novel takes a particularly exalted view of it. At another East–West meeting of writers, held in Vienna in 1967, Claude Simon explained his own concept of the work of art's contribution to the revolutionary movement: 'En revanche, au sein de l'immense et incessante gestation du monde, et dans l'ensemble de l'activité de l'esprit, toute production de celui-ci, à condition d'apporter quelque chose de neuf, joue son rôle, le plus souvent de façon invisible, souterraine, mais cependant capitale' (reported in La Quinzaine Littéraire, 1 May 1967).[19]

The apparent indifference of the New Novel to public events or to particular political attitudes masks a genuine moral commitment, therefore. On the same occasion as he spoke the words quoted above Simon also brought together two quotations, the first from Trotsky: 'In order to transform life, we must first of all start by knowing it'; the second from Proust: 'Nous ne connaissons vraiment que ce que nous sommes obligés de recréer par la pensée.'[20] This recreation is one which the writers of the New Novel demand of their readers that they should share, since it is a priceless and a secret process which they are objectifying in front of them, as they read. The lesson is not the narrow one of some sectarian movement in a particular society, but a universal one, in which the structures and function of consciousness itself are invoked.

The New Novel offers no final or easy salvation, because it implies that time must ultimately put an end to the conscious existence of the individual. But the mechanism of the universe has

---

[19] On the other hand, within the immense and unceasing gestation of the world, and within the activities of mind as a whole, anything that the mind produces, provided that it contributes something new, plays its part, most often in a way that is invisible and subterranean yet of the first importance.

[20] We only truly know what we are obliged to recreate in our minds.

some 'play' in it, which enables us to perform our *actes de reprise* and explore the limits of our existential freedom. This is our own 'play' or 'recreation'. The relationship between personal freedom and impersonal necessity on which the New Novel depends for its tension is cunningly reflected by Robbe-Grillet, in the film of *L'Année dernière à Marienbad*, by the old Chinese game of nim. The result of the game is pre-ordained, for the player who makes the first move must lose; yet during the course of the game he is able to make a series of free choices, within the rules of the game. Right up until the moment he acknowledges defeat he is free to invent his future. The virtue of the New Novel is that it embodies the extent of our creative freedom without any attendant illusions.

D

CLAUDE SIMON

I

CLAUDE SIMON has not attracted the patient attention or the critical argument which his dense and manly novels deserve. There are various reasons why this should have been so: he is a considerably older man than Robbe-Grillet or Butor (though younger than Nathalie Sarraute), he has written very little in the way of formal polemics or criticism of other writers, and his career as a practising novelist extends back in time far beyond the frontier normally taken as marking the New Novel off from the Old. Moreover, it has remained quite easy to treat Simon as a naturalist, as a novelist who insists on writing *about* something and has never wholly accepted the generalities or the austerity of the *nouveau roman*'s extremists.

The fact remains, however, that in his mature novels Claude Simon has moved very close to the theoretical standpoint of the other New Novelists. He has not strayed from or diluted the ideological position which he held when he started out as a novelist, with *Le Tricheur*, which was written in 1941 though not published until 1946. But he no longer conveys this position in the same way; he has gone over, in fact, from being an explicit writer, ready to conceptualize his philosophy in an abstract language, to being an implicit one, whose philosophy must be deduced from its objective configurations in the minds of his fictional narrators. This important transition from one narrative mode to the other can be dated convincingly to the mid-1950s, between the publication of *Le Sacre du printemps* in 1954 and that of *Le Vent* in 1957. This latter novel was the first which Simon published with the progressive house of Éditions de Minuit and this fact alone at the time was enough to move him closer in the public mind to the other high priests of the New Novel. The fact that Simon began his career as a novelist only mildly experimental in intention has certainly made it easier to elucidate the structures and meanings of his later, far more secretive books.

But there is one intimate and disturbing conviction that Claude Simon has never sought to keep secret and which quite dominates his fiction: the conviction that the human individual and the world are both in process, that they are irredeemably subject to transience or molecular exchange. In his novels Simon holds fast to his sense of the instability of matter to the point where he is led to undermine the fictitious stability which the order of a work of art imposes on the flux of experience.

The picture of matter which he proposes is a mercantilist one, from which the notion of increase has been excluded, no doubt because it might be held to mirror an optimism that is quite alien to Claude Simon: 'il supposa que devait jouer simultanément une autre loi . . . selon laquelle le niveau du contenu dans les divers contenants doit être partout égal, en vertu de quoi l'Histoire se constituait au moyen non de simples migrations mais d'une série de mutations internes, de déplacements moléculaires . . .' (*Le Palace*, p. 12).[1]

Such a view, which erects exchange as the principle of the world-process at the expense of creation, is not a simple or a comfortable one for men to live by. There is evidence from his novels that Claude Simon is a lapsed and disappointed revolutionary; by denying us, as he does, any hope of an ultimate transcendence of the human condition along the plane of history, he is perhaps defining himself as a man who still accepts Marxian prescriptions about the reifications endemic to a market economy while now doubting man's will to re-humanize them.

Simon is not, obviously, the first twentieth-century novelist to try and expose the illusion of stability which so many people find so comforting, and which he himself links, as his predecessors have done, most notably Sartre in *La Nausée*, with the complacency and vanity of the bourgeoisie, that thinks itself immortal.

[1] he supposed that another law must operate simultaneously . . . according to which the level of the content in the different containers must be everywhere the same, by virtue of which History was constituted by means not of simple migrations but of a series of internal mutations, of molecular displacements . . .

But Simon is not limited by class considerations; he is attacking the foundations of everybody's world, including his own, and salvation, such as it is, depends not on the adoption of some handy creed, but on the brave acknowledgement that this is the way things are.

'Reality' then has two degrees of intensity in Simon's novels: there is 'everyday' reality, with its consoling intimations of immortality, and 'real' reality, which reinstates all the constituents of our world and our experience in time. Real reality is a disturbing and an aggressive order of things, that few people will be strong enough to live with: 'le propre de la réalité est de nous paraître irréelle, incohérente, du fait qu'elle se présente comme un perpétuel défi à la logique, au bon sens . . .' (*L'Herbe*, p. 99).[2] This logic and common sense are what the phenomenologist condemns as acquired and inadequate habits of ordering experience and not personal, authentic modes of perception. Simon goes on to say in *L'Herbe* that books have always been written in terms of an inadequate logic and that to present things as they really are will demand new structures and a new syntax. The *nouveau roman*, that is to say, represents a gain in realism.

The concept of a 'secret' reality, accessible only to the initiated, is discussed at some length in Simon's early book of themes and ideas, *La Corde raide*, where he talks, for example, of: 'Une réalité artificielle supplantant, remplaçant l'autre. L'autre difficile et secrète, apparente et pourtant invisible' (p. 12).[3]

Later, when he writes of what might be called the epistemology of painting, he criticizes the many artists who have been satisfied with the first of these realities and have never made the attempt to penetrate as far as the second. They have attempted to transform reality rather than to show it. The one great artist whom he singles out, as having struggled all his life to get behind the 'décor', is Cézanne, who went as close as anyone could to the heart not of *the* matter but of matter itself: 'il avait découvert, non plus arbres,

---

[2] the property of reality is to appear to us to be unreal, incoherent, from the fact that it presents itself as a perpetual challenge to logic and common sense . . .

[3] An artificial reality supplanting, replacing the other. The other difficult and secret, apparent and yet invisible.

visages, maisons, bouteilles ou fruits, mais ce quelque chose d'autre, sans raison, ni postulat de raison que sont arbres, visages, maisons, bouteilles, fruits . . .' (ibid., p. 114).[4]

The achievement of Cézanne, so far as Simon is concerned, is to have been able to paint the external world from, as it were, the standpoint of nature itself, and to strip it of all those human and, more particularly, those aesthetic associations that generally obscure its integrity and its independence of consciousness. Simon is not alone in paying this homage to Cézanne as the forerunner of an implicit mode of communication in which it is by attentive description that the artist (or writer) creates the expression he is seeking; the philosopher Merleau-Ponty is also fond of calling on the same painter as an example of a proper phenomenological method: 'Dans ses œuvres de jeunesse, Cézanne cherchait à peindre l'expression d'abord et c'est pourquoi il la manquait. Il a appris peu à peu que l'expression est le langage de la chose elle-même et naît de sa configuration' (*Phénoménologie de la perception*, p. 372).[5]

The parallel with what Simon himself attempts is a close one; description is no longer, as it was once thought to be, primarily illustrative in purpose, it is creative. The writer does not use the expression he wants to convey as a starting-point but instead works towards it as a goal. A state of mind thus comes to be expressed by a full and detailed configuration of its elements.

Simon has always known what picture of reality it was which he needed to present in his novels, and as his technique has grown more assured and consistent so the force of the confrontation for his readers has increased, to the point where exposure to his insistently shifting world has become a suitably uncomfortable experience. At the same time, there is a limit to this discomfort, because the poles of Simon's unshrinking materialism are not creation and destruction, but disintegration and reintegration.

---

[4] he had discovered, no longer trees, faces, houses, bottles or fruit, but that something other, without reason or postulate of reason, which are trees, faces, houses, bottles, fruit . . .

[5] In his early work Cézanne was trying to start by painting the expression and that is why he missed it. He learned gradually that the expression is the language of the thing itself and arises from its configuration.

Some sort of solace is therefore to be had from the undeniable presence of the phenomenal world as a whole. As Merleau-Ponty puts it: 'il y a certitude absolue du monde en général, mais non d'aucune chose en particulier' (ibid., p. 344).[6] Substantial manifestations that are apparently endowed with their own lasting unity and separateness are thus an illusion, or at least relative to the individual mind that contemplates them. What Simon tries to do, like Cézanne, is to make us aware that such isolated manifestations, or things in the widest sense of that word, are a relative and artificial stasis of a substance constantly in flux.

Simon's proliferating style of writing, with its tangents, its references, and its repetitions, therefore matches, however insufficiently, the endless possibilities of the causal relationships that can be established between isolated phenomena. It is aimed at fixing our attention not only on the present configuration of elements but also on all the other configurations which the present one has necessarily abolished. In Simon we become conscious of just how inadequate a weapon language is, in the battle to immobilize a fluid reality. What he is trying to carry out is the task prescribed by the phenomenologists of re-situating objects in the flux, in the immediate certainty of their first appearance in the conscious mind.

Simon goes to unusual lengths to block up all our escape routes from this uncomfortable presence of the flux. The traditional road to timelessness has always led vertically upwards into the sky, our most convenient symbol for the void, molecularly speaking. But in Simon's novels things happen in the sky as well. *La Route des Flandres* for example is dominated by the rain, slanting endlessly down on the scene of the rout of the French cavalry in 1940, and frequently invisible until it can be seen against some suitable background, like a roof or a wall, the change of viewpoint being the device whereby the mind moves inward from appearance to reality.

In this novel Simon makes many comparisons between the rain and the destructive processes of time itself, and the analogy becomes blunter still once the rain has been transformed—another

[6] there is absolute certainty of the world in general but not of any one thing in particular.

sign of substantial continuity—into the mud that slowly engulfs
the bodies of men and animals along the Flanders road:

une goutte d'eau qui se détache d'un toit ou plutôt se scinde, une partie
d'elle-même restant accrochée au rebord de la gouttière (le phénomène
se décomposant de la façon suivante: la goutte s'étirant en poire sous
son propre poids, se déformant, puis s'étranglant, la partie inférieure—
la plus grosse—se séparant, tombant, tandis que la partie supérieure
semble remonter, se rétracter, comme aspirée vers le haut aussitôt après
la rupture, puis se regonfle aussitôt par un nouvel apport, de sorte
qu'un instant après il semble que ce soit la même goutte qui pend,
s'enfle de nouveau, toujours à la même place, et cela sans fin, comme
une balle cristalline animée au bout d'un élastique d'un mouvement
de va-et-vient) (p. 25).[7]

Here Simon has made surprising connections between the
faulty perception of a natural phenomenon and the illusive hopes
of a suffering humanity. The first optical illusion which he describes is that of the upper part of the drop of water which 'seems'
to rise after its separation from the rest of the drop, to enjoy an
'aspiration'; but in actual fact the movement of the water is, as we
would all recognize in this case, a relentlessly downward one,
deprived of any melodramatic intensity because it is only a drip,
not a waterfall; the second illusion in the passage quoted is the
second drop of water which 'seems' to be only the reappearance
of the first one, seems, therefore, to offer a promise of timelessness.
The microscopic scale on which Simon has chosen here to teach
his lesson is quite characteristic of him, because the lazy or dishonest mind might easily take refuge from the threat of time in
phenomena supposedly too trivial to betray its machinations.
In the same way the most potent symbol for the withering and

[7] a drop of water that is detached from a roof or rather is divided, one part
of it remaining clinging to the edge of the gutter (the phenomenon being
decomposed in the following manner: the drop extending into a pear-
shape under its own weight, becoming deformed and then throttled, the
lower part—the fatter one—separating and falling, while the upper part
seems to go back up again, to be retracted, as if sucked upwards immediately after the break, then immediately swells up again with a new
deposit of water, so that a moment later it seems to be the same drop
which hangs, is inflated again, always in the same place, and so on endlessly, like an animated crystalline ball on the end of an elastic, with a
to-and-fro movement).

impersonal passage of time in *Le Vent*, a novel set in south-west France, is the wind itself, which blows through the town for two hundred and sixty-five days in the year. Like the Flanders drizzle, the wind does not remain an invisible force, but is continually filled with spiralling clouds of dust and detritus, whose frantic, futile motions are an apt epiphany of History itself.

Perhaps the subtlest and most surprising of all the ways in which Claude Simon has set about denying us the consolations of vacancy is in a later novel, set in Barcelona, where the air is full not of dust but of pigeons. One of them, indeed, settles on a window-sill at the very start of the novel and perches like an evil omen in front of the narrator's inward eye. The restless, circular flights of the pigeons in *Le Palace* are one of this novel's several symbols for the circularity of the historical process itself, which is the main theme of the book: 'les centaines de taches claires et frémissantes s'entrecroisaient en dents de peigne sur des plans différents de gauche à droite ... comme un rideau mouvant par delà lequel, à travers la glace du bar, il lui semblait le voir intact ... le frémissant voile de pigeons ondulant, fléchissant, retombant, s'affaissant enfin, la muraille froide de la banque réapparaissant de nouveau ...' (p. 23).[8]

This is a much more significant passage than any naturalistic interpretation could ever reveal. Without ever for a moment having to warp the processes of nature for his own didactic ends, Simon has turned the pigeons into the humble but menacing messengers of his philosophy. Two quite separate temporal continua are involved in the passage quoted, the 'present' and a 'past', fifteen years before, when the narrator of the novel, now revisiting Barcelona, had been a Republican volunteer in the city, and when a building that is now a bank was the headquarters of the left-wing organization to which he had belonged. Thus the use of the pigeons as a 'rideau' or 'voile' is crucial, because they form an obstacle interposed between reality and the eye; at such

[8] the hundreds of bright, quivering spots interlocked like the teeth of combs on different planes from left to right ... like a moving curtain beyond which, through the glass in the bar, he seemed to be able to see it intact ... the quivering veil of pigeons undulating, sagging, falling, finally subsiding, the cold wall of the bank reappearing once more ...

moments we have the illusion of immobility because memory replaces perception, and it is only when the pigeons again settle that things return to what they actually are, or what they have become. In this particular case the image of revolt and the heroic attempt to direct the course of history to human ends have degenerated into an image of frozen rigidity (the downward movement is again accentuated by the behaviour of the birds) and an attempt to preserve the elusive stuff of life in a strong-room. Banks, and Simon has made this point even more directly in a subsequent novel, *Histoire*, belong to the mineral kingdom and not the vegetable; they stand for death and not for life.

It is clear that Claude Simon is obsessed by time in its negative, regressive role. The movement he detects within the substantial scene is one extremely hostile to all human pretention. Time regarded as a possible agent of progress or improvement in the individual or common lot does have a part to play, but this part, too, is a discouraging one. The favoured 'heroes' of Simon's novels are men who have made a crushing discovery: that time operates independently of human aspiration, so that progress, when it comes about, does so in a wholly fortuitous manner which is a further bitterly ironic comment on the optimism of reformers.

If Simon sees matter as a whole as a fixed container, whose contents undergo an unceasing osmosis, then he is bound to take a different view about matter in its secondary form, once it has been sectioned up (temporarily, of course) in accordance with human needs. Inanimate objects are capable of reminding us of our mortality, paradoxically, by being inanimate. In *La Corde raide* he writes: 'La mort se tient à côté de tous ces gens dans les choses. Les choses sur lesquelles ils s'asseyent, les choses dans lesquelles ils boivent, patientes, ironiques, méprisantes. La même table, la même banquette et les fantômes successifs, éphémères, de ceux qui viennent s'y asseoir, s'agitent, vivent et disparaissent, remplacés par d'autres' (p. 176).[9]

The object, then, will have a sinister part to play in his novels:

[9] Death stands beside all these people in things. The things they sit on, the things they drink out of, patient, ironic, scornful. The same table, the same seat and the successive, ephemeral ghosts of those who come and sit there, move about, live and die, replaced by others.

that of messenger, bearing the news of mortality from a previous historical epoch or simply a previous generation. It is given the status of a fossil, open to interpretation in all its uncomfortable lack of ambiguity. Simon, as one would expect, is fond of presenting objects in inventories, or heterogeneous collections, which suppress the idea of function and so stress their impersonality with regard to the human race that created them. In an early novel, *Gulliver*, for example, there is a long description of the random possessions of Herzog, an exiled Jewish intellectual, who has just been telling his visitor how he lost his belief in historicism:

Bert laissa errer son regard sur les enseignes d'artisans, les nymphes 1900, les peintures naïves ou d'aliénés, les automates, les reliures romantiques, les idoles polynésiennes, les images d'Epinal, les Républiques quarantehuitards coiffées du bonnet phrygien, aux effigies multipliées à profusion sous forme de bouteilles, de pressepapiers, en terre cuite, en fer forgé, en plomb, dressés de place en place au milieu du chaos, semblables aux incarnations d'une protéiforme, mythique et perplexe divinité . . . (p. 65).[10]

The divinity invoked, of course, is, in a sense, matter itself, but more striking than that is the type of object that Simon's description here, as so often, lingers on. The two periods of architecture and design from which he likes to choose his examples are the Baroque, and its more domestic relation, the Rococo, together with the Art Nouveau movement of the turn of this century. The resemblance between these styles lies, broadly speaking, in the fact that they abandon the straight lines and plain surfaces of more functional styles for a great amount of ornamentation and tension between structural elements. It is common for art historians to describe the Baroque as a painterly style of architecture, and Claude Simon can equally well be described as a painterly novelist. As a young man he studied painting under André Lhote and he

[10] Bert let his eye roam over the craftsmen's sign-boards, the 1900 nymphs, the paintings by primitives or mental patients, the automata, the romantic bindings, the Polynesian idols, the coloured picture-sheets, the Republics of '48 in their phrygian bonnets, with the profusion of effigies in the shape of bottles and paperweights, in terracotta, cast iron or lead, rising here and there in the midst of the chaos, like the incarnations of a protean, mythical and perplexing divinity . . .

has publicly expressed his regret at not having succeeded as an artist.

In his presentation of the world in his books, Simon is adamant, as I have suggested, in refusing any definition in time or space to isolated fragments of matter. His preoccupations are very close to those of Baroque architects, as summarized by that style's first great analyst, Heinrich Wölfflin: 'Unlike the contour, which gives the eye a definite and easily comprehensible direction to follow, a mass of light tends to a movement of dispersal, leading the eye to and fro; it has no bounds, no definite break in continuity, and on all sides it increases and decreases.'[11]

Simon in his mature novels has certainly suppressed all but the barest suggestion of contour. To return for a moment to the language of philosophy rather than that of the fine arts, he builds up his books in terms of successive fields of consciousness, or what Merleau–Ponty, in his notes on the novelist, called screens—by which he means that each actual perception (or memory) is the condition, or the stimulus, for the appearance in consciousness of a whole pseudo-world of other images. Whatever appears as an isolated element in Simon, therefore, and in his later novels this is always an image lodged in the memory, is the centre of a vast number of possible associations. It is clear that any one memory image, provided that it carries a sufficiently provocative emotional charge, might be an agent for the resurrection of a whole lifetime.

Simon sees the Baroque as the aesthetic expression of minds obsessed with transience. It is in the Baroque that we are made acutely conscious of the instability of forms, which appear to be forever on the point of disintegration; it is a style that lacks altogether the rectilinear confidence of the early Renaissance. Wölfflin makes an interesting leap into Hegelianism to draw attention to the way in which the Baroque can incarnate the relativism of an existentialist age: 'The baroque never offers us perfection and fulfilment, or the static calm of "being", only the unrest of change and the tension of transience.'[12]

These are precisely the implications of the term as it is found in Claude Simon. He uses it for example in the title of: *Le Vent:*

[11] *Renaissance and Baroque*, London, 1964, p. 31.
[12] ibid., p. 62.

tentative de restitution d'un retable baroque, where he indicates the
tension that underlies the novel, a tension also referred to in a
citation from Paul Valéry, as being between the forces of order
and those of disorder.
The Baroque embodies the last precarious stand made by the
will to order. The whole of *Le Palace* is dominated by the exuber-
ant architecture and fittings of the eponymous palace, before the
war a luxury hotel for rich South Americans. At the start of the
novel the narrator imagines the crucial moment of the building's
transformation into a revolutionary headquarters. Two files of
men wind up and down the staircase, one carrying out the extravagant and frenetic furnishings of the past, the other carrying in
the stark and functional equipment of the present. The contrast is
brutal, and it bears out what Simon first said about the Spanish
Civil War in *La Corde raide*, that it was an uprising not against a
particular regime but against the whole condition of man on
earth. Thus, when the revolutionaries take over, their first act is to
remove the evidence of their ultimate defeat, the futile curlicues
of a Gaudi-esque age. Fifteen years later, in the moment of the
narrator's final surrender, just before he commits suicide, it is
the building, now a bank but referred to here in its past as a
palace, which overwhelms him: 'à moins qu'à ce moment . . .
l'ombre du palace ne soit elle-même parvenue jusqu'à lui, le
recouvrant, le dispensant de bouger, l'absorbant, s'étendant sur
lui comme un linceul . . .' (p. 215).[13]
   Still in the same novel there is another striking example of all
that Simon hopes to convey by dwelling on a certain aesthetic
style like this: the extremely long and complete description he
gives of the label on a cigar-box. A superficial reading is sure to
see this as a move in the direction of an arid *chosisme*, but what
really matters is to note at what moment and in what circumstances the narrator's attention is focused on the cigar-box. In the
first place he chooses to examine it just after throwing away the
previous day's newspaper, discarding, that is to say, reading-
matter of a starker, more functional kind. In the second place he

[13] unless at that moment . . . the shadow of the palace had itself reached him,
   covering him, absolving him from moving, absorbing him, spreading
   over him like a shroud . . .

has been given the cigar-box by an American volunteer with the Spanish Republicans, who plays the part of what might be called the Wise Old Man in this novel, a part that Simon has written into most of his novels; the Wise Old Man's function is to initiate some naïve younger man, in this case the narrator, into the secret that life has no linear purpose. In the third place the box is, as by now we would expect, empty; it has lost therefore its own function, and the message it conveys is one of negativity, of absence, death, or what one will. The episode is a complex one, because it follows another well-known baroque mannerism, of which the *nouveau roman* is very fond, the *mise en abyme*, whereby the pattern of the whole is reflected or mirrored in certain of its parts. It is, as it happens, an extension of a parallel episode in *L'Herbe*, where the dying Aunt Marie, who can teach the next generation a lesson without even returning to consciousness, has passed on to her niece Louise, the narrator, a box of odds and ends, which the girl spends a long time trying to interpret; this interpretation is an intuitive one, for she is finally able to deduce from the attentive study of a photograph that the lesson of the dying aunt's life has been one of renunciation. Simon has used a photograph, or a whole series of them, in the same way in *Histoire*, a novel constructed around the discovery by the narrator of an old bundle of picture postcards sent years before his own birth by his dead father to his dead mother; these postcards are found piled in significant disorder in a chest of drawers in the family home and can be equated without difficulty with the contents of a memory.

There is one manufactured object in particular which acts as a *memento mori* in our lives, and that is a clock. Paradoxically, it is not the passage of the hands around the clock-face which Simon uses as a reminder of transience but the simple presence of the object itself. The clocks he describes are stopped; what he conveys is that it is our own intimate *temps vécu* that is under the threat of cessation, not impersonal or cosmic time, which we must suppose to continue without us. The clock in fact will survive those who consult it. In *L'Herbe*, for example, there is the description of a clock in a seedy hotel room, used, it is suggested, by many generations of furtive adulterers. It is built into the body of a semi-recumbent shepherdess, and dates, inevitably, from the eighteenth century: 'le tout . . . dans ce style rococo et poudré, comme si décidément toutes les pendules semblaient avoir été fabriquées en série par ce même siècle philosophique. . . .' (p. 90).[14]

There is added point to the presence of this clock above the adulterers' bed, because the act of sex, for Simon, is perhaps the most powerful reminder of all of the body's ultimate defeat by time. Moreover, the historical pattern that he alludes to in the passage from *L'Herbe*, by showing the clock itself to be the product of a doomed and frivolous age, shortly to be followed by the stern rectilinear morality of the French Revolution, is the same one as appears in *Le Palace*. The final flowerings of a desperate aesthetic like the rococo must inevitably lead, so it would seem, to a total revolt against the human condition; after which the whole cycle can start all over again.

This perdurability of the inanimate, which Claude Simon makes so much of, represents, in relation to novelistic tradition, a reversal of values; the presence of human beings is here guaranteed, as it were, by the presence of their artefacts. As physical survival comes to dominate the ethical philosophies of the modern world it is probable that the underlying resentment that Simon expresses, that objects should outlast their creators, will become a more potent force in people's attitudes.

What survives the human and social disintegration in *Le Palace* is the topography of the main square of the town; while all the characters and events of *Histoire* emerge as it were from the woodwork and the furnishings of the house in which the narrator, the last representative of a once prolific family, is now living alone.

Simon does not attempt to make the isolated object or fact stand out from the surrounding fictions with anything of the geometrical fervour of Robbe-Grillet, but he is making the same point; objects are irreducible facts and any attempt to turn them into permanent possessions is doomed.

In what ways, then, does he relate this alarming spectacle of the external world to the individual consciousness that experiences it?

[14] the whole thing . . . in that powdered rococo style, as if all clocks definitely seemed to have been mass-produced by that one philosophical century . . .

In the course of time, Simon's novels have become more and more rigorous adventures of the memory, as he has accepted the programme of the *nouveau roman*, whereby writing is shown to be concerned not with things themselves but with images in the human mind. 'Intentionality' is much more potent and revealing as an organizing principle amidst the litter of what our minds have retained than it is amidst the richness of immediate perception.

On the other hand, in a novel the act of perceiving and the act of remembering can quite simply be made homologous, provided that the novelist suppresses all explicit indications as to which is which. Epistemologically, the writing of fiction introduces a mode which is, in the words of one of the most perceptive critics and rigorous practitioners of the New Novel, Jean Ricardou, 'par-delà le réel et l'irréel'. It is not hard for a writer to conceal the different-iation between the visible and the invisible, at least until such time as the invisible elements become recognizably fantastic. With Claude Simon perception constantly stimulates memory, and one memory stimulates many more. Thus the articulation of his novels must often seem involuntary, and the feeling is strengthen-ed that their narrators are helpless victims, in danger of being crushed by the weight of their own past.

Each perception can be compared with Husserl's definition of an apprehension: 'The apprehension is a singling out, every per-ceived object having a background in experience. Around and about the paper lie books, pencils, ink-well and so forth, and these in a certain sense are also "perceived", perceptually there, in the field of intuition.'[15]

If the act of perception is taken as extending only as far as the moment when a sense-impression becomes an impression in the reflective consciousness then the relationship of the background objects to the one that has been singled out by an act of attention remains a public, or spatial one; but as soon as this impression recedes into the past it can be succeeded by other impressions whose relationship to the first is a wholly private and associative one, susceptible of explanation not by the laws of geometry but by the more problematical ones of dynamic psychology.

Simon introduces episodes into his novels which themselves

[15] *Ideas*, p. 117.

reflect in miniature (in what amounts to a *mise en abyme*) the conditions of the act of perceiving or remembering. In *Gulliver*, for example, there are no less than ten descriptions of car rides taken at night, with an emphasis laid on each occasion on the headlights of the car, as they pick out a rapidly unreeling ribbon of landscape by the side of the road. One is reminded that Merleau-Ponty describes an act of attention as revealing our world to us 'comme un projecteur éclaire des objets préexistants dans l'ombre' (*Phénoménologie de la perception*, p. 34).[16] Simon's use of a motor car is also intended to embody man's inability to escape from mechanical necessity; the flux of consciousness is a movement through time—indeed it is the succession of images that constitutes our inner time. (In *Le Palace*, in case there was any doubt of this, the chauffeur who drives the Republicans' car recklessly through the streets of Barcelona is directly identified with death itself.)

Increasingly in his novels, Simon has come to use artificial light to exemplify the field of consciousness when this is filled not with an immediate perception of the present, as might be held to be the case with the headlights in *Gulliver*, but with a reproduction of the past. The property of artificial lighting which he is therefore led to stress is its considerable power of distortion; his lighting effects are always theatrical, illuminating human faces from below, for example, as if by the footlights of a stage, so that the shadows of their features are inverted—or magnifying figures that should be human to the point where, this being memory, they are huge and portentous: 'leurs ombres déformées démesurées projetées sur le mur par la lanterne qui pendait à la hauteur du premier dans la vaste et lugubre cage d'escalier équipée à l'électricité et pourvue d'une ampoule trop faible qui les éclairait d'en-dessous étirait deux silhouettes noires géantes et courbées par leur fardeau . . .' (*Histoire*, p. 225).[17]

Since the burden in question is the dead body of the mother of

---

[16] the way a searchlight lights up objects pre-existing in the shadows.
[17] their deformed, exaggerated shadows thrown onto the wall by the lamp that hung level with the first floor in the huge lugubrious well of the staircase equipped with electricity and provided with an inadequate bulb which lit them from below elongated two gigantic black silhouettes bent under their burden . . .

E

this novel's narrator, and since the direction of the movement described is, once again, downwards, it is obvious that Simon constructs a passage like this to embody not only an epistemological statement about the way in which experiences, as they recede into the past, undergo ever more profound modifications of contour and balance, but also a metaphysical statement or conviction about the cheerless issue of all individual life.

One important distinction needs to be made here between sequences of perceptions of the external world and sequences of memories. The first are aligned in cosmic or public time, the second are a-temporal in respect of cosmic time and aligned only in the private time-scale of individual consciousness. In the memory what took place fifteen years before may, indeed will, lie alongside what happened yesterday, and the contiguity, which plays such an important part in a psycho-analysis or in a psycho-analytical interpretation of a dream, is what finally enables us to evaluate our own past and present.

The discontinuity of remembered experience is made very evident in Claude Simon's novels. One of his favourite expressions of it is the old silent picture, with its jerky movements and its abrupt cuts from one sequence of images to another. In *Histoire* he writes of the 'shattering discontinuity' of these films, so underlining the powerful emotional effect that a similar technique of presenting images can have in a novel, where the narrator, apparently unable to stem the flow of memories, finds his most disturbing secrets being revealed by the contiguity of apparently heterogeneous scenes from his past. Not that the tempo of this re-presentation ever matches that of the actual human mind; Simon frequently allows a single such scene to extend for twenty or more pages before there is a transition to another, brought into being because it shares the same emotional tone or some physical constituent with the previous one.

This discontinuity of the memory is paralleled by the temporal and spatial discontinuity of our perceptions. Because we are prisoners in time and space, the amount of direct evidence we can have of other lives and places is severely restricted. As Sartre's Roquentin discovered in the Bouville library, we are forced to project our own obsessions into the gaps in our knowledge, if we

are to turn a number of isolated facts into a coherent pattern.
Claude Simon has been aware of the implications of this right from
the start of his career. In his first novel, *Le Tricheur*, where the
story is told from several viewpoints, there is one character, a
Jewish watch-salesman—the obvious representative of impersonal, public time—whose knowledge of what is going on is
wholly external. Apart from one brief and futile attempt at intervention he remains an observer pure and simple, he sees what
anyone might see, granted his location in time and space. He sees,
for example, Louis, the central character, leave his hotel room and
later return to it, and sees him standing by the window before
going to bed. He does not know what we know, that in the
interval, the time-gap, Louis has committed the murder that
represents his hopeless attempt to correct the operations of chance,
and that by the time he stands in his window he has come to the
realization that the attempt *was* hopeless, and that he must hence-
forth accept the meaningless flux of existence.

There is nothing at all original about this technique, which
Simon has used to stress the terrible and ironic gap between
behaviouristic fact—our visual experience of the world and of
other people—and its invisible, problematical hinterland of
motive and feeling. It is simply the old device of dramatic irony,
whereby the reader is let into a secret denied to a protagonist, and
granted, as it were, the power to intervene in the pattern of events
by becoming morally involved in an individual's fate. Simon has
continued to rely in all his novels on this same divorce between
what is known and what is only imagined, but if it was only an
incidental element of the structure of *Le Tricheur* it has since become the keystone; in that book we are left in no doubt that what
Louis had been doing in his interval of invisibility actually took
place—the murder of the priest is given the same veridical status
as the events in the life of the watch-salesman. But in a novel like
La Route des Flandres we are made very aware all the time that what
links the few certain facts of George's reconstruction of his early
war experiences is pure fabrication, the stuff of fiction indeed. Near
the end of this novel Georges describes the group of four horse-
men, which includes the main characters of the story (with the
exception of the girl Corinne): 'les quatre hommes reliés entre eux

par un invisible et complexe réseau de forces d'impulsions
d'attractions ou de répulsions . . .' (p. 302).[18]

The elaboration of this invisible network is the substance of the
novel, but there is never any suggestion that what we end up with
is a definitive picture of their relationship. Simon makes things
doubly problematical in this novel, as he does elsewhere, by introducing more than one perspective on the events he is involved
with. These additional perspectives—what the jockey Iglesia
and George's fellow-prisoner Wack have to say or add—are also
part of the substance of the narrator's memory, so that we end up
with the complicated situation whereby we have to suppose that
Georges's own obsessions have also distorted what he remembers
of the obsessions of others. In point of fact this final complication
is not introduced into the novels until they have become wholly
interior and concerned with the images of a single memory: with
L'Herbe that is to say, since in Le Vent it would still seem that
what we have to deal with are the narrator's perceptions and not
his memories. But if we accept Simon's multiple perspectives at
their face value, as independent imaginings provoked by the same
set of phenomena, then their effect is to show up the relative
nature of all such reconstructions—the presence of other perspectives in fact prevents us from attributing too much finality to
the central one.

The obvious difficulty with this sort of structure concerns the
choice of the original facts, the necessary elements in and out of
which the fiction will weave its insubstantial thread. In Simon's
case there is clearly a large element of autobiography involved in
the selection of the facts, as well, presumably, as of the emotions
that lend them significance. The process is reminiscent of that of
Henry James, who built the baroque magnificence of *The Spoils
of Poynton*, as he admits in the Preface, from a single chance
remark overheard at a party. Claude Simon himself has claimed
to lack any ability to invent and a number of the themes and
even the characters of his later novels are present in embryo
in *La Corde raide*, where there is certainly no suggestion that
they are fictional. He has drawn heavily and directly on his

[18] the four men linked among themselves by a complex and invisible network of forces impulsions attractions or repulsions . . .

own life; his books have clearly involved him in a lot of self-exploration.

But this self-exploration is conducted in accordance with the precepts of the *nouveau roman*, in a succession of mental pictures and not in the abstraction of a conventional analysis of mental states. Simon has no conception of the self as somehow independent of its experiences. It is nothing more than the sum of its past: 'Je est d'autres. D'autres choses, d'autres odeurs, d'autres sons, d'autres personnes, d'autres lieux, d'autres temps . . .' (*La Corde raide*, p. 174).[19]

Consciousness in fact must always be consciousness *of* something. The phenomenological attempt to grasp the structure of pure consciousness involves, as we have seen, the bracketing of the natural world but not its abolition. All that happens, to adopt the language of the cinema, is that in the *nouveau roman* the camera angle takes on much more importance and is seen to determine ultimately the contents of each shot.

To say that I am the sum of my past is also to say that this past is ever-present, available for retrospective examination if a suitable stimulus be provided. Moreover, the past extends right up to the present moment, which is itself turned into the past by a simple act of retention. By itself this present moment is utterly meaningless, but it can be related to the past and, in a manner of speaking, orchestrated, by being set into an apparently meaningful sequence. Writing, for Claude Simon, is a prolonged act of retention, as he tries to keep a hold on the thoughts that have passed through his head since the moment he began writing. The pattern that characterizes his later novels therefore, where his technique has reached maturity, is a circular one, as the memories spread like ripples, out from the moment of composition. Once the process is under way the narrative line, the line that is to say of cosmic time, advances hardly at all. In *La Route des Flandres* there is time for Georges, the narrator, who is remembering his wartime past as he lies in bed with Corinne, the widow of his commanding officer, to be accused of not really loving her and to be attacked with a handbag; in *Le Palace* the present advances to

[19] I is others. Other things, other smells, other sounds, other people, other places, other times . . .

the point where the narrator commits suicide in an underground lavatory. In *Histoire* the present finally vanishes altogether, since the events of the narrator's day, as he goes about his business, emerge in undoubted sequence but are described in the past tense. But because Simon's narrators are shown as still embedded in time it means of course that any final hope of stability is suppressed —the present moment or the moment of composition is not to be the still centre from which they view a turning world, for it too is turning and with it their perspective on the past. This is a pattern made very clear in Michel Butor too. In his original review of *L'Herbe* Claude Ollier, himself one of the most uncompromising of the New Novelists, saw this novel as a desperate search for just such a still centre, one where time must have a stop, or where, in Sartrian terms, the impossible coincidence might be achieved between the *en-soi* and the *pour-soi*: 'la quête d'un moment privilégié, la saisie, dans le mouvement général, d'un instant d'immobilité, qui serait à la fois le centre de gravité, voire le but secret, de l'action . . .' (*N.N.R.F.*, January 1959, p. 137).[20]

Certainly the narrators of Simon's later novels have no hope of ever catching up with the present moment, because they are engaged on the impossible task of reflecting on an experience as it happens. Simon is fond of drawing attention to this inevitable gap between the act of perception and the act of reflection, with what one might call his separation symbols, membranes, partitions, and the like, which represent the final barrier that prevents the questing consciousness from merging with its experience: 'et entre sa paume et la peau soyeuse du bras, encore quelque chose, pas plus épais qu'une feuille de papier à cigarette, mais quelque chose s'interposant, c'est-à-dire la sensation du toucher éprouvé légèrement en retrait . . .' (*La Route des Flandres*, p. 238).[21]

The last few words make it clear that what we have to deal with is a time-lag, and it is this time-lag which will keep the narrator, or

---

[20] the search for a privileged moment, the apprehension, within the general movement, of an instant of immobility, which would be at once the centre of gravity, indeed the secret objective, of the action . . .

[21] and between his palm and the silky skin of the arm, still something, no thicker than a cigarette paper, but something interposing itself, that is to say the sensation of touch experienced after a slight delay . . .

the novelist, going, perpetuating a struggle which he knows to be a hopeless one. Simon in fact recognizes that even the present tense is a convention, and that the distortion of the outside world, which may begin with our perception of it and be aggravated by the processes of memory, is given further impetus still when we start to verbalize on the contents of that memory. And the further the lived present has receded into the past then the greater this distortion is likely to be—everyone must have had the experience of wondering whether some of the contents of his memory are fact or fiction, for in the perspective of time these categories seem easily to be reversed. The effect of this recession in time is, para-doxically, an increase in intensity, as the tangled complexities of the present moment or even the immediate past are refined down to the often mythic simplicities of the retained image.

The novelist who, like Claude Simon, deals in memory, has every right, by simple reference to our common experience, to introduce into his books figures that are caricatures of living human beings, reduced to little more than a single function. Because they are no longer caught up in the present flux of becom-ing they are free to be hypostasized as essences. Louise, the central figure in *L'Herbe*, reflects on this process in connection with two of Simon's most monumental figures, Pierre and Sabine, the one a mountainous, complaining body, the other a bedizened and pathe-tic queen of tragic opera, whose voices reach her from the next room: 'comme si elles lui parvenaient non pas simplement assourdies par l'interposition d'une mince épaisseur de briques mais de très loin dans l'espace ou le temps, ce recul leur conférant une sorte d'existence propre, les décantant, les dépouillant de tout ce qui dans la réalité (le contact direct avec la réalité) vient gêner notre perception . . .' (p. 168).[22]

It is the thin screen of bricks—the wall of a room—which reminds us therefore that a great deal of what is not immediate perception will be false, because it represents a gross impoverish-

---

[22] as if they were reaching her not simply muffled by the interposition of a thin partition of bricks but from far away in space or time, this remoteness conferring on them a sort of personal existence, decanting them, stripping them of everything which in reality (direct contact with reality) confuses our perceptions . . .

ment of reality as well as the intrusion of *a priori* judgements into the phenomenal scene.

In Simon's novels, as in those of Robbe-Grillet, the direct evidence of the eye can offer a temporary guarantee of moderation or balance in the mind, but as soon as some obstacle intervenes between the eye and its objective then the monsters and the myths are unleashed. This point is concisely made in *Histoire*, where the narrator is describing a horse-race, during the course of which horses and riders vanish behind a fold in the ground: 'puis les toques englouties elles aussi, le minuscule chapelet des pastilles multicolores disparaissant, puis un temps pendant lequel on pouvait les imaginer, apocalyptiques, galopant toujours . . .' (p. 64).[23]

What we have to deal with, therefore, is not the unity and equilibrium of perception, but the often gross and melodramatic distortions of a reality that has dissolved into a collection of images. The importance of the image that has survived is achieved at the expense of all that has not survived, all that we might have been able to call on to fill the gaps that now exist in our picture of past events. The unity of the flux can never be restored to our individual past; our attempts to set it in motion again must remain at a level of derisive artificiality. Writing of the 'unreal' world of the image Sartre says: 'Il faudra, si je veux le [the image] transformer, créer en fait d'autres objets; et, entre les uns et les autres, il y aura forcément des trous. De là un caractère discontinu, saccadé de l'objet en image: il apparaît, disparaît, revient et ce n'est plus le même; il est immobile et c'est en vain que je veux lui donner un mouvement . . .' (*L'Imaginaire*, p. 260).[24]

The adjective 'saccadé' is one which Claude Simon himself is constantly using to describe the motions of his human figures. In this way he establishes the distance between us, or the narrator,

[23] then the caps swallowed up as well, the tiny rosary of multicoloured lozenges vanishing, then an interval during which they could be imagined, apocalpytic, still galloping . . .

[24] If I want to transform it [the image] I will need to create in fact other objects; and, between these and the others, there will necessarily be gaps. Hence a discontinuous, staccato character of the object as image: it appears, disappears, returns and is no longer the same; it is motionless and I seek in vain to endow it with movement . . .

and them, and also draws attention to the fact that our equipment for recording the passage of experience, like that of the early cinema, is patently inadequate. But if the cinema was able to develop high-speed cameras and thus preserve an illusion of continuity, this is something denied to the human power of retention. With Claude Simon it is time that always turns out to be the enemy, time that undermines the very basis of our existence. He is concerned to show that every person and thing is trapped inescapably within the flow of time, and also to show how it is time that prevents us from making more than a token effort to recuperate our past. There is no such thing as stability or certainty in Simon's world—'Rien n'est sûr, rien n'est fixe',[25] he told an interviewer. These are the convictions he has set out, as a novelist, to make us share, and the attack he makes on our complacency is at the same time an attack on the complacency of the traditional forms of fiction, which assume that the gaps in our knowledge of the past can be filled by a remorseless and unambiguous logic. Simon will establish no definitive sequence of cause and effect, because to do so would involve playing the role of God. Like Robbe-Grillet or Butor he will limit himself to the play of the individual mind, presented in all its uncertainty and necessary relativity. He is not, as we shall see, without positive recommendations as to how we can best face our inevitable fate, but the foundations of his books, like the foundations of his philosophy, are rigorously negative. He will not allow the shadowy compensations of agnosticism to mitigate his severity.

II

As Simon's novels have become more explicitly confined within a single mind so they have also become more theatrical, and the human figures that jerk and gesticulate across the screen of consciousness are presented like actors in a poorly synchronized film, sometimes grotesque, sometimes imposing, but never wholly authentic presences. Moreover, most though not all the characters

[25] Nothing is certain, nothing is fixed.

of the novels are made doubly unauthentic because they are deprived of the self-knowledge which would keep them conscious of their ultimate annihilation and so make them more keenly involved in the natural world around them and less confident of the validity of their own actions.

Simon's chosen heroes, on the other hand, whose privileges I will enumerate later, are permitted the cruel but dignified recognition which came to Don Quixote only on his death-bed, that wisdom begins where knight-errantry ends, with a surrender of the will to the state of things as they are. At the centre of Claude Simon's world-view there stands some intimate disappointment; from the evidence of what he has put into his novels it might seem that this disappointment had to do with his experiences in Spain during the Civil War, although it is customary nowadays to date all such critical turning-points to early childhood, and to the subject's relations with his parents. What was enacted in Spain for Simon may therefore have been prepared years before; the important thing is to recognize that the metaphysical stance he has adopted, which professes the futility of all idealistic human endeavour, is an emotional and not a rational one.

The dialectical relationship between the permanence of substance and the ephemerality of its separate forms is reflected on the human plane as the relationship between the permanence of organic life as a whole and the passing away of individual men and women. Individuals replace one another unceasingly and their behaviour also bridges the generations, because the actions and interactions in which Claude Simon is interested are the instinctive ones, those basic, bodily encounters between people which he uses to divert our attention from any possible consolations to be had in the undeniable intellectual advance of the modern world. Simon's novels are full of scenes in which the characters are shown as acting out, in slightly changed circumstances, age-old patterns of behaviour. The sight of Barcelona's crowded trams, for example, reminds the narrator of *Le Palace* only too directly of the lorry-loads of militiamen driving frantically round the city years before: 'et peut-être était-ce toujours les mêmes (les mêmes camions, les mêmes gladiateurs) tournant et retournant autour des pâtés de maisons, comme dans ces opéras où les figurants à peine sortis de scène se dépêchent de galoper derrière le décor pour rentrer par le côté opposé . . .' (p. 224).[26]

By extension we are to see this as the pattern of history itself, with each generation going blindly through the motions of its predecessors, performers in a costume drama which we, the privileged onlookers, can never wholly take seriously. The only crime the actors are guilty of is their lack of self-awareness; they are made to look foolish because they think they are the first to have played these roles. Simon's novels contain many examples of this cyclical view of history, especially within the basic human unit of the family. By his technique of juxtaposing the present with different segments of the past he is able to show very powerfully how one conditions the other, and show us heredity as one of the forces that diminish the amount of freedom we have when we act.

There is a fine example of this in *La Route des Flandres*, where the death of de Reixach, the leader of the little group of cavalrymen that has survived the destruction of their regiment, and the husband of the woman with whom the narrator is sleeping as the events of the book occur to him, is presented more as a case of suicide than of death in action. The death of this particular de Reixach keeps merging in Georges's mind with that of one of his ancestors—a common ancestor as it happens—during the Revolutionary wars. This previous de Reixach's death has been handed down in the family as suicide following a military defeat, but there is a strong suggestion that it was the direct result of his having discovered his wife's infidelity. The parallels with the present situation are precise, since the second de Reixach may well suspect that his own wife has been unfaithful to him with his jockey Iglesia. It is difficult of course to decide whether it is the present that is conditioning Georges's view of the past or *vice versa*, and a further difficulty arises if we take the view that neither de Reixach's death need be seen as suicide, since all we have in either case is evidence of Georges's own obsessions, shedding the same light on both remote past and recent past. But even this would not

---

[26] and perhaps they were still the same ones (the same lorries, the same gladiators) turning and returning round the blocks of houses, like in those operas where as soon as they leave the stage the supporting cast go galloping off behind the scenery so as to come back on the other side . . .

seem to invalidate Simon's point, that all human activity is repetitive: it simply reminds us that any such final view of history depends on our own situation in time and space.

The pattern is similar in an earlier novel, *Le Vent*. Here Montès, the central character of the book though not in fact its narrator, returns to a part of France from which he had been removed thirty-five years before by his outraged mother, a few months after her wedding, when she discovered her husband making love to the maid. The events that follow Montès's return include an episode that mirrors this previous one. Hélène, the elder daughter of Montès's 'uncle', whose status in the novel is as the absurd representative of a bourgeois sense of propriety and order, discovers her maid in bed with a gypsy and drives her from the house. Both episodes embody the same simple conviction, that the order of respectability can never cope with the chaos of desire.

A final example can be found in *L'Herbe*, where Louise, the narrator, receives what amounts to a message from the dead, in the shape of a photograph belonging to her Aunt Marie, who lies dying upstairs. From studying it the girl concludes that the aunt had renounced many years before her chance of happiness with a young suitor in order to look after her brother, Pierre, who is now Louise's father-in-law. It is a similar act of renunciation to the one that Louise finally makes herself. At the start of the book it seems likely that she will leave her husband and escape the forces of heredity that weigh her down, but by the end she has accepted that her lover will never in fact come for her, and that she will never go after him. Nothing else has happened to suppress her apparent chance of escape, because Simon is not dealing with simple chains of cause and effect. But her whole stance towards her future has been tilted by the message she has received from the past, the intimation of mortality, and from now on she will accept, rather than indulge in futile gestures of revolt.

Here then we have an essential stage in the development of Simon's heroes, the recognition that our actions are determined from outside, and that our own reason or wills are puny instruments when they are compared with the juggernaut of blind chance. This recognition is to some degree cathartic, in that it represents an end to conflict, but such a term leaves out of account another side to Simon's determination, which is that we should apply ourselves heart and soul to the attentive study of what is, once we have stopped worrying about what might be. From this point of view Simon's first novel, *Le Tricheur* already looks forward to his mature fictions. Whenever Simon has used the verb 'tricher' he has always invoked its primary definition: that of correcting the operations of chance. As Ludovic Janvier points out in *Une parole exigeante* Simon recognizes three temptations towards the acceptance of fate: gambling, nature, and women; and those who resist these temptations, through trickery, revolution, or chastity can never finally hope to triumph.

Louis, in *Le Tricheur*, is determined to act, to impose his own will on the course of events. On the face of things his act is as nearly gratuitous as it could be, for he has decided to kill a priest in the town to which he has eloped. And yet the choice of victim proves itself to have been pre-determined by his own past, so that the murder of the priest suddenly turns from being an *acte gratuit* into a conditioned symbol of revolt against his heredity, centred on his mother. Louis's father had been killed in the First World War and his mother, now dead, had wanted him to become a priest. Ultimately the sacrificial victim is killed, and by Louis, but not of course in the manner he had planned. What had been intended as a bold and premeditated killing, face to face, with a revolver, turns into a furtive assault from behind, with a brick. The act no longer seems to be the end of a chain of reasoning but an instinctive movement over which Louis has no control:

A partir de ce moment, ça m'a pris et je n'ai plus pu l'arrêter. Je ne crois pas que ça se voie, mais ça secoue tout mon corps et j'entends battre mon cœur et c'est comme si je pouvais sentir le sang couler dans mes artères les parcourant des frissons, et je ne peux pas l'arrêter et je sens que maintenant c'est en dehors de moi, comme si la volonté était arrivé au sommet de son ascension, bloquée là avec un déclic qui ferme la porte par derrière et maintenant les forces courent toutes seules vers l'accomplissement . . . (p. 246).[27]

[27] From that moment on, it trapped me and I could no longer stop it. I don't think it shows but it shakes my whole body and I can hear my heart beating

So much, one might say, for what Simon calls in *La Corde raide*, 'les élégantes solutions offertes par M. Gide' (p. 36).[28] There are obvious parallels between the passage quoted above and another, more famous fictional murder, committed at much the same time, that of the Arab in *L'Etranger*. At the moment when he commits his crime, Louis, like Meursault, is not an autonomous agent but more an intermediary, controlled from outside, divorced from his action by a gap that Simon bridges with the necessity of a natural law and Camus with the connivance of a metaphorical Nature.

The central theme of Claude Simon's fiction is certainly this recognition that chance wins in the end, and that to try and fight it is a foolish waste of our short time on earth. Implacable necessity undermines all illusions of freedom of action, the a-temporal world of the mind must ultimately succumb to the temporal rule of the body. All attempts to shape the future come unpleasantly unstuck in Simon's books, especially in those cases, like *Le Tricheur*, where the protagonist's aims are achieved in a quite different way from that which he had intended. Cause and effect, the arrogance of ratiocination, may be applied to the past, inaccurately as we know by reference to the complexity of the present, but to apply it to the future is the height of absurdity.

Such is the lesson learnt in Simon's second novel, *Gulliver*, by Bert, who suddenly realizes, at a moment when he is busy playing the role of God and promising to provide railway tickets to help two people leave town, that one of the two is the girl with whom he is in love, Eliane de Chauvannes. His shock at this discovery turns him into a typically will-less Simon hero, last shown wandering defeated through the town, as night falls: 'il continuait, insensible au froid, insensible à la douleur qui lui brûlait

---

and it's as if I could feel the blood flowing in my arteries making shivers go through them, and I can't stop it and I feel that now it's outside me, as if the will had reached the top of its ascent and was locked there with a click that shuts the door behind it and now these forces are moving unaided towards their fulfilment . . .

[28] the elegant solutions offered by M. Gide.

l'orbite, à suivre au hasard rue après rue l'interminable dédale de tranchées noires, dans la nuit tombante envahissant le ciel tragiquement vaste, tragiquement vide' (p. 373).[29]

It is worth noting that the agency chosen to defeat Bert's own plans for Elaine is a railway train, another straightforward symbol for the mechanical necessity, barely exteriorized in his case, which defeats Louis in *Le Tricheur*.

The same recognition is made even more forcibly in Simon's third novel, *Le Sacre du printemps*. The central character, Bernard, is a mathematics student, and the figures he manipulates reflect his youthful idealism, his hopes of manipulating the world itself by premeditation. It is at the moment when he wipes them off his blackboard that he begins to admit defeat. The main thread of the narrative concerns Bernard's attempts to raise enough money on a ring to pay for an abortion. The girl, whom he fancies he loves, has in fact stolen the ring from her mother, and as the book develops it becomes the ironic, circular symbol of all those who would try and shape the future to their own ends. Ultimately the abortion is procured, because the girl is knocked down by a car and loses her child, a form of conveyance which, as we have already seen, Simon is fond of introducing as a symbol of immutable necessity. In this novel he is quite explicit about what lesson he is trying to teach us, it is not simply configured in events or images as in his later novels. Bernard's stepfather has made the great discovery during the Spanish Civil War—this must be taken as an indication that Simon himself lost his faith in revolution on the same occasion—and he has a long monologue near the end of the novel, when he explains to Bernard, who has hitherto despised him utterly, the significance of what has happened to him:

Voilà: le hasard, ou si tu préfères le vent, ou si tu préfères les engrenages bien réglés, ou le type de Calcutta, ou d'Antony, s'est, ou plutôt se sont chargés de réussir ce que vous vous êtes donné tellement de mal, toi depuis quarante-huit heures, elle depuis huit mois, pour

---

[29] he continued, indifferent to the cold, indifferent to the pain that was burning his eye-socket, to follow haphazardly street after street the interminable maze of black trenches, as the darkness gathered, invading the tragically vast, tragically empty sky.

rater. Plus besoin de bague maintenant ni de quoi que ce soit . . .
(p. 247).[30]

The ring, the traditional symbol of eternity, has passed down
from one generation to the next and its lesson has been learned. It
ends up, quite useless, in Bernard's pocket, though not before he
believes it to have been stolen by the girl-friend of the fence to
whom he is trying to sell it. The ring having disappeared after he
has slept with this girl himself, he is able to attribute her infidelity
to calculation but with his discovery of it still in his own pocket he
is forced into a final revaluation, recognizing that she was only
satisfying the instinctive needs of her body, that it is desire, not
mathematics, that drives society on.

The quotation from *Le Sacre du printemps* introduces the wind as
one of many possible synonyms for chance, for the blind energy of
matter which refuses to be controlled. It is not surprising that
Simon should have taken it as the title of his fourth novel, set in a
Southern French town where the wind blows almost incessantly.
The figure ripe for conversion in *Le Vent* is Montès, whose attempts
to intervene in the life of the town to which he comes, or rather
returns, are quite disastrous. Although there is nothing so clear-
cut as a single effect resulting from a single cause in Simon's later
fiction it can be safely said that because of Montès's presence two
murders ultimately take place. To use a well-worn critical analogy,
he is a catalyst.

Up until such time as he has learnt his lesson Montès is naïvely
anxious to impose order on chaos: 'cette volonté d'ordre, de
stabilité, de cette conception obstinément boy-scoutesque et
optimiste du monde à quoi il s'accroche, qu'il cherche à toute
force à préserver, à tenir pour vraie contre l'évidence même . . .'
(p. 149).[31]
Le Vent is so organized as to hint that Claude Simon believes

---

[30] There: chance, or if you prefer the wind, or if you prefer the well-regulated
gears, or the chap from Calcutta, or from Antony, has, or rather have
undertaken to effect what you, yourself for the last forty-eight hours and
she for the last eight months, had been taking so much trouble over
messing up. No more need of a ring now or of anything else . . .

[31] that will to order, to stability, to that obstinately boy-scoutish and optimistic conception of the world that he clings to, that he tries might and
main to preserve, to maintain as true against the evidence itself . . .

that the will to order is not simply helpless in the face of chaos but actually provokes chaos, for the whirling dance of particles around the figure of Montès is a very melodramatic one. Once it has begun to subside, after the death of Rose and her gypsy husband, and after Montès's failure to get custody of her two children, he goes to the railway station—a reminder of the ending of *Gulliver*—with Maurice, a pathetic fertilizer salesman, desperate for respect, who is certainly a failed blackmailer and possibly also an informer:

Et c'est pourquoi, je suppose, peu lui importait de savoir, de tirer au clair le rôle (néfaste, ignoble ou simplement fatal) que Maurice avait pu jouer dans tout cela, alors qu'il venait de voir ce monde, cet ordre au mythe duquel il s'accrochait avec une espèce de crainte superstitieuse et fétichiste, lui éclater sous le nez comme ces ballons d'enfant, ne lui laissant même pas entre les doigts les dérisoires réliques de quelques lambeaux de caoutchouc. Que Maurice fût une canaille ou non, cela avait peut-être une importance pour lui, Maurice, mais certainement pas (ou plutôt, à ce moment, certainement plus) pour Montès (p. 208).[32]

The moral equivalent therefore of Simon's prescribed acceptance of the flux is indifferentism. The sequence of adjectives in the first bracket in the passage above shows a decline from vigorous condemnation to complete permissiveness. Any moral stand represents a useless taking of sides against nature. What we have in *Le Vent*, as always with Simon, is the triumph of necessity, and to say that this is good or evil, just or unjust, is quite alien to his intentions. He is trying to establish a fundamental truth and, like Robbe-Grillet, he criticizes the philosophers of the absurd for erecting the absurd itself into an idol, and for positing a nonexistent ideal order of things against which reality can be measured and found wanting. In *La Corde raide* he admits that he himself took a long time to make the vital discovery that forms the

[32] And that is why, I imagine, he was not really worried about finding out, about elucidating the role (ill-fated, ignoble or simply fatal) that Maurice might have played in the whole thing, when he had just seen that world, that order to the myth of which he had clung with a sort of superstitious and fetishistic fear, burst in his face like those children's balloons, not even leaving him with the derisory remains of a few scraps of rubber between his fingers. Whether Maurice was a swine or not may have had some importance for Maurice himself, but certainly not (or rather, at this moment, certainly no longer) for Montès.

F

fulcrum of his world-view, the discovery, he writes: 'qu'il n'y avait rien à corriger, seulement à prendre . . .' (p. 64).[33] He connects this with what he learnt from Cézanne, that there was in Nature a great deal to 'take': 'cette somptueuse magnificence du monde, pourvu que l'on parvînt à en être conscient' (p. 64).[34]

It would be dishonest then to stress exclusively the negative side of Simon's novels; they are not an attempt to show us (despite *Le Palace*) that the logical way to acknowledge necessity is to commit suicide. What he wants us to do is simply to live in the constant presence of death, so that our awareness of the world we live in may be heightened and more truly personal. This of course is the Romantic ethic of so many twentieth-century writers, and has a religious dimension that gives it a very medieval ring. It is significant that *La Route des Flandres*, a novel by a man who offers us not the slightest hope of salvation outside time, was reprinted by the Club du Livre Chrétien. Claude Simon could be said to present us with a world that it would be simple to redeem, by a single irrational gesture, but this he has so far shown no signs of making.

The point where he parts company from the religious view of life's vanity is in his treatment of death. No trumpets sound for the departing hero in Simon because there is no other side for him to go to. The sky, as we have seen, is liable to be full of dust, or rain, or pigeons—reminding us perhaps of the materialist philosopher's consolation, such as it is: 'rien ne périt, tout change'. Death, for Claude Simon, as for Oscar Wilde's prison doctor, is but a scientific fact, a simple re-distribution of substance. But this disintegration, with its Lucretian overtones, is not a modern Epicureanism, inviting us to a life of sensual satisfactions, for Epicurus, like anyone else, believed what he wanted to believe, and no doubt looked forward to dissolution as enabling him to escape the attentions of some very capricious immortals. Simon's atheism is of a gloomier, post-Christian sort, and he sees the extinction of the individual as a wholly negative fact, as 'scandalously inconvenient', as he says in *La Corde Raide* (p. 53).

[33] that there was nothing to correct, simply to take.
[34] that sumptuous magnificence of the world, provided that one managed to become aware of it.

In this book he writes of his own experience of death during his war service in Flanders, death seen no longer as something abstract, happening to other people, but as something personal and immediate, so immediate that it is the continuation of life that seems remote and impersonal. He is at pains to de-sanctify the experience: 'J'ai été plusieurs fois assez près de la mort, mais si j'imagine comment cela serait passé si les choses avaient été jusqu'au bout, je ne vois rien que de très médiocre . . .' (p. 48).[35]

Death is simply a cessation in time, perhaps violent, perhaps not, it is in no sense a fitting or a holy conclusion towards which all life gracefully moves. If it endows a life retrospectively with significance then this can only be for other people, since we cannot live through our own death. From Simon's own experiences it would seem that the last contents of consciousness will be as heterogeneous as those of any other moment of life, but that their emotional tone will have changed: they will be more clamant and more intense.

The two novels most wholly under the sign of death are *L'Herbe* and *La Route des Flandres*. The first is dominated by the comatose body of Aunt Marie, who lies poised in a vegetal state, preceding her final absorption into the mineral world. Her raucous breathing seems to be audible all over the house, and through the closed shutters of her bedroom only a T of light is allowed to enter, the initial letter of the word 'temps':

retrouvant en face d'elle exactement à la même place sur l'oreiller le crâne nu, la main décharnée et jaune—la patte de poulet—allant et venant sans trêve, défroissant sans fin les plis imaginaires du drap sur la poitrine aussi plate qu'une poitrine d'homme, comme si, au fur et à mesure qu'elle prenait possession de ce corps la mort avait pour effet . . . de le dessexuer . . . (p. 112–3).[36]

---

[35] I have been pretty close to death several times, but if I imagine how it might have been if things had gone on right to the end, all that I can see is very mediocre . . .

[36] finding in front of her again in exactly the same place on the pillow the bare skull, the yellow fleshless hand—the hen's claw—moving to and fro without respite, endlessly smoothing out the imaginary creases in the sheet above the chest that was as flat as a man's, as if, as it took possession of the body, death was having the effect of depriving it of its sex . . .

Death presented like this cannot be seen as either dignified or melodramatic, it is just one more transformation among the many, and one which was foreshadowed in the moment of conception. *La Route des Flandres* is full of the deaths of men and animals, de Reixach, Wack, and above all that of the horse, which reappears three times in the course of the book, and around which, according to Simon himself, the whole construction of the novel revolves, in a pattern he likens to an ace of clubs. This horse, like Aunt Marie, is neither fully animal nor fully mineral:

le cheval ou plutôt ce qui avait été un cheval était presque entièrement recouvert—comme si on l'avait trempé dans un bol de café au lait, puis retiré—d'une boue liquide et gris-beige, déjà à moitié absorbé semblait-il par la terre, comme si celle-ci avait déjà sournoisement commencé à reprendre possession de ce qui était issu d'elle, n'avait vécu que par sa permission et son intermédiaire (c'est-à-dire l'herbe et l'avoine dont le cheval s'était nourri) et était destiné à y retourner, s'y dissoudre de nouveau . . . (p. 27).[37]

This first reminder that all flesh is fated to return into the ground comes to Georges, the narrator, just after the moment where he has made the crucial abdication from all attempts to organize the experiences he is remembering into any logical pattern. And what is equally important is that the whole of *La Route des Flandres* is brought to mind by the act of love, since Georges is now, some years after the war has ended, sleeping with Corinne, the widow of his wartime commander.

The sexual act, described with some frenzy and great frequency in Simon's novels, is an especially provocative reminder of mortality. The entry into the woman parallels the entry into the earth: Georges's position as he straddles Corinne is what jerks his mind back to a moment when he took cover in a ditch, to escape what he thought must be an inevitable German bullet. The

---

[37] the horse or rather what had been a horse was almost completely covered— as if it had been dipped into a cup of white coffee, then taken out again—in a liquid grey-beige mud, already half absorbed seemingly by the earth, as if the latter had already begun to take possession once more on the sly of what had issued from it, had lived only by its permission and its mediation (that is the grass and the oats on which the horse had been fed) and was destined to return to it, to be dissolved in it once more . . .

woman's pubic hair, always a focus of attention in the descriptions
of naked women, is constantly likened to vegetation or under-
growth to establish a more visceral equation between woman and
nature. In *L'Herbe*, where the almost tropical exuberance of the
vegetation is an urgent threat to all illusions of permanence and
stability, Louise, the narrator, is made love to in the grass. After
it is over she becomes aware of the crushed grass slowly straight-
ening itself again, resuming its inexorable growth. For the act of
sex involves an illusion of timelessness and of escape from our
unwanted solitude, but because, in our post-coital return to the
limits of self, we are made aware of the final frustration of our
hopes of a definitive communion; the act as a whole is a metaphysical one:

puis cela reflua se précipitant maintenant en sens inverse comme après
avoir buté contre un mur, quelque infranchissable obstacle qu'une
petite partie de nous-mêmes aurait réussi à dépasser en quelque sorte
par tromperie c'est-à-dire en trompant à la fois ce qui s'opposait à ce
qu'elle s'échappe se libère et nous-mêmes, quelque chose de furieux
frustré hurlant alors dans notre solitude frustrée, de nouveau empri-
sonné, heurtant avec fureur les parois les étroites et indépassables
limites . . . (p. 265).[38]

Simon is among those who see the sex act as the 'little death',
but it is an urge we must accept, just as we must accept the big
death. Those with a will to order, like Max in *Gulliver* or Bernard
in *Le Sacre du printemps*, can try chastity to stop the march of time,
but the results are disastrous. In *Histoire* the world itself, so reassuring and orderly in appearance, is described as capable of
suddenly returning to original chaos 'comme une vieille putain
retroussant ses jupes' (p. 66).[39]

Another aspect of sexual gratification which Simon naturally
stresses is the de-personalization which it involves: it is an act in

[38] then it flowed back rushing now in the opposite direction as if after
stumbling against a wall, some impassable obstacle that a small part of us
might have succeeded in getting past somehow by deception that is by
deceiving both what was opposed to its escaping to its being freed and
ourselves, something furious frustrated howling then in our frustrated
loneliness, once again imprisoned, striking furiously against the walls
the narrow and impassable limits . . .
[39] like an old whore lifting her skirts . . .

which the man turns into a mythical aggressor, the servant rather than the master of his sexual organ, itself often likened to a ram or a Cyclops. The orgasm, like war or commerce, is simply an act of exchange, subject to laws which it is beyond men to dominate.

But if sexual intercourse is one of those violent activities that connive at essential disorder, procreation is shown to be an attempt at preserving order, because it is clearly intended as controlling, at any rate in part, the future. This is brought out forcefully in *Le Vent*, where Hélène, the resplendently pregnant daughter of a very bourgeois family, discovers her maid in bed with a gypsy lover. She is appalled that this should be happening in the very next room to where her own children lie asleep, as if these children had in fact been produced by some discreet parthenogenesis. There is a stark confrontation between order and chaos: 'regardant, sans le voir, le corps, entièrement nu, de l'homme debout en face d'elle, brun, bosselé de muscles, avec, au milieu, cette espèce de tenon, de potence, de bourgeon de chair érigé de la touffeur fauve et moite, et la fille, la boniche, essayant de se couvrir sous le drap, mais sans doute elle (Hélène) ne la voyant pas plus que l'homme, c'est-à-dire dans leur réalité physique, violente, priapique . . .' (p. 114).[40]

The principle which Hélène represents is one which Claude Simon shows to be doomed, because it is an attempt to arrest the flux. The inevitable end of all such attempts will be defeat, either in acceptance or in suicide. Since the family might be thought to be a social unit capable of preserving some sort of stability amidst the wreckage, Simon always shows families at a moment of collapse or at least of decline. de Reixach, in *La Route des Flandres*, whose figure is frequently overlaid by that of his Conventional ancestor, has really signed his own death warrant by marrying Corinne, who represents the very opposite principle to himself, as is shown by what the jockey Iglesia has to say about

[40] looking, without seeing it, at the body, entirely naked, of the man standing facing her, brown, its muscles protruding, with, in the middle, that sort of tenon, the gibbet, the burgeoning flesh erect in the damp, tawny hair, and the girl, the maid, trying to cover herself with the sheet, but she (Helen) no doubt not seeing her any more than the man, that is in their physical, violent, priapic reality . . .

her: 'elle était non seulement une femme mais la femme la plus femme qu'il eût jamais vue, même en imagination . . .' (p. 40).[41]

It is inevitable, therefore, that Corinne will be unfaithful to de Reixach and that years later, after the war, it should be this overt messenger of chaos who brings the disorderly events of the novel into Georges's mind as they lie in bed together. No wonder de Reixach's last act is to brandish his sword uselessly at the German sniper who shoots him, an anachronistic, hereditary gesture that is his last, futile word against the fate that has crushed him.

The introduction of Corinne, like a germ of anarchy, into an ordered, traditional society is a pattern that can be traced right through Simon's novels. In the first of them, *Le Tricheur*, the artist Gautier, a man who has been near enough to death in the Great War to see through all the pretence of life, marries Cathérine, the daughter of an old family in decline, concerned these days with preserving a decent 'façade'. In *Gulliver* it is the grandmother who clings fiercely to the established order and code of behaviour, her two degenerate grandsons who live entirely by their instincts, their pygmy-sized minds derisively asked to control giants' bodies. The same conflict is repeated in *Le Palace*, where it is the unnamed Schoolmaster and Policeman who cling desperately to the hopes of a new order held out by the Republican uprising, and the cynical, worldly-wise American on the other hand who teaches the idealistic young student narrator an oblique lesson in acceptance, by means of the cigar-box already alluded to and some nocturnal love-making. In *Histoire*, again, the narrator's Uncle Charles is presented as a figure altogether alien to the grandiose life-style of the rest of his crumbling family.

Simon's view of society, therefore, like his view of matter, is a bleak one. Society represents a tension between the warring telluric forces of order and anarchy, and it is the forces of anarchy that are given the upper hand. The final victory will be theirs because we inhabit a Heraclitean universe in which all coagulations of matter, institutions as well as individuals, are destined for dissolution. Law and order are at best a convenient fiction, invoked to serve an immediate need, but without any lasting

[41] she was not only a woman but the most womanly woman he had ever seen, even in his imagination . . .

validity in times of stress. In *Le Tricheur* the hero Louis recalls having seen a simple-minded hunchback struggling in the hands of two policemen on a Sunday afternoon; the respectable bourgeois passers-by, out for their family walk, join in on the side of order with a desperation that is intended no doubt to indicate the futility of their gesture. While in *La Route des Flandres* the disintegration of the hierarchies of society in time of war is shown as total; de Reixach's upraised sword, or the local mayor's shotgun, are the last puny and insufficient weapons brandished to stay the disaster.

Human and social relationships are everywhere based on aggression in Simon's novels. There is the aggression of sex, the aggression of war, and the aggression of trade, which hardly need to be differentiated. This aggression is instinctive and inevitable, and authentic people will feel a need for it, to identify themselves with the world-process, like the girl Cécile in *Le Vent*, who finally gives herself to her boy-friend in real desperation. One of the most overt symbols for the totality of human endeavour which Simon has used is the rugby match in *Gulliver*, an angry brawl in the mud and drizzle, which ends, rather predictably, in a draw or, in French, a 'match nul', without either side having scored any points. In this way all finality is avoided, the to-ing and fro-ing will go on, without lasting advantage, the human equivalent of the closed world of matter, to which nothing will be added or taken away.

But just as the permanent constituent of that world, the totality of substance, is constantly being divided, by human needs or aspirations, into the separate configurations of our everyday experience, so the undifferentiated and blind libido which underlies all human activity will take on different forms according to historical or geographical circumstances. In particular the energy that once found an outlet in war now finds one in commerce. When Simon traces the history of a particular family this is the essential evolution; as we move towards the present-day the battlefield is abandoned for the market-place, and the great-grandson of the general becomes a shopkeeper. There is no suggestion of course that what we have here represents some sort of moral progress, nor that the law is irreversible and reveals a gradual entropy of human energy. It can operate within a single lifetime, as well as within successive generations; when they lay down their arms Simon's warriors tend to become business-men. There is the stepfather in *Le Sacre du Printemps*, a volunteer in the Spanish Civil War and now an antique dealer; Max Verdier, in *Gulliver*, also involved in the Civil War and later an arms dealer; the de Chavannes twins in the same book, resistance fighters then black marketeers; and above all the prisoners in *La Route des Flandres*, where the institution of the camp, following the collapse of the French army in Flanders, reads like a parable of the formation of human society itself. This allegory is foreshadowed in *La Corde raide*, where Simon reflects on his own prison camp experiences:

> Un monde, un monde libre, anarchique et pourtant parfaitement construit, et qui, sans souci des bornes qui le limitaient, faisait que sentinelles, barrières, règlements, s'effaçaient, devenaient seulement quelque chose de semblable aux habituelles fatalités et obligations qui pèsent sur toute réunion d'humains, mais extérieurs, et sans plus d'influence sur son développement que la maladie, les accidents ou la mort naturelle . . . (p. 135).[42]

Once the prisoners have become accustomed to the inevitable restrictions, directly compared as these are to the restrictions imposed on us by necessity itself, their life is dominated by exchange. In *La Route des Flandres* this exchange centres round the table where the prisoners sit playing cards, and the astonishingly heterogeneous assortment of objects they have managed to bring into captivity with them become the stakes. The exchange therefore is controlled quite directly by the operations of chance, and not by the decisions of the individual reason or will. It is presided over by the gods of commerce, two mythic figures of great presence, the one a Jew, the other simply a Mediterranean of indeterminate origin: 'le chef de jeu donc, le tenancier—ou banquier—un Maltais (ou Valencien, ou Sicilien: un mélange, un de ces produits bâtards et synthétiques de ports, de bas quartiers et

---

[42] A world, a free world, anarchic and yet perfectly constructed, and which, heedless of the boundaries that marked its limits, caused sentries, fences, regulations to be effaced, to become simply something like the habitual fatalities and obligations which weigh down on any gathering of men, but external, and with no more influence on its evolution than sickness, accidents or natural death . . .

d'îles de cette mer, cette vieille mare, cette antique matrice, creuset originel de tout négoce, de toute pensée et de toute ruse . . .)' (p. 218).[43]

These two figures are more than heightened embodiments of certain racial characteristics, they preside coolly and indifferently over the blind grubbings of mankind like harlot and procurer, exploiting instincts that will never die. They are no more to be resisted than the sexual impulse or the furies of war. In *Histoire*, it is Lambert, the narrator's school-friend, who presides over long passages of the book as an unsympathetic god of exchange: first as a malicious punster, lubriciously distorting the Latin sentences of the Mass in the school chapel (exchanging meanings that is to say); as a stamp-collector; and later as a shady trafficker during the German occupation. Lambert, needless to say, understands clearly the principles by which he lives: 'il sortait de ses poches pour nous épater cet inépuisable assortiment de billes de timbres en double de porte-mines de stylos de briquets . . . à échanger ou à revendre . . . et plus tard les journaux cochons, et plus tard encore ces déclarations sentencieuses débitées d'un air supérieur méprisant et sévère sur la constitution bio-chimique du cerveau ou les lois économiques des passions humaines . . .' (pp. 45–6).[44]

One reason why so many of these figures in Simon's later novels take on a simplified, superhuman stature is simply that they are seen as memory-images, pared of the pettiness of immediate perception. But there is of course another reason too, which is that they draw attention to the cyclical, repetitive movements of human history. They are the mythical figures who return again and again to remind us that nothing has changed fundamentally, that the superficial formulations of society may be different, but

[43] the chief gambler, therefore, the casino owner—or banker—a Maltese (or Valencian or Sicilian: a mixture, one of those bastard and synthetic products of ports, slums and islands in that sea, that old pond, that ancient matrix, the original melting-pot of all trade, all thought and all cunning . . .)

[44] he produced from his pockets in order to amaze us that inexhaustible assortment of marbles stamp swaps pencil-cases pens lighters . . . to exchange or to sell back . . . and later on smutty magazines, and later still those sentencious statements uttered with a superior scornful and stern air about the bio-chemical constitution of the brain or the economic laws of human passions . . .

that the basic urges of human behaviour remain. More than most novelists Simon deals in a very few 'types'; his heroes, whom I have already considered, his Wise Old Men, like the stepfather or Ceccaldi, in *Le Sacre du Printemps*, Iglesia the jockey, the American in *Le Palace* or Uncle Charles in *Histoire*; his Stop-the-World types, like Max Verdier, Suñer in *Le Sacre*, the Schoolmaster in *Le Palace*, or de Reixach. This typology is inevitable because everything and everybody must be polarized into the two possible camps, they must either fight disorder or accept it, and it is the function of the Wise Old Men to ferry converts from one camp to the other.

What Simon has to set out to achieve therefore is a large degree of depersonalization, because what concerns him is not our differences (apart from this one basic difference) but our underlying equality as members of the same race, confronted by the same ultimate fate. With his technique of casting systematic doubt on whatever evidence he is offering us about the past he can surround any human figure with a nimbus of uncertainty that effectively isolates him in one set of circumstances and one function. The one reasonably stable piece of evidence we have is his recurring presence in the field of consciousness, and it is this, paradoxically, that confers on the figure in question an air of unreality, like the revolutionaries whom the student remembers from Civil War days in Barcelona:

se tenant donc là, insolites, et même légèrement incroyables, légèrement irréels, légèrement désuets, parmi les fantômes potelés des servantes culbutées et des baigneuses surprises, comme s'ils étaient eux-mêmes quelque chose de pareil à des spectres prêts à réintégrer (ce qu'ils firent) l'endroit d'où ils étaient sortis; cette espèce d'inépuisable et vague réserve où se tiennent ceux que nous n'avons rencontrés que quelques heures ou que quelques jours, sans passé, sans avenir, échappant à ces fatidiques servitudes auxquelles sont habituellement soumis les humains, c'est-à-dire principalement de passer par des phases successives (l'enfance, l'adolescence, et à la fin l'inévitable décrépitude), de changer de visage, de vêtements, d'avoir un nom ... (*Le Palace*, p. 33).[45]

[45] standing there then, out of place, and even slightly unbelievable, slightly unreal, slightly antiquated, amidst the dimpled phantoms of tumbled maidservants and girls surprised while bathing, as if they were themselves

The memory then is the one realm in which we are to a certain extent free, since its images can become the playthings of the reflective consciousness. The memory generalizes in haste what is given to is as particular, and represents therefore a gross distortion of our actual experience. It is here that there intervenes a fundamental doubt as to Claude Simon's intentions as a novelist; is he using the novel to give us an authentic view of the world or not? In his later novels at least his vision of the cosmos is refracted through the consciousness of his narrators and one is left with the old problem of how closely one should identify this narrator with the novelist himself. The memory, he acknowledges, is a grossly distorting mirror of reality, but it is by studying these distortions that we can reconstruct the preoccupations which generate them. It would seem inevitable, therefore, that we should identify Simon's narrators absolutely with himself, for it is hard to believe he is proposing that we should take his world-view as wholly relative, and dependent on the fact, say, that Georges is sleeping with Corinne, when *La Route des Flandres* passes through his head. Rather one would think that Simon had put his narrator in this position in time and space in order to confer on his retrospective vision something more than a relative validity, and one that *does* offer us a final view of things. In a way, then, there is a point of stability in Simon, which is simply the recognition that stability or certainty are impossible and that everything is in a constant state of change. Since this recognition is made in every one of his novels it would be perverse to suggest that this did not represent some sort of irreducible absolute, a zero-point, by reference to which it is possible to organize our lives.

Simon is much concerned, though the point does not emerge very defiantly from his novels, with the existentialists' quest for

---

something similar to spectres ready to resume possession (which they did) of the place from which they had come; that sort of inexhaustible and vague reserve that contains the people we have only known for a few hours or a few days, without a past, without a future, eluding those fateful tyrannies to which human beings are habitually subject, that is principally to pass through successive phases (childhood, adolescence, and finally inevitable decrepitude), to change their faces, their clothes, to have a name . . .

authenticity. For him, this means allying oneself with the processes of nature in a way that may not seem obvious. In *La Corde raide* he makes it quite clear how much he admires the honest craftsman: 'Probablement le monde doit changer et se transformer, et il change et se transforme chaque fois qu'un homme accomplit quelque chose de bien fait, chaque fois qu'un ouvrier fait une table qui est une table dans sa vérité de table . . .' (p. 71).[46]
Here he fails to account truly for his own values: it is hard to see how the recommended alliance between man and nature, in the transformation of matter, can ever lead to aesthetic judgements of the nature of 'quelque chose de bien fait'. *All* work, however badly or well it is done, is surely acceptable on the premises from which Simon has started. At the heart then of his positive prospectus for how we should spend our days there lies an intuition, able to distinguish between the behaviour that is theatrical, or inauthentic, and the behaviour that is the expression of the real self. As the stepfather says in *Le Sacre du Printemps*, in the long speech which teaches Bernard a final lesson about life: 'le seul authentique service que l'on puisse rendre aux autres c'est d'être exactement soi-même' (p. 264).[47]

This is how he himself had come to realize that there was more worth in the gun-runners, the mercenary dockers, and the prostitutes with whom he came into contact during his experiences in Spain than there was in him, a young middle-class foreigner playing at being a revolutionary. Claude Simon's answer to the problem of acting in good faith is to remain as far as possible on an instinctive level (assuming anyway that work is an instinct and not a rationalization). Small wonder that he himself has always been presented to us, in the biographical notes sent out by his publishers, as a grape-farmer as well as a novelist. His profound recognition, displayed time and again in his novels, that all intellectual systems aimed at ransoming or ordering the past are hopelessly illusory, makes it strange that he should ever have set out to write books. From this point of view he is, like Robbe-Grillet, an anti-

[46] Probably the world has to change and be transformed, and it changes and is transformed each time a man achieves something that is well made, each time a workman makes a table which is a table in its truth as a table . . .
[47] the only authentic service we can render others is to be exactly ourselves.

novelist, using the novel to show us that the attempts of language to cope with reality are doomed. Simon shares the common human desire to rescue the past from oblivion but he refuses to share the illusion that it can ever be finally satisfied. There is thus a profound contradiction, or tension, in his novels, between the urge to reconstruct the past as densely and plausibly as possible and the perpetual recognition that any sort of certainty dies with the event.

III

The weapons with which Lewis Carroll's odd landing-party pursued the Snark were not well adapted to their purpose; to threaten the life of a monster with a railway-share is to make a gesture whose puny insufficiency reminds us uncomfortably of the metaphysical standing of godless man, hoping perhaps to derive from the Stock Exchange the sustenance he can no longer get from the cathedrals. It is a gesture that might also remind us of the insufficiency of language, itself articulated in time, to offer us anything but a derisory caricature of the glories (or complexities) of immediate experience. It is this insufficiency to which the *nouveau roman* is constantly drawing our attention, and nowhere more openly than in Claude Simon.

The only member of the Bellman's party, as it happens, who finally got to grips with the animal they were pursuing was the man who had forgotten both his name and his belongings, and who relied on his courage alone. But as everyone knows he softly and silently vanished away, an unfinished cry on his lips. The Snark proved to be a Boojum, and language failed at the last to imprison the reality of this discovery. Lewis Carroll's poem does not need to be restricted to any such exact meaning, but it is an accurate parable of the problems we have in expressing what is in our minds. Writing of Claude Simon, Merleau-Ponty says that in his novels 'Il s'agit de faire parler ce qui est senti',[48] a programme of appalling complexity; words can never, in the last resort, match either the intensity or the continuity of feelings, they are bound to

[48] What is felt has got to be made to speak.

remain a very rough approximation, and since to isolate a single
feeling or sequence of feelings is itself a gross distortion of our
conscious experience, it would seem that the attempt to preserve
a written record of it is peculiarly futile, or arrogant.

Language, therefore, for Claude Simon, belongs among those
naïve, fetishistic systems to which we cling in our need for reassurance. It is like the mathematics of Bernard in *Le Sacre du
printemps*, which represents his attempt at controlling the course
of time and which leads him to an ultimate equation: $x = 0$, what
is not known is nothing, it is the *néant*. The belief that language is
something more than an inadequate and ephemeral system of conventional notation is one which Simon gives to the illiterate to
hold, like the peasant father of Pierre, in *L'Herbe* and *La Route des
Flandres*. Pierre himself still subscribes to the inherited magic of
language, just as his wife, Sabine, subscribes to the gaudy magic of
the rings she wears on her fingers—there is a grim humour in the
episode in *L'Herbe* when she flushes one of them down the lavatory on a train journey. But Pierre's writing is reduced by Simon
to an empty ritual. He sits all day in his summer-house, covering
sheet after sheet of paper, but the effect is nil. The words ought to
be able to counteract the operations of time on his body, as he
grows grotesquely fat, but instead, by a bitter twist, they become
the waste product of his sedentary, almost motionless life. Writing
—we are never told what he writes about—is his only *raison
d'être*: 'la voix de son père, empreint de cette tristesse, de cet
intraitable et vacillant acharnement à se convaincre elle-même
sinon de l'utilité ou de la véracité de ce qu'elle disait, du moins
de l'utilité de croire à l'utilité de le dire . . .' (p. 36).[49]

But despite Pierre's desperate attempts to hold on to his belief
in the power of language, this is not passed on to his son Georges,
who reflects, in *L'Herbe*:

parce que je voudrais n'avoir jamais lu un livre, jamais touché un livre
de ma vie, ne même pas savoir qu'il existe quelque chose qui s'appelle
des livres, et même, si possible, ne même pas savoir, c'est-à-dire avoir

[49] the voice of his father, marked by that sadness, by that stubborn but
vacillating desperation to convince itself if not of the usefulness or the
truthfulness of what it was saying, then at least of the usefulness of
believing in the usefulness of saying it . . .

appris, c'est-à-dire m'être laissé apprendre, avoir été assez idiot pour croire ceux qui m'ont appris que des caractères alignés sur du papier blanc pouvaient signifier quelque chose d'autre que des caractères sur du papier blanc, c'est-à-dire exactement rien . . . (p. 152).[50]

The two great inadequacies of language, when it comes to recording our immediate experience, are that it is logical and that it is impersonal; it cannot hope to record fully what is chaotic and unique. 'The This of sense', says Hegel in *The Phenomenology of Mind*, 'which is "meant", cannot be reached by language, which belongs to consciousness, i.e. to what is inherently universal.'

Setting out to undermine the pretentions of the spoken or the written word, Claude Simon leaves little standing. He does not argue simply that language cannot do more than hint at the richness and complexity of an individual's relationship with the external world, he also argues that language cannot cope with a mental world either.

Each of Simon's later novels is therefore a record of language slithering about in a frantic attempt to keep its footing in a mental reality; its justification is as an incantation, neither useful nor harmful, providing we are kept constantly aware of its futility. It is hardly surprising that every time we are allowed into the summer-house where the self-doubting sorcerer Pierre sits continuing his alchemy it is dusk, and the words quickly merge into the background until they are indecipherable. Simon is clearly not going to allow us any chance of resurrecting the Proustian illusion that art is somehow absolved from the necessity of final disintegration; he has introduced a fifth-column into his own books, whose mines are timed to explode, not in a few years, like those of the new generation of 'throwaway' artists and writers, but here and now, as we read. What Simon almost seems to be demanding is that the print of his novels should be destroyed behind us, by some process of electrolysis, so that all we would be left with at the end would be our own discontinuous and imperfect recol-

[50] because I wish I'd never read a book, never touched a book in my life, or even known that there exists something called books, or even, if possible, known, that is to say learned, that is to say allowed myself to be taught, have been idiot enough to believe the people who taught me that characters lined up on blank paper could signify anything at all except characters on blank paper, that is precisely nothing . . .

lections of a vanished text; in this way the process of reading and that of living would be brought closer together.

By denying himself a form of consolation which creative artists have often relied on in the past, Simon takes another step towards allying himself with the ordinary man, whose powers of expression are not sufficient to enable him to objectify himself in a work of art. Writing, Simon says, is as simple as talking, it need take no account of the reactions of other people; what matters is that the writer, like everyone else, should act in good faith.

According to Simon to write is merely to keep a record of the continuous present, forever a step behind the mind as it were, and it is the process of composition itself which determines the direction which the imagination (or the memory) will take. Yet novels as complex as the ones we are concerned with do not give any impression of resulting from a sort of automatic writing, they are formidably elaborate structures with a satisfying shape to them, and they have been written over considerable periods of time.

There is no need, however, to be suspicious of Simon's own declaration about the genesis of what is, to date, by far the longest novel he has written, *Histoire*: 'Tout est parti des cartes postales',[51] because he also admits to the great number of alternative continuations presented to him as he writes, so that the ultimate shape of the novel is revealed, unexceptionally, to result at least in part from a conscious process of selection.

In *Histoire*, indeed, Simon has shown, more clearly than ever before, just how the act of writing is itself a metaphorical transposition of the process of exchange. The narrator of the novel is concerned with getting money and, after a fruitless visit to a bank manager in search of a loan, he sells a chest of drawers that is part of the furniture of the old family home in which he still lives. This chest of drawers contains the postcards that have given rise to the novel and can therefore be taken as a metaphor for the human mind itself, as the container of memories. The exchanging of the piece of furniture for bank-notes is thus a very complex act indeed; it is the exchange of substance for a fiduciary equivalent, still

[51] It all began with the postcards.

G

material (paper), yet of a purely symbolic value; the exchange of the past for the present; the exchange of the matter of the external world for its symbolic expression in words.

The whole of *Histoire* is dominated by the intimations or realizations of such acts of exchange, all of which are shown as representing a loss to the narrator. At the moment when he is lunching in a restaurant, for example, he sees the sequence of events as threefold: the writing by the waitress of his order, the mastication of the food, the arranging of the bank-notes with which he pays for his food in a drawer of the till: 'Mangez et buvez ainsi décomposé selon les trois règnes fondamentaux c'est-à-dire écrit, bio-chimique et économique . . .' (p. 147).[52]

It is the narrator's Uncle Charles in this novel who is accorded the status and prestige of the writer himself; he plays the part of the older man who has learned the lesson of life. Like the stepfather in *Le Sacre du printemps*, Uncle Charles pours scorn on his nephew's idealistic 'boy-scout' intervention in the Spanish Civil War. The narrator remembers his uncle in two different *milieux*, the family home in south-west France and an artist's studio in Paris, where he had gone as a young man in order to paint. In the family home he is represented as sitting in a permanently darkened room, surrounded by disorder and distilling alcohol; this activity is an obvious enough metaphor for the function of the novelist, likewise surrounded by what Simon refers to as 'le foisonnant et rigoureux désordre de la mémoire' (p. 273).[53] The darkness (or artificial light) in which the uncle sits stands for that momentary illusion of escape from time which the apparently a-temporal world of the memory can offer; but the exclusion of the destructive sunlight is no more complete in this case than in that of Aunt Marie in *L'Herbe*, for in both cases the menacing set-square or 'T' of natural light penetrates the closed shutters. Moreover, Uncle Charles is distilling alcohol, the agent of intoxication, the effects of which on the consciousness are to reveal to it the disturbing nature of a reality denied by familiarity: 'quand le monde visible se sépare en quelque sorte de vous perdant ce

---

[52] Eat and drink thus broken up in accordance with the three basic kingdoms, that is writing, bio-chemistry and economics . . .

[53] the abundant and rigorous disorder of the memory.

visage familier et rassurant qu'il a (parce qu'en réalité on ne le regarde pas) . . . les objets cessant de s'identifier avec les symboles verbaux par quoi nous les possédons . . .' (p. 177).[54]

Among the postcards sent by his father to his mother which the narrator finds in the chest of drawers in *Histoire* there is also a photograph showing his Uncle Charles in an artist's studio in Paris. This photograph clearly obsesses the mind of the narrator more completely than any of the other images he has discovered; he returns to it on numerous occasions throughout the novel and lends it a spurious but revealing animation by imagining the events that preceded and succeeded the scene portrayed by the camera. This shows a painter at his easel, not Uncle Charles, but a large Dutchman, whom Simon turns into the artist in general, or, by obvious extension, the novelist who uses, like himself, 'pictorial' techniques. He makes several direct comments on the relationship between the artist and the scene he is painting: 'la toile sur le chevalet lui apparaissant, de là où il se trouve . . . réduite presque à un simple trait, un peu plus épais que le montant du chevalet, comme la simple indication d'un plan, un écran, une séparation symbolique . . .' (pp. 277–8).[55]

This screen can be taken equally well as an easel, as a sheet of paper, or as human consciousness itself, none of which ultimately can do justice to the splendours of the material world when they attempt to reproduce them. Predictably, Simon stresses the grossly material body of the artist in the photograph, which he contrasts with his slender paint-brush, 'cet infime et dérisoire prolongement'.[56] But he ends on a note, if not of optimism then at least of a gentleness he has shown few signs of anywhere in his previous novels: 'Restant donc là . . . à regarder non pas un fragment d'incertaine réalité et un tas de viande flamande séparés par un écran, mais en quelque sorte deux parties du Hollandais . . . se

---

[54] when the visible world is somehow separated from you losing that familiar and reassuring face which it has (because in reality we do not look at it) . . . objects ceasing to identify themselves with the verbal symbols by which we take possession of them . . .

[55] the canvas on the easel appearing, from where he stands . . . to be reduced almost to a single line, a little bit thicker than the upright of the easel, like the simple indication of a plane, a screen, a symbolic separation . . .

[56] that trivial and derisory prolongation.

rejoindre et se réconcilier sur une mince trame de fils de lin . . .'
(p. 278).[57]

This proposition, that the painter (or writer) is able to achieve a
reconciliation on the canvas or the page of manuscript between
the body that is dragging him remorselessly downwards into the
earth and the immaterial vision of reality imprinted in his consciousness is the most direct suggestion that Claude Simon has yet
made that writing is for him a form of existential therapy.

Simon's decision to be a writer can also be understood as an act
of commitment to a doomed and otherwise speechless humanity.
In his books he has returned over and over again to the same
historical situations—the Spanish Civil War, the 1940 defeat of the
French Army, bourgeois family life in a town in south-west
France; and since the publication of *L'Herbe* he has underlined the
obsessive impulses of the creative imagination by dealing with the
affairs of a single family. *Histoire*, in particular, which takes up
once again several of the themes already treated in *La Route des
Flandres* and *Le Palace*, exploits a Balzacian *retour des personnages*;
but Simon, like Balzac, could quite easily rename the characters
in his earlier novels to fit in with this scheme, because their
relationships and functions are the same as those of the later
books.

As a preface to *La Corde raide* Simon has quoted Dostoevsky:
'Cependant il me semblait que tout cela méritait une sérieuse
attention, surtout pour celui qui n'est pas venu en simple specta-
teur, mais se range lui-même sincèrement et de bonne foi parmi
cette racaille' (p. 9).[58]

This book, moreover, is dedicated to some of his Catalan
friends from Civil War days. Simon has himself made the un-
nerving, stoic discovery that we must accept and even co-operate
with the meaningless flux and reflux of matter, and in his books
he is concerned to convey this discovery to us. The one great act

[57] Remaining there then . . . looking not at a fragment of uncertain reality
and a heap of Flemish flesh separated by a screen, but somehow at two parts
of the Dutchman . . . joining together and being reconciled on a thin tissue
of linen thread . . .

[58] However, it seemed to me that all this merited serious attention, especially
for a man who did not come simply as a spectator, but who sides sincerely
and in good faith with this riff-raff.

of sympathetic communication that takes place within the novels, as I have said, is that between the different incarnations of the Wise Old Man and the idealistic young one. This communication, explicit in an earlier book like *Le Sacre du printemps*, but more subtly conveyed in the language of things in *L'Herbe* or *Le Palace*, is another *mise en abyme*, a miniature reproduction within the text of what Simon sees as the purpose of his own books. This purpose is undeniably a moral one. Simon's morality is based of course on a thorough-going materialism, and he might himself shrink from applying the term 'morality' to anything except artificial codes of behaviour based on a certain idealism.

The power of the honest word, then, is not to suspend the passage of time but to recognize it. The word is made flesh, but like all flesh it is destined to perish, with a greater or lesser rapidity. It is simply an imprint left behind by reality as it passes, an artefact among other artefacts, with the status at best of a fossil. This is why Simon makes considerable use of newspaper headlines in his novels—the word in its most quickly perishable form. He shows them dislocated at once from their function, by placing them in such a position that the observer's view of them is interrupted. The process of their disintegration is of course a gradual one, as the meaning slowly drops away from the words, and as the world slowly reconstitutes itself, to deny any lasting validity to this ephemeral record. In *Le Palace*, for example, the student is constantly glimpsing newspaper headlines, first of all complete—'Quién ha muerto a Commandante Santiago?'—then reduced to 'Quién ha muerto a Comman', and finally, later on the same day, 'Quién ha muer'. In *Histoire* there is a different headline with a similar function as well as a similar theme, since it records the suicide of a girl who has jumped from a high window.

Since the effect of time (and language) is to turn a once living reality into a random assortment of fossils, or images, surviving in the memory, the work of the novelist might be compared to that of a palaeontologist, attempting to reconstruct a lost civilization from a few scattered relics. The gaps in his knowledge can be filled in by the imagination, as long as everyone is shown that the products of the imagination are hypothetical and not historical, and that they create a hypothesis which is only one of the infinite number of possible hypotheses, an arbitrary reality sub-tended by the preoccupations of the individual consciousness.

Two of the most striking features of the way in which Claude Simon writes are his use of alternatives and his refusal to move forward in a straight line. His novels are constructed as sequences of scenes of varying length; some of these remain completely static, others jerk into motion. Each scene is connected to the next one by means of what might be called a 'hinge'—some sense-datum common to both of them (Simon has himself described the memory and hence his novels as possessing 'une architecture purement sensorielle'), a common psychological substratum, based no doubt on Freud's own dictum, 'In a psychoanalysis one learns to interpret propinquity in time as representing connection in subject-matter', or a common linguistic content, such as a word with two divergent meanings, or a homophone. In his earlier novels Simon remained more truly cinematic, in that he generally relied on sense-impressions to lead from sequence to sequence; he has since become more linguistic and in *Histoire* it is more often a word that effects the same transformation.

Simon sometimes implies that these sequences of memories, privileged as they are by taking place wholly within the mind, are outside time altogether. Uncle Charles, for example, in *Histoire*, inhabits in his shuttered study 'un univers fixe où le temps ne s'écoulait pas à la même vitesse si tant est qu'il s'écoulât . . .' (p. 49).[59] What these sequences truly are, of course, is a-chrono-logical.

Unlike Robbe-Grillet Simon does not exaggerate the distinc-tions between images that are to be construed as facts and those that are to be construed as fiction. He is determined to avoid what to him would be an illusion of stability. Yet certain elements of his novels can be distinguished as co-ordinates, round which the narrator's, or the novelist's, imagination can play with freedom, and betray to us its intentions. It is only in Simon's more mature novels, starting with *Le Vent*, that these co-ordinates take on their true importance, trapped as they now are in the quicksands of systematic doubt and repetition. But he has never allowed any of

[59] a fixed universe in which time did not pass at the same speed, if indeed it passed at all . . .

his novels to unfold simply in the traditional pattern, where cosmic time and phenomenological time can be taken as one. The facts even of *Le Tricheur* are not presented in the order in which they happen. The form of this novel, like that of the one that followed it, *Gulliver*, is very close to that of the detective story. By varying the point of view Simon manages to finish the novel twice so to speak, the first time with a hole in the narrative, later to be filled when he recounts Louis's murder of the priest. *Gulliver* begins with a crime, the murder of the de Chavannes's family servant by a gang of Resistance *épurateurs*, and the rest of the novel explains the event in great detail by assembling information from various sources about the people involved and their past. But in these early novels the reconstruction of what we might call the invisible reality, the elements that have to be invented to fill in the gaps of the 'visible' reality, are given straightforwardly and not swathed in uncertainty. Hearsay evidence would seem just as valid as direct evidence. In the later novels this is not so. On the first page of *Le Vent*, for instance, the narrator, a very shadowy figure in this novel, introduces one of his prime sources of evidence for the story we are about to read, the local lawyer:

Et tandis que le notaire me parlait, se relançait encore—peut-être pour la dixième fois—sur cette histoire (ou du moins ce qu'il en savait, lui, ou du moins ce qu'il en imaginait, n'ayant eu des événements qui s'étaient déroulés depuis sept mois, comme chacun, comme leur propre héros, leurs propres acteurs, que cette connaissance fragmentaire, incomplète, faite d'une addition de brèves images, elles-mêmes incomplètement appréhendées par la vision, de paroles, elles-mêmes mal saisies, de sensations, elles-mêmes mal définies, et tout cela vague, plein de trous, de vides, auxquels l'imagination et une approximative logique s'efforçaient de remédier par une suite de hasardeuses déductions . . .) (p. 9).[60]

[60] And while the lawyer was speaking to me, launching himself once again— perhaps for the tenth time—on this story (or at least what he knew of it, or at least what he could imagine of it, having only had of the events that had taken place in the last seven months, like everyone else, like their own hero, their own actors, that fragmentary, incomplete knowledge, made up of a sum of brief images, themselves incompletely apprehended by the eye, of words, themselves wrongly understood, of sensations, themselves ill-defined, and the whole thing vague, full of holes, of gaps, for which the imagination and an approximate logic strove to compensate by a series of hazardous deductions . . .)

Thus the story of *Le Vent* is provided by evidence, itself not always reliable, from eye-witnesses plus a great deal of imagination. Apart from the lawyer, the narrator meets Montès himself and a number of other townspeople, and to the chaos of what he hears from them he will lend his own order, so that what we have to deal with is one man's imagination at work on the evidence of a lot of other people's imaginations. No wonder it is hard to determine just what the co-ordinates are in Simon's later novels. So much relentless undermining of the text throws us back ultimately on the present moment, on the sound of a voice, talking to us out of the dark.

We are told very little about the narrator in *Le Vent*, except that he is in the area to write a thesis on romanesque churches; what he finds himself writing, of course, as the sub-title of the novel shows, is something belonging to another and altogether, in Simon's terms, less reassuring aesthetic order, the Baroque. He may have had hopes of writing a book to match the simplicity of the earlier style, but events dictate otherwise, or rather the impossibility of separating events from the placenta of doubt in which they are born and then reborn. In the same way neither Louise in *L'Herbe*, Georges in *La Route des Flandres*, the student in *Le Palace*, or the narrator in *Histoire* are more than partly externalized. But they have learned, or are learning, the lesson of renunciation and they are there, refracting reality for us. Simon, like Butor, but unlike Robbe-Grillet, has not eliminated the intermediary consciousness of a narrator altogether, however closely he may identify himself with him or her. This identification is not, as we have seen, difficult for him to effect, because these narrators operate from a single, consistent viewpoint, the sombre viewpoint of Claude Simon. It might seem that by providing us as he does with an intermediary Simon is in danger of admitting a point of stability into his shifting universe, but this he has tried to avoid by allowing the narration to oscillate between the first and third person. The result is bewilderment, the reader having been wilfully disorientated.

These first and third persons can only be conjugations of the same person, and the problem is to decide why the shift takes place when it does from one to the other. A possible solution is provided to this question in *Histoire*, when the narrator suddenly switches into the first person as he is describing a scene we know to belong in the comparatively distant past, involving not himself but his uncle. This momentary identification is, therefore, a dynamic or affective one, a gage of the profound links that the narrator is in the process of discovering between his own situation and that of his uncle. Such an identification is, at the same time, the guarantee that the scene being described is largely the product of the narrator's imagination and the product of his fascinated contemplation of the photograph of his uncle in Paris, for identification of this sort is a cumulative effect and certainly not an instant displacement of consciousness.

A change from the third to the first person, then, should draw attention to a change in the degree of intensity of the images in the narrator's mind, and is a subtle indication to the *lecteur averti* that the narrator's most intimate concerns are being explored.

Histoire, apart from this single disconcerting shift, remains firmly rooted in the third person, but Simon's previous novel *Le Palace*, offers no such stability, since, for all the obvious interiority of the experiences which are recorded, it seems to lead to the suicide of the third-person narrator. If this episode, right at the end of the novel, is meant as a projection of the imagination into the future, then this would be the only time Simon had ever indulged himself in such a feeble stratagem—his concern, after all, is with the dynamic interplay of past and present. Instead, the only plausible conclusion as to his intentions is that this suicide has been deliberately made *impossible*, so that it should operate as a final lever of alienation between the reader of the novel and its narrator.

Another possible conclusion about Simon's modulations of the point of view is that he wants to stress the ultimate solipsism of the novelist who can only, since he is alone as he writes, explore the virtualities of his own being at the same time as he records the actualities of other people's. The action of another individual may be accurately registered, but its nimbus of intention is a projection by the observer. There is a striking passage in *Histoire* that can be invoked to support this view, when the narrator, himself waiting in a bank to try to borrow some money, observes the shadow-play of two figures removed from him by the characteristic symbol of separation—a glass partition. Inevitably, it is a freak of lighting which alerts us to the significance of the disposition of the figures:

la curieuse disposition de sources lumineuses qui a pour résultat de projeter à l'intérieur de la tête de l'un des interlocuteurs le buste du second, faisant que celui-ci semble occuper le centre même des pensées de l'autre, comme si ce dernier en parlant s'addressait non pas à la personne assise en face de lui mais en quelque sorte à l'image réduite de celui-ci projetée sur sa rétine ou formée dans son cerveau par son système optique . . . (p. 75).[61]

The only point from which it is always possible to examine Simon's novels is that of the reader himself. In the *nouveau roman*, as Maurice Blanchot has said, 'tout doit se déployer . . . comme dans la simultanéité d'un tableau'.[62] The time taken to read the novel, our own 'temps vécu', is the time it takes our eye to travel over the canvas of the artist. The direction which it takes cannot be wholly predicted, however skilful a painter may be in controlling our responses by the structure of his work; to that extent we are more the prisoners of a writer than we ever can be of a painter, even when we are invited by William Burroughs and other 'fold-in' writers to shuffle the pages of their books like a pack of cards and determine our own sequence of events. If we are ever to be made free of the writer's dictates and entirely responsible for the order of what we read then it would seem that we must be given not lengthy syntagma like whole pages to juggle with, but the final reduction of the original into isolated words, or perhaps even morphemes. Until such a time as that the novelist, however humble, must go on presenting us with images arranged in a certain order, while at the same time drawing our attention to the fact that this order is purely relative and transient.

Claude Simon of course needs to seek an order, a structure, to match that of the continuous present, at the moment when it

---

[61] the result of the curious arrangement of the sources of light being to project the bust of the second speaker inside the head of the first, in such a way that the former seems to occupy the very centre of the other's thoughts, as if the latter as he talked was addressing himself not to the person sitting opposite him but somehow to the scaled-down image projected on his retina or formed in his brain by his optic system . . .

[62] everything must be deployed . . . as in the simultaneity of a painting.

turns into the past. If he were to be perfectly rigorous about this he would have to start each novel in mid-sentence, mid-clause or even mid-word, and leave it in the same state of suspension, for only in this way can he show that what we are about to read is an arbitrary instant of a particular consciousness, detached quite artificially from the instants that precede and succeed it. But although Simon's sentences are long they are not endless. He accepts the need for a few signposts, like chapter divisions and even punctuation, but at the same time he makes it quite clear that these are conventions, without equivalent in the chemistry of the brain. In *La Route des Flandres* and *Le Palace*, for example, the divisions between chapters are in a sense nullified, because the first few lines of the succeeding chapter merely repeat the last few lines of the first one, a neat reminder of the phenomenological insistence that each state of consciousness is imbricated within the next and that each moment contains the sum of all those that have preceded it. The text of *Histoire*, all 400 pages of it, is broken up now and again but to no apparent system, since the novel is really one continuous sentence.

Simon makes, as one would expect, the same contemptuous use of words that normally express a logical connection between two isolated phenomena. Professor Guicharnaud marks as one of the three chief characteristics of his prose: 'A superabundance of logical tools such as "donc", "de sorte que", etc., but stripped of their normal functions, emphasizing the desperate effort of reason to affirm order, actually the débris of reason's defeat.'[63]

While this is true it does not take account of the subtlety which Simon often shows in his use of a word like 'donc'. Gone certainly is its normal function as a monolithic rationalization of a sequence of events; yet it can still retain the power to disclose the true determinism that Simon sees as marking what we do, as an example like the following from *La Route des Flandres* may show:

Georges déclarant qu'il avait décidé de s'occuper des terres, et soutenu (quoiqu'il fît semblant de ne pas l'entendre, quoique affectant de leur parler à tous deux également, et tourné cependant ostensiblement vers elle seule et se détournant ostensiblement de son père, et cependant s'addressant à lui, et ne tenant ostensiblement aucun compte d'elle ou

[63] *Yale French Studies*, no. 24, p. 105.

de ce qu'elle pouvait dire) soutenu, donc, par la bruyante, obscène et utérine approbation de Sabine . . . (p. 233).[64]

The effect of the long parenthesis here is to add weight to the word that discloses just how Georges's decision has been conditioned: 'soutenu', which needs to be read in conjunction above all with the epithet 'utérine', since Sabine is the mother of Georges, and the representative in his life of the force of heredity. The use of 'donc' is ironic only to the extent that nothing of what we have learned from the bracket of the visible disposition of the three characters involved, Georges, his father and his mother, justifies its use. In fact to judge by appearances this conjunction is wildly out of place, but we have of course already been alerted to the notion that appearances are deceptive by the repetition of the conditional 'quoique' and the adverb 'ostensiblement'. And while Georges's body is turned towards his mother, his voice is directed at his father; in Simon's scheme of priorities between body and voice (or language) it is the first which always wins. It is the woman, therefore, who stands for the pull away from the reason and towards the earth and death. 'Donc' may have lost its normal function but it would seem, in a case like this, to have acquired another, more visceral one.

This passage from *La Route des Flandres* also serves to introduce another of the highly characteristic typographical devices of Simon's books—the brackets he uses so freely, and which sometimes give birth to brackets within the brackets. This sort of proliferation models the tendency towards dispersion of the human mind; the brackets are an indication that each moment of Simon's text is a focus of multiple associations, that he has selected one of these associations when he might with equal necessity have selected another.

Thus the brackets are just one of the ways in which Simon can avoid any tendency towards a chronological flow in the narrative;

[64] Georges stating that he had decided to look after the property, and supported (although he pretended not to hear her, although affecting to be talking to both of them equally, and yet turned ostensibly towards her alone and turning ostensibly away from his father, and yet adressing himself to him, and paying no attention ostensibly to her or to what she might say) supported, then, by the noisy, obscene and uterine approval of Sabine . . .

the proliferating clauses that crowd in between the subject of a sentence and its verb, to the point where the connection between the two is quite lost to view, are the principal agent of destruction. He makes it obvious that there is absolutely no limit to the potential number of these interruptions or digressions, because they are the actual substance, the gelatine, in which people and events are trapped, the insufficient but menacing paradigm for time itself. Things cannot be said to begin or end in Simon, they appear and disappear. There are a large number of references in the novels to things appearing as if by magic; one minute they are visible and the next they are not. What he is dealing with in fact are not events but states.

To preserve the impression of stasis it is clear that the key to Simon's narrative technique must be his use of the verb, and the most striking and most commented-on feature of his books is their obsession with the present participle, which is no doubt why he has so often been compared with William Faulkner. Granted Simon's preoccupations, the present participles are inevitable, for only by using them can he prevent the narrative from going somewhere, and from giving us an unwanted impression of logical succession. To an interviewer he said: 'L'emploi du participe présent me permet de me placer hors du temps conventionnel.'[65]

Conventional time is cosmic time, and Simon depends on the present participle to situate the action in the mind's time, in the here and now. This form of the verb, used as a narrative device, denies the action it describes any recognizable beginning or end, and preserves the discontinuity of memory. A movement conveyed in a present participle is an element in a mental picture, it is an image and thus a denial of chronological reality. By stringing together sequences of present participles, Simon conveys a succession of movements in which one movement merely replaces the other, divorced from any external temporal reference and its implications of a narrow, non-dynamic causality.

Moreover, the present participle also has the effect of diminishing the importance of the agent in any action. By using it Simon withdraws the primacy from the agent and gives it to the act, which is thus partly depersonalized—a procedure that is bound to

[65] The use of the present participle enables me to place myself outside conventional time.

remind one of what is involved in Husserl's *epochè* or 'eidetic reduction' where the act of perception becomes more important than either the perceiver or the perceived.

The present participle rejects the idea of finality, in both the temporal and the purposive sense but it is not a neutral, inexpressive form, because it can easily turn the agent into a victim, struggling with forces outside his control or forces able to divert his energy towards ends of their own. A random example from *Le Palace* shows how, by alternating between an active verb and a present participle, Simon delimits the authority of man over matter: 'se cognant aux meubles dans l'obscurité il atteignait la chaise, tâtonnant sur le dossier, puis sur le siège, puis par terre à la recherche de son pantalon qu'il saisit enfin, tournant et retournant un moment le tas d'étoffe flasque pour trouver la ceinture et qu'il réussit enfin à passer' (p. 188).[66]

The moments of achievement are recorded in one imperfect and two *passés simples*, the moments of failure with the present participle, and if it is the present participle that ultimately seems to dominate Simon's narrative technique then this is because his theme is defeat, defeat not just for the recognizable individual but for the great mass of humanity, without exception.

There is also good reason for him to make use of the past participle. The past participle, used adjectivally, contains of course the evidence of an action; it is a very handy tool for a writer who sees inanimate objects as the repository of the past, as fossils with a message for the present. A description of the palace itself in the novel that bears its name provides a good example: 'comme si les pierres taillées, transportées, entassées et louées ensuite contre les bénéfices tirés de la vente de la sueur racoltée dans les champs de tabac . . .' (p. 188).[67]

The effect is vertiginous, as the participles open up avenues in time and space, avenues that Simon is concerned to acknowledge

[66] banging into the furniture in the darkness he reached the chair, feeling along the back, then on the seat, then on the ground hunting for his trousers which he finally got hold of, turning the heap of limp material this way and that for a moment so as to find the belt and which he finally succeeded in getting on.

[67] as if the stones, shaped, transported, piled up and then let against the profits derived from the sale of sweat harvested in the fields of tobacco . . .

but not to explore. What he wants us to feel above all is that this building is an end-product, the result of a process which, if we tried to follow it back in time, would lead us into impossible ramifications and involve eventually a large part of the human race. By using a succession of past participles, as he does here, just as he uses successions of present participles, he manages to turn them into a narrative device. The function of the building in this novel is to represent to the student the weight of the past and the threat of disintegration, and it is the participles that make this threat a potent one, by giving the masonry a history and showing it as the petrifaction of a vast complex of human interaction. The building has survived and the people have gone; Simon's lesson is not a new one.

Like all such doomed efforts to overcome time Simon's style is essentially baroque, in its restless refusal to draw straight lines or to recognize some ultimate point of stability. His is a literary structure frozen miraculously at the moment of collapse, an ephemeral moment of equilibrium between the forces of order and the forces of chaos. Like a seventeenth-century architect he introduces light to remind us of the dark, and he patterns small details to remind us of the pattern of the whole. This is a painterly style and it suggests that Simon believes more in pictures than in words. Certainly in his later novels the agonized self-questioning of the narrators—'comment savoir?', 'comment était-ce?'—makes one more than ever conscious of the utter fragility of the logos's power to make any sort of order out of chaos.

By deciding, after *Le Sacre du printemps*, to change from an explicit to an implicit way of writing, Simon qualified himself to be discussed in terms of the *nouveau roman*. It was the same decision that has enabled him to make us share more fully his own experience of the flux. The number of indications in his later novels that stop us indentifying absolutely with the narrator are reduced to a minimum; we can fill our own field of vision with the disturbing contents of his. But if we then want to satisfy a basic human need and order these contents for ourselves into some sort of logical pattern, we must of course reassemble it. In this way Simon destroys the last remaining chance of finding a point of rest, for it would seem that the process of reading and reflecting on what we have read must itself add to the ceaseless 'va-et-vient' of particles.

MICHEL BUTOR

'*my past is given only by memory and is characterised in memory* as *my past, a past present—that is: an intentional modification.*'

E. HUSSERL. Cartesian Meditations.

I

IF, for Claude Simon, the novel has come more and more to be built in the image of his baroque palace, a wave improbably frozen for a moment before it crashes down and engulfs us, then for Michel Butor, more overtly a moralist, it is a cathedral, or at least a column towards a future cathedral, a monument into which we will be able to withdraw in search of purification from our sins. Butor, like Simon, is concerned above all else with the great weight of the past, accumulated as it is behind each of our actions in cosmic time. And again like Simon he is engaged on a quest for authenticity, to find the form of self-expression that will enable us to become fully human and rise above mere biological necessity.

But Butor is an altogether more hopeful writer, and suggests that if we set about assuming our own past sincerely we can indeed bring about a revolution, in the rational conduct of our own lives. In this he represents the optimism inherent in the phenomenological programme, where the word is seen as having a privileged position among the possible forms of self-expression.

Each of Butor's more substantial literary works is primarily a sermon to this text: that it is only by bringing into the light of language and syntax the speechless urges which breed in oblivion, that we can hope to make the world a more rational place to live in. Before he became a writer Butor was a teacher in France, but more especially abroad, and the didactic will is strong in him to teach the human race a lesson. This lesson is a hidden one, how-ever, and hard to uncover, since it is implicit in the structure of what he writes, never conceptualized. As a critic, Butor himself has been impressively assured and lucid in exposing the secret lessons taught by other writers of the past, by a thorough and self-effacing examination of their texts, and it his own type of criticism that his novels demand and deserve. These novels, and other pieces of writing that must be classed as fiction, are without doubt the most formidably intellectual of all the fabrications of the *nouveau roman*. They lack the sensual intensity of Claude Simon's novels or the bawdy humour of Robbe-Grillet's, and are so austere-ly exemplary that it is no surprise that since 1960 Butor should have moved farther and farther away from the novel as such, into experiments such as his opera, *Votre Faust*, or his extremely complex stereophonic radio productions, *Réseau aérien* and *6 810 000 litres d'eau par seconde*. He is very self-consciously a man of his time—he once told an interviewer that he did not want to *be* contemporary but to *become* contemporary, an elegant distinction showing a refusal to be lulled into any essentialist fallacies; he has clearly come to regret the limitations of the novel form.

Butor has published only four texts that can be classified as novels: *Passage de Milan, L'Emploi du temps, La Modification*, and *Degrés*. But he has been by far the most prolific of the three writers studied in this book, as poet, critic of writing and painting, librettist, stereophonic playwright and journalist, as well as novelist. All his work, however, shows the same preoccupations as the handful of novels, even when he becomes a critic of writers as apparently remote from the present as Montaigne.

Butor himself sees no great divergence between his activities as novelist and his activities as critic, because of his awareness of the tradition of the French novel. For him, a novel must be a form of criticism because it stands in a certain relationship to all the novels that have preceded it or, if not all the novels, then at least those that the novelist himself has read. The new novelist writes a novel because no existent one, so far as he knows, says what he wants to say; his aim is to correct or supplement the existing stock of novels by invention. Hence we have, says Butor, 'critique et

H

invention se révélant comme deux aspects d'une même activité'.[1] for just as the creator criticizes by inventing, so the critic invents by criticizing, since he selects those elements of the reality confronting him—the work or *œuvre* of an artist—and arranges them in such a way as to explain that artist's intentions.

It is a striking achievement of Butor to have been able to apply this same sense of the dialectical movement in artistic creation to painting, to the point where it becomes possible to add to the concept of the anti-novel that of the anti-picture, one which is painted in order to decry certain pictorial conventions which the artist sees as outmoded. Butor's prime conviction as a critic, therefore, is the valuable one that all artistic creation takes place in an artistic atmosphere, that the creator's impulse must come in part from the desire to modify a view of reality which is no longer in accord with the facts of reality. This is especially true of the present day and of contemporary writing, when, Butor writes, 'Toute invention littéraire se produit à l'intérieur d'un milieu déjà saturé de littérature' (*Répertoire* 3, p. 7).[2]

There are already so many novels in existence that no one has the time to read them all, yet still writers suffer the compulsion of adding to the number. Why? Butor's answer, which is the justification of the novels he has written himself, is that the need for renewal is constant if we are to live in the present and not in a congealed moment of the past; and that a literature, or literature *tout court*, is a monument built in time, a cumulative and continuous undertaking of right-minded men. It is, as it were, the inscription which men add to the material world.

Butor has investigated, often in very unexpected ways, the physical properties of the printed word and its role in our physical environment. In an essay called 'Le Livre comme objet', for example, he links the dignity and the ethical possibilities of the book with its capacity to survive the act of reading: 'De l'objet de consommation au sens le plus trivial du terme, on passe à l'objet d'étude et de contemplation, qui nourrit sans se consumer, qui

[1] criticism and invention proving themselves to be two aspects of a single activity.
[2] All literary invention is produced within an environment already saturated with literature.

transforme la façon dont nous connaissons et habitons l'univers' (*Répertoire* 2, p. 92).[3]

The book thus acquires a third dimension. Having read it, or even while we are still reading it, we can turn back to a previous page (or turn on to a later one), a freedom for the reader in respect of the author denied to the audience in a cinema or a theatre, but one which we take for granted, as Butor is ready to point out, in respect of the books we use most and analyse least, telephone directories and dictionaries.

Butor has criticized writers for not exploiting this extra dimension, and for adhering blindly to a rigid linear progression from page to page. He has not ignored it himself, in fact he has grown increasingly ready to make use of it. His four novels are still to be read in a traditional sequence, line after line, but the same is quite untrue of subsequent works, like *Mobile*, a 'study for a representation' of the United States, or *6 810 000 litres d'eau par seconde*, which sets out to recreate the scene of Niagara Falls with some completeness; here the reader is invited to determine his own route through the text, which is laid out in such a way as to make a consecutive reading almost completely nonsensical. Butor's arguments are extremely convincing in favour of more and more thoughtful and elaborate layouts of the printed page, with the writer seeking a personal but by no means hermetic notation to suit his text.

The denial of the straight line as the main principle of textual organization is open to interpretation as originating in a metaphysic, as being an attempt to deny time or chronology. It is revealing that what is, to my mind, the best single essay on any of Butor's novels should have been written by Michel Leiris,[4] a writer who, in his own intricate and intense volumes of auto-analysis, *L'Age d'homme* and *La Règle du jeu*, shows how an a-linear arrangement of autobiographical material is able to provide an illusion of invulnerability against time. But this is an

---

[3] From the object of consumption in the most trivial sense of the term, we pass to the object of study and contemplation, which nourishes without being consumed, which transforms the way in which we know and inhabit the universe.

[4] 'Le Réalisme mythologique de Michel Butor.'

illusion which Butor is quite ruthless in excluding from his novels.

He himself talks about replacing the narrative line with a 'surface', and this surface is, in a sense, the space which the writer encloses and gives a meaning to with his forms. Butor equates the book very directly with a sacred structure in the first of several essays he has written on Victor Hugo: 'Victor Hugo romancier.' In a chapter of *Notre-Dame de Paris* called 'Ceci tuera cela', Hugo makes a prophecy which we are intended to recognize as history by withdrawing in effect from the Middle Ages and foreseeing that the cathedral will one day be replaced by the book, that print will replace architecture as the repository and disseminator of our ethical systems.

But the repository is more than just a place of storage, it is also a stronghold, a focus of our defence against the forces of inhumanity. Oral forms of expression are uttered, transmitted but ultimately denatured or forgotten altogether; printed ones are humanity's greater hope, since together they will constitute a massive work of reference for future generations. All forms of expression—this is a notion central to Butor's high-minded philosophy of the arts—are defences against oblivion.

So the power that menaces the novelist's carefully and hopefully elaborated edifices is the power of forgetfulness. It is the waters of oblivion that wash murkily around their foundations. Like Robbe-Grillet, Butor makes use of water in his novels, to stand for what is without form, the darkness that precedes expression, the ground against which whatever exists must stand out. To the extent that he is a novelist of memory this ground might be identified with the whole of the past, the totality of what is potentially recuperable but as yet unrecorded.

This pattern, of the work of art representing something built amidst the waters of oblivion, is one which Butor has brilliantly exposed in his essay on Proust: 'Œuvres d'art imaginaires chez Marcel Proust.' He shows how each imaginary work of art in Proust, be it one of Elstir's paintings or the famous Vinteuil sonata, reflects Proust's philosophy of the genesis and structure of his own novel. The painting which shows a church apparently surrounded by water, thanks to the surprising point of view taken by the painter of his subject, is a simple transposition, a *mise en abyme* of *A la recherche* itself, a similar monument patiently erected by the narrator as he strives to find his way back to a paradise of childhood. The Fall, in Proust as in Butor, can be equated with forgetfulness.

The most useful example of such a structure in Butor's own books is not a novel but a short, unclassifiable book called *Description de San Marco*, where his attempts to re-erect the cathedral in print lead him into the field of concrete poetry. The particular building lends itself admirably to what he is trying to do because of its geographical situation: Venice is a city built in the water and constantly threatened by it. The Cathedral stands solidly against this threat, and in the vestibule Butor draws attention to the prophet's finger pointing towards the interior—it is in fact Moses pointing towards the Promised Land. The building, like the legends it enshrines, represents a victory over the formless element:

> L'eau
> Moïse tiré des eaux
> Venise surgi des eaux
> Cercueil venu des eaux d'Egypte
> Contenant le corps de Saint-Marc (p. 60).[5]

Apart from being a penetrating exercise in the iconography of St. Mark's, revealing the triple analogy between Moses, Venice, and the body of the city's tutelary saint, this passage is also a *mise en abyme* of Butor's own book or, if one prefers, his book is itself conditioned by the reality it is trying to picture. *Description de San Marco*, a book conceived and documented in Italy but printed and published in France, is itself a piece of architecture housing something—memories—that would otherwise have receded slowly into nothingness; the book is intended as a sufficient recreation of the actual structure of the cathedral, able to stabilize the memory and prevent it from relapsing into increasingly distorted views of the vanished reality. It would be interesting to know whether, at the time when he wrote *Description de San Marco*, Butor was

[5] The water
Moses pulled from the water
Venice arisen from the waters
A coffin come from the waters of Egypt
Containing the body of Saint Mark.

acquainted with the classical memory systems of the Greeks and Romans, which recommended the placing of images to be remembered in well-known buildings, so that they might be recalled in the desired order as the mind was allowed to circumambulate the chosen site. Since, as Frances Yates shows in her remarkable book on *The Art of Memory*, these systems became integrated during the Renaissance with the Hermetic traditions of Egypt, and since Butor, as I hope to show, is certainly profoundly acquainted with the traditions and devices of Hermeticism, it seems probable that he is, both in this case as well as in books like *Mobile*, exploiting this ancient practice quite knowingly.

He selected St. Mark's in Venice not, presumably, because of its intrinsic architectural merits, but because of its strange suitability for him as a model or exemplar. As a writer he is concerned to teach not a particular lesson, valid for this situation or that, but a method that is valid for any possible situation whatsoever, a method to live by, no less. What he is saying in *Description de San Marco* is certainly no different from what he says elsewhere in his books; it has been summed up by Ludovic Janvier: 'il s'agit de faire attention . . . d'éviter la submersion' (*Une Parole exigeante*, p. 149).[6]

Turning now to Butor's earliest novel, *Passage de Milan*, it is not hard to collect evidence of the earnestness of his ambitions. This neglected book is extraordinarily complicated, like its successors, but it is a most profitable source of insights into Butor's definition of the novel itself. The narrative starts at dusk and ends at dawn the following morning, so that the book is constructed as a mental journey through the darkness of the night, with its attendant threats of nightmare and even madness. Moreover, the night begins with a crucial transition, equally dependent on the time of day, from a mode of direct observation to one of reflection: 'Depuis des années que l'abbé l'observait au moment des pages brunissantes, renonçant lentement à fermer ses volets, avant de s'installer près de sa lampe à contempler le passage des vitres de la transparence à la réflection . . .' (p. 7).[7]

---

[6] we have got to pay attention . . . to avoid being submerged.

[7] For years past the *abbé* had observed it at the moment when the pages turned brown, slowly deciding not to close his shutters, before settling down by his lamp to contemplate the glass passing from transparence to reflection.

The *abbé*, like Delmont in Butor's third novel *La Modification*, is not, it seems, eager to exchange the natural light of day for the artificial 'lamp' of the reflective consciousness, to be forced, that is, to look inwards and take stock of his beliefs. Yet from the moment when he settles down to the task there is nothing he can do, for the inexorable process is under way; from this point on whatever may take place outside the *immeuble* in which he lives is relegated to the inferior realm of contingency, while what takes place within the *immeuble* is sanctified by the imposition of significance, or necessity. During the earlier part of the night the *abbé's* mind is not altogether closed to the outside world, since certain visitors will be admitted to call on the inhabitants of the *immeuble*.

The *abbé*'s home, for as long as the novel lasts, is really his own mind, but it is not altogether clear in *Passage de Milan* whether these callers represent fresh sense-impressions, which no prolonged act of reflection can altogether exclude, or simply memories called into being by the process of association.

At the moment when he stares from his window, the *abbé* Ralon looks out over a junk-yard: 'où l'attention découvrait des planches usées, des madriers, des lattes, et puis des pierres et des ferrailles, matériaux plus jamais utilisables, penserait-on . . .' (p. 7).[8]

This scene, several parallels for which occur in Robbe-Grillet's novels, presents the debris or, more specifically, the building materials out of which the novel will be erected: none of these materials are new, these are old images, revealed to the mind by an act of attention. They already possess a significance for the consciousness that contains them and so demand to be re-animated or re-humanized, in such a way that the past ceases to be a dumb and lifeless fatality. In the course of the twelve hours that follow the *abbé*'s disconnection from the external world, he has got to erect these relics, this menacing ossuary of his past existence, into a structure that will lead him to the light once more. A prolonged act of attention is demanded of him, one that lasts twelve hours by virtue of a necessary convention: that this act of

[8] where the attention could make out worn planks, beams, slats, and then stones and old iron, materials, one would have thought, that could never be used again . . .

attention be recognized as itself subject to the processes of cosmic time.

All that can be seen standing in the *abbé*'s junk-yard when he surveys it are two scrawny trees, enclosed by a fence and plastered with *affiches*. The tree as metaphor for a man is not a new one, and these two trees surely represent the *abbé* himself and his brother, Alexis, who, as the novel proceeds, becomes more and more of a *dédoublement* of Jean Ralon, he being also a priest but a teacher and not a writer. The fence surrounding them is the temporary safeguard of Jean Ralon's withdrawal into the reflective consciousness, but more important are the *affiches*. On the naturalistic level these are acceptable as posters, but on the more profound, the mythical or ontological level, they are the labels which we apply to everything and especially to human beings, ourselves included, in order, generally, to cloak their real, disturbing and immediate presence behind the comfortable illusion that we have classified them; these labels are a dangerous denial of individual freedom, and if they are not peeled off then we succumb to the blandishments of habit, denying the potent and revolutionary possibilities for change of the present moment. Such is the perpetual alertness demanded of the existential hero of Butor's world.

The complex events that constitute *Passage de Milan* are designed for this purpose, to restore Jean Ralon to a fuller and more wholesome state of self-knowledge. By the end of the night, after its disturbing and revelatory dreams, the *abbé* has become aware for the first time of the insincerity of his Christian profession. He imagines himself, for example, being addressed by his crucifix: 'il dira de ses lèvres de cuivre: tes rêves sont plus sincères que tes prières, va donc vers ces dieux qui te tourmentent, et ne perpétue plus ce mensonge de consacrer mon corps et mon sang avec des mots qui ne viennent que de la surface de ton cœur' (p. 285).[9]

It would be perfectly reasonable but not particularly helpful to interpret *Passage de Milan* as the book that embodies Butor's own rejection of Christianity—his own rejection indeed of any

---

[9] it will say with its lips of copper: your dreams are more sincere than your prayers, go therefore towards those gods that torment you, and do not perpetuate further this lie of consecrating my body and blood with words which only come from the surface of your heart.

absolute world-view, in favour of a fertile appreciation of the virtues of cultural and ethical relativism.

The journey towards the light, therefore, is one taken into the depths of the subconscious. That this is a dangerous and costly journey goes without saying, for Butor never suggests that we shall enjoy what we find if we undertake it. In *Passage de Milan* it is a journey involving a death; but this death is ultimately a beneficial one, since it is the death of what had been threatening the stability or rationality of Jean Ralon's being. The girl who dies is Angèle Vertigues, who is celebrating her twentieth birthday with a party. This party is, in effect, what links the *immeuble* where the events take place in *Passage de Milan*, with the outside world, since it is the guests to the Vertigues's apartment, together with those to another entertainment with precisely similar connotations on another floor, that constitute the influx of alien images into Jean Ralon's consciousness. The party itself is a scene of refreshment and of movement—it provides a buffet supper and a dance. The dance in particular is a direct reflection of the movement of the novel itself—the *jeu*, in which the dancers or characters are free to move within the limits laid down by the rules. The nature of this movement, which must ultimately break free of the artificial restrictions placed on it, and lead to giddiness or vertigo, is clearly linked with the name of the girl in whose honour the dance is being held and who becomes a sort of ritual victim. (The buffet supper can also be taken as representing the function of the novel, as is the case also with Robbe-Grillet, but Butor takes a much sterner view than Robbe-Grillet of the purpose of this refreshment, which to him is a guarantee of a more rational praxis later on.)

The death of Angèle Vertigues is an indication, therefore, that the novel has done its job. The first part of her name must be associated with the death of Jean Ralon's Christianity, the second with the death of the confusion that has caused him to act irrationally or hypocritically. The murder of the girl constitutes a new moment of stability in Ralon's life; its ambiguous function casts the mind back to something written by Roland Barthes in *Le Degré zéro de la littérature*: 'l'ordre, que ce soit celui du continu poétique ou celui des signes romanesques, celui de la terreur ou

celui de la vraisemblanc, l'ordre est un meurtre intentionnel'
(p. 36).[10]

The murderer in *Passage de Milan* is Jean Ralon's nephew Louis
Lécuyer. Together with his two uncles, Jean and Alexis, Lécuyer,
the 'squire', makes up a family triangle, the same pattern of kinship to which Butor returns in *Degrés*. He kills the girl at a moment
when the dance is all but over, when she is in the embrace of a
would-be burglar called Henri Delétang; the weapon, significantly, is a candle-holder. The name De l'étang (of the pond) has a
sinister sound in view of the threat of water to which I have
already referred, and it is appropriate that the burglar's schemes
should be foiled by a candle-holder. Lécuyer, with his subservient
status revealed in his surname, belongs to the class of servants in
Passage de Milan—at one point in the novel the status and interaction of all the characters are represented by a painting of sets of
playing-card figures, kings, queens, and valets. These valets
circulate in the *immeuble* by their own staircase, separated from the
main staircase used by the kings and queens by a thin pane of
glass. Just before he kills Angèle, Lécuyer breaks this glass and
cuts his hand as he does so, in order to get from one staircase to
the other. This shedding of blood should alert the attentive reader
to the anthropological notion of a *rite de passage* or initiation cere-
mony, raising the status of Lécuyer as high as that of his uncles;
likewise, in *Degrés*, much stress is laid on the fact that the young
nephew, Pierre Eller, is to be initiated by means of what we are
reading, into his uncle's secrets.

As a result of what he has done Lécuyer is finally ejected from
the *immeuble* and sets off for Egypt, whence the *abbé* Ralon had
himself once come (and where Butor himself had spent a year
teaching French not long before he wrote this novel). Butor's
own visit to Egypt occasioned his first great feeling of *dépayse-
ment*, by his own admission, and made him aware that other perspectives on life are possible, different from those imprinted in our
minds by our own country's cultural and social traditions. With
Louis Lécuyer setting off for the East therefore (the Orient or
source of light), the *abbé* Jean Ralon is revealed as having come

[10] order, whether it be that of the poetic continuum or that of the signs of a
novel, that of terror or that of plausibility, order is an intentional murder.

to terms with his past, and as having acknowledged the persistent vitality of the Oriental gods who have tormented him during the night.

Right at the end of *Passage de Milan*, it is the other brother, Alexis, the teacher, whose name may be intended to remind us of Alexandria, the home of gnosticism and alchemy, who pronounces a final absolution over the dead Angèle Vertigues: 'Alexis qui fait un signe de croix furtif, et qui murmure: "Et lux perpetua" . . .' (p. 286).[11]

The departure from Europe of the youngest apex of the Ralon triangle, the boy orientated towards the future, is an optimistic conclusion for *Passage de Milan*, effected by the conjunction of the two uncles, the writer and the teacher. Butor has clearly divided the function of the novelist, as he sees it, between the two of them. Jean Ralon spends his time bent mysteriously over signs that no one else can understand; in fact he is reluctant to recognize his responsibility as a mentor or oracle for the uninitiated, as his mother complains, referring to the cries of birds which she is forced to treat as omens (the 'milan' of the title is a kite, while, be it noted the word 'butor' in French means a bittern): 'et mon fils si savant ne saura pas, ne voudra pas m'interpréter leurs cris, ce qui m'a forcé malgré moi à les écouter . . .' (p. 57).[12]

If superstition is to be replaced by true knowledge, therefore, Alexis Ralon must be added to Jean Ralon, so that the signs can be interpreted and communicated, thus saving future generations from the blindness of the past.

At the end of *Passage de Milan* the *immeuble*—the *abbé*'s consciousness that is—is returned to the necessities of daylight, the interlude of play is over: 'Apparais enfin dans ton extérieur, grande pile de veilles et de sommeils, te voilà rendu à ta destination diurne, élément d'une rue qu'on ne regarde pas' (p. 281).[13]

From these last few words it is possible to grasp the true

[11] Alexis who makes a furtive sign of the cross and who murmurs: 'Et lux perpetua' . . .
[12] and my son learned as he is cannot or will not interpret their calls for me, which has forced me to heed them in spite of myself.
[13] Appear, then, in your externality, great pile of vigils and of sleep, for you have been returned to your diurnal destination, an element of a street that no one looks at.

importance of the notion of the *regard*. It is the act of attention, the *acte de reprise*, in which the mind withdraws from involvement in the flux of the phenomenal scene and investigates the process of signification. The *regard*, for Butor, is not an indulgence but a vital necessity; he, at least, could only feel flattered at being enrolled into a critic's *école du regard*.

In *Passage de Milan* all the main themes of his subsequent novels are stated, even if they are not worked out with the same apparent rigour. The hero or narrator is launched on an auto-analysis. This requires that he should be cut off from full self-knowledge, by some mental block or complex, but that he should also be brought to the point of examining this block and raising the censorship that it has imposed on his tongue. Butor's novels are certainly based on the Freudian proposition, whether this has been empirically proved or not to the satisfaction of all psycho-analysts, that the formulation of psychological distress in words is itself a cure. Certainly, it seems not to be eccentric in analytical circles to hold the view that the contribution of psycho-analysis to therapeutic medicine lies in precisely this, that it offers a semantic system whereby the patient can be helped to make order out of the chaotic experience that is threatening to overwhelm him. Order, in fact, is both a death and a resurrection.

In his second novel, *L'Emploi du temps*, which is again a work of extreme complexity, Butor makes one thing at least rather clearer —that the fabrication of a novel is a necessary activity for a man bewildered and threatened by a reality he is unable to understand. Butor does not seem to doubt that in the contemporary world, with its massive provision of information about itself and the great speed of its technological revolutions, all men of good faith must feel thus bewildered. The experience in his own life from which, with very many reservations, *L'Emploi du temps* can be said to stem, was the two years which he spent as a *lecteur* in the University of Manchester. I say 'very many reservations' because a number of superficial and often preposterous interpretations have been made of this novel, which try to turn it into a guidebook to Manchester. But it is quite evident that not a single one of the many topographical details which the novel contains has been inserted gratuitously; to read *L'Emploi du temps* as in any sense an exercise in descriptive naturalism is to misread it hopelessly.

Butor has himself admitted that the experience of Manchester for him was one of exile—he found himself in a country whose language he could read but not communicate in. But if *L'Emploi du temps* is a guide-book it is a guide-book to life itself and not to a particular town in the north of England. In the novel Manchester has been completely rebuilt as Bleston, with reference not to any maps but to Butor's own structural needs.

For this book Butor has used a first-person narrator: Jacques Revel, a Frenchman who is sent to Bleston for a year's *stage* by his firm. According to Leon S. Roudiez, the dates of Revel's stay in Bleston correspond precisely with those of Butor's own first year in Manchester, so that from this point of view there is no attempt at disguise. But Revel spends only one year in Bleston where Butor had spent two in Manchester, and he is not an academic but a translator. Very little is said in *L'Emploi du temps* about Revel's working-life at the firm of Matthews & Co., because the real work which he does in Bleston is to write the book we are reading. But the firm he is attached to is an export business, and his own responsibility is with the translation of correspondence. Revel, therefore, is Butor the novelist, not Butor the French university *lecteur*. He is in the export business because he is exporting a piece of England to France, or a bit of his own experience into ours, and giving comprehensible form to signs that neither he nor we could understand if it were not for his presence as mediator or interpreter.

Until Revel starts on his book, the town of Bleston has represented to him a huge and violent threat of total disorientation and submersion; it is a perfectly formless and subjective emotion which has to be expressed objectively. The name which Butor has given to his narrator is itself a sign of his function—Reve(i)l—the agent who can bring what is dark in Bleston partially but not wholly into the light of the waking state. The year he spends there is divided into two unequal periods; the seven months from the first of October when he arrives, and the five months from the first of May when he begins to write his book. These are five months that can be placed under the sign of Apollo, the bringer of light and harmony, and it is pertinent to remember also that Maia herself was the mother of Hermes, the god of eloquence. These mythological parallels are not as forced as they may seem, because Butor is never a man to exclude a support of this kind for the structures of his novels; for him any serious work of art is partly interpretable as a new myth in an endless series, designed to give us a fresh measure of control over our lengthening past.

The equation between Revel (or Butor) and Apollo is made clearer by what he has written in a book containing a number of travel essays, called *Le Génie du lieu*, about his visit to Delphi. He stresses above all the peace-making responsibilities of the oracle during the wars between states in Ancient Greece. Nowadays we are more likely to see these wars as taking place first in the individual subconscious, and only later as finding expression, if the conflicts are not resolved, in harmful public irrationalisms. Of Apollo himself Butor writes: 'Il est Loxias, c'est-à-dire l'oblique, l'énigmatique, celui par qui l'énigme prend forme, au lieu de demeurer illimitée, contagieuse et destructrice' (p. 77).[14]

What is enigmatic about the therapy which Butor, the bringer of light, offers us, is simply that it is implicit in the structure of the novel. In a sense it does not matter what the exact configuration of this structure may signify, because its mere existence is a guarantee of a new stability, but if we want to understand the specific case, of Revel in *L'Emploi du temps* for example, then there is a great deal of hard detective work involved.

It is evident that Revel, the foreigner in a country whose signs he cannot properly understand, has more than a merely personal significance for Butor. His relationship with the city of Bleston reflects man's relationship with the universe. It is only through man and the powers of his consciousness that the universe can be given a meaning. For Butor, man is a negative capability, able to reflect everything that exists except, as it were, for the organ of reflection, his own eye. In a recent work, classified by its author as a *capriccio*, *Portrait de l'artiste en jeune singe*, Butor describes the

[14] He is Loxias, that is the oblique one, the enigmatic one, the man through whom the enigma acquires a form, instead of remaining limitless, contagious and destructive.

difficulty he has always had in determining the physical properties of other people's eyes—'l'œil m'aveugle sur lui-même' (p. 16).[15] The eye is the one element of the natural world that resists objectification, for the sound, old-fashioned reason that it is 'the window of the soul', the evidence of the Other. But if the eyes of other people represent a challenge to the man who would objectify them, then his own eye represents the impossibility of the subject becoming an object for itself.

Because the eye of the subject, the reflective agent, must remain forever a subject, it is therefore an alien presence in the world, judged from the standpoint of objective reality itself. Butor has all along been fascinated by this ontological situation, which can also be transposed into a geographical or cultural situation—the existence in the midst of one order of phenomena of a phenomenon of quite another order. In *Le Génie du lieu*, for example, he dwells on the Christian chapel half-hidden amidst the proliferation of columns in the great mosque at Córdoba in Spain; in *Portrait de l'artiste en jeune singe* he introduces a Hungarian and describes his country, with every ethnic justification, as 'cette flaque d'Asie demeurée après les mascarets d'invasion' (p. 21).[16]

The forces against which the Butor hero struggles so bravely can be differentiated into two, into what Ludovic Janvier calls 'le lieu qui enchante, le monde qui disperse' (*Une Parole exigeante*, p. 150).[17] Enchantment is what will seal his lips and reduce him to the level of an animal; it is the power of a scene or picture which involves the spectator to the point where he is incapable of withdrawing from it or determining his intentionality—Butor has a habit of referring to pictures in his novels as 'traps'. Dispersal will bewilder the hero by the realization that nowhere is there to be found any final stability, that the possible perspectives open to the mind are infinite. Here Butor is close to Claude Simon, in that the acceptance of relativism seems to fill him with a certain anguish, but in his case this soon turns into the determination that the task he has set himself, and us, must be the task of all right-thinking men. The threat of dispersal is transformed into a call for co-

[15] the eye blinds me to itself.
[16] that puddle of Asia left behind after the tidal waves of invasion.
[17] the place which enchants, the world which disperses.

operation. By weight of numbers relativism itself is disguised almost as an absolutism.

The role of the narrator in Butor's novels is thus to be the individual consciousness *through* which reality is expressed; he is, apparently, a passive figure. This passivity is also accentuated by the fact that he has not been allowed the capacity to comment explicitly on his achievements—his passivity is a challenge to the readers of the novel to supplement it with their own activity. But in point of fact the narrator is extremely hard-working and creative in the course of the novel—he draws up a map of his experience which is a model of the sort of map we should all be able to make from our own particular and irreplaceable vantage-point. Thus the map of Bleston which Revel offers, and which is provided as a frontispiece to *L'Emploi du temps*, is hardly adequate as a guide to the city; it is full of blank spaces because it records only the efforts of a single individual to set in order a past that, like all our pasts, involves many other individuals. The maps of these other individuals will supplement his own, or may even contradict it.

The reason why Butor has been criticized for minimizing the importance of the hero in his novels is surely his determination to define the authority of the human mind as rigorously as possible. His is the ontology of *L'Être et le néant*—consciousness adds nothing substantial to the universe, it is a negative form awaiting a content, a blank screen. Its creation therefore is a synthesis, a pattern created out of the pre-existing world-stuff: 'Cette totalisation de l'être n'ajoute rien à l'être, elle n'est rien que la manière dont l'être se dévoile comme n'étant pas le pour-soi, la manière dont il y a de l'être' (*L'Être et le néant*, p. 230).[18]

Butor makes this clear in *L'Emploi du temps* in a very intricate *mise en abyme*. Revel sees the book which he has just begun to write —the one we are reading—as a talisman which will protect him against the forces of darkness threatening to destroy him, which have kept him silent for the first seven months of his stay in Bleston. Soon after the novel is started he buys himself a handkerchief, a white one, made in the image of the book, a 'signe

[18] This totalization of Being adds nothing to Being, it is nothing more than the way in which Being is unveiled as being not the for-itself, the way in which there is Being.

protecteur' as he calls it, fabricated 'dans la matière de Bleston' (p. 53).[19] Shortly afterwards he uses this handkerchief to wipe the mud off himself after he has slipped down in the doorway of the Old Cathedral. The handkerchief, or novel, is used therefore to get rid of the evidence of the Fall. There is nothing remotely theological about Butor's schema, the Fall, as I have already said, being simply oblivion or forgetfulness, and the book not, as in the case of Proust, an attempt to recover a lost paradise, but an attempt to recover the lost events without which the present moment has no meaning.

One thing that emerges very clearly from *L'Emploi du temps* is that Butor sees the novel as able to embody a specifically modern myth, to help us find our way about the contemporary world. Bleston *is* the modern world, and for Revel it presents itself first and foremost as a nightmare, or as a prison—his first lodgings are in a hotel with the sinister name of L'Ecrou. Expression—the search for a language—and escape are, therefore, one and the same thing.

Revel's early encounters with the scene of his alienation are un-equivocal in their sense of menace: 'Dès les premiers instants cette ville m'est apparue hostile, désagréable, enlisante, mais c'est au cours de ces semaines routinières, quand j'ai peu à peu senti sa lymphe passer dans mon sang, mon présent perdre son étrave, l'amnésie gagner, que sourdement s'est développée cette haine passionnée à son égard . . .' (p. 38).[20]

For as long as Revel is implicated in his routine he is helpless, because he is acting blindly, unaware of his passage through time which demands of him a constantly renewed stance towards the world. The blindness of habit and the blindness of amnesia are one; the 'lymph' that passes into the bloodstream is a small but deadly tributary from the waters of oblivion, like the River Slee which is such a forbidding part of the townscape of Bleston. What is lost through this amnesia is the sense of the uniqueness of the

[19] a protective sign . . . made from the stuff of Bleston.

[20] Right from the first moment this town appeared to me to be hostile, unpleasant, a quicksand, but it was during those routine weeks, when I gradually felt its lymph passing into my bloodstream, my present losing headway, amnesia gaining on me, that there developed secretly this passionate hatred against it . . .

I

present moment, which is not just the repetition of past moments but a projection beyond them, an existential challenge and a responsibility. Once we lose headway in our journey through time we are adrift, at the mercy of tides and currents we have the power to utilize, if not fully control.

In the house of James Jenkins in *L'Emploi du temps*, where this fellow worker from Matthews & Co. lives with his mother, there is a particular engraving which shows a fallen king fleeing through a forest, watched by wolves. Jenkins himself is a true son of Bleston: in fact he tells Revel he has never once been outside the city limits, and his knowledge of other places is derived from the films he has seen at the News Cinema. He is in league with the town, through whose streets he drives in a black car. Yet Jenkins's father had been the man responsible for the New Cathedral of Bleston, a structure mirroring Revel's own. Jenkins is a man who has not risen to the responsibility of his lineage, therefore. Revel sees the engraving on the occasion of his first visit to the Jenkins house, an occasion which marks his first penetration of the secret life of the town: 'j'avais réussi à m'introduire dans une des fêlures de ce mur de verre trouble qui me séparait de la ville' (p. 52).[21] The engraving of the fleeing king is thus a reminder of his own responsibility *vis-à-vis* Bleston itself, to save it (and himself) from the wolves by lending the city his tongue.

His task is to explain Bleston to itself, to bring order to it from inside. He appreciates that the city has a secret desire to be cleansed, through the only possible agency, that of human attention. In *Le Génie du lieu* Butor talks of having felt an 'impérieuse nécessité d'introduire un peu d'ordre et de clarté dans la confusion menaçante' (p. 164),[22] when he found himself confronted by Egypt. But this feeling, as he shows in *L'Emploi du temps*, need not be an immediate reaction to the experience of exile, it may be dangerously delayed; the eyes may be too fascinated to close, but until they are closed no attempt can be made at the recuperation of the past or the ordering of the present.

[21] I had succeeded in introducing myself into one of the cracks in that wall of cloudy glass which cut me off from the town.
[22] an imperious necessity to introduce a little light and order into the threatening confusion.

The struggle that matters is the one between fascination and abstraction. At the start of *Portrait de l'artiste en jeune singe* Butor singles out not only eyes but also hair as 'objets peut-être justement trop fascinants pour moi, ils m'attirent tellement que je ne puis en abstraire la couleur, surtout dans le souvenir' (p. 15).[23] It follows that only those elements of reality which threaten to annul our powers of abstraction are worth countering by the patient elaboration of a novel.

Revel's own confrontation with Bleston is mirrored in *L'Emploi du temps* by two other works of art, both produced there by visiting French artists of previous centuries. The first is the Vitrail du Meurtrier, a stained-glass window in the Old Cathedral portraying the murder of Abel by Cain, the second a series of eighteen tapestries in the local museum, recording the story of Theseus.

Cain is presented in the window as the father of the arts as well as the murderer of his brother, and as the founder of a new city. But such is the arrangement of the stained glass that this new city is the real city of Bleston, visible through the window. One of the possible etymologies of the name Bleston is 'Abel's town', so that the work of art, the Vitrail du Meurtrier, thus becomes the transformation of the city from Abel's town into Cain's. The artist is the fratricide because the building of a new city, an imaginary one, involves the suppression of the old or real one. Michel Butor's most sympathetic and perspicacious critic to date, Jean Roudaut, makes the excellent point in his book, *Michel Butor ou le livre futur*, that whereas the murder of the father—the Œdipus myth which is also involved in *L'Emploi du temps*—embodies the murder of the past and the will to oblivion, the murder of the brother must be seen as a stage of growth.

Standing in front of the Vitrail du Meurtrier, staring at a scene which shows the posterity of Cain at work, as weavers, blacksmiths, and musicians, Revel ponders: 'Bleston, ville de tisserands et de forgerons, qu'as-tu fait de tes musiciens?' (p. 75).[24] The lack is one which he is on the way to filling himself; the book that he is

---

[23] objects indeed that are perhaps too fascinating for me, they attract me so much that I cannot abstract their colour from them, especially in memory.

[24] Bleston, town of weavers and of blacksmiths, what have you done with your musicians?

now writing will bring a measure of harmony to a dissonant city, by, as it were, scoring it, finding for its expression a new notation of great intricacy or even secretiveness. The day before Revel sets out on his book he burns the street guide to Bleston which he had bought on his arrival in the town, but he is forced to buy another one to replace it, because even when it is completed his own book will not suffice on its own to still the threat posed by Bleston.

L'Emploi du temps represents the temporary judgment of one man, not the Last Judgment of God, or of all men. Revel is very scrupulous in the way in which he disposes his papers about his work-table as he writes, a table he several times refers to as his 'rampart' against the town: on the left are the guide-books and maps he has relied on in the past, on the right the accumulating pages of manuscript that will one day complement or correct them. This pattern is repeated in the dispositions of the interior of the Old Cathedral in Bleston, where it had originally been intended to portray the Last Judgment in stained glass in the apse. To the left of the apse is the Vitrail du Meurtrier, to the right plain glass, replacing stained glass that had portrayed the story of Abel. This window had been destroyed many years before by a mob, whose archbishop had failed to pacify it, because some secret guilt had removed his powers of speech at the critical moment— he, like Jean Ralon, was a priest who had abdicated from his true responsibilities. But Revel has recognized his own sacerdotal obligations to his flock, and his book will come to fill the gap left by the incapacity of the historical archbishop. By the time he leaves Bleston the view through the plain glass is dominated by a vast new department store. This is an apt metaphor for the novel as Michel Butor practises it; for him the novel is a working model of reality which can structure the commerce of the mind. 'La vertu intrinsèque du modèle réduit', writes the structural anthropologist Claude Lévi-Strauss, 'est qu'il compense la renonciation à des dimensions sensibles par l'acquisition de dimensions intelligibles' (*La Pensée sauvage*, p. 36).[25]

Butor is in no doubt that the transformation of sensibilia into intelligibilia is a vital therapy which the novelist is still capable of

[25] The intrinsic virtue of the scale model is that it makes up for the loss of tangible dimensions by the acquisition of intelligible dimensions.

demonstrating to people how to apply to their own lives. There is a robust psycho-analytical dimension to his work, but one of a particular, non-reductive kind. Something which Butor stresses is that the past must not be destroyed altogether, but brought under control, comprehended in fact or, to use the alchemists' term, transmuted. Butor has inherited the great admiration and sympathy shown by many Surrealists for the alchemists, and, above all, for the tradition of the hermetic text, intended as instruction for the initiate, yet so disguised as to face him with taxing problems of interpretation and, moreover, incomplete in some vital detail.

The problem with Butor's own texts is to decide whether they are, to employ the helpful distinction drawn by another contemporary French writer of alchemical inclinations, Raymond Queneau, hermetic or merely 'hermeneutic', whether they are, that is, susceptible of a total elucidation by anyone but the man who wrote them. I have always assumed that they are, that Butor's *mystification* has a pedagogic intention, but the question may seem a little academic since books like *L'Emploi du temps* or *Portrait de l'artiste en jeune singe*, with its display of geological symbolism, are sufficiently opaque to resist a full interpretation in the time available to the most willing and persevering reader.

The aim of Revel in Bleston, or of the novelist at grips with his past, is thus sublimation or purification. One of the least naturalistic features of *L'Emploi du temps* are the fires that are constantly breaking out all over the town. But these fires both destroy and provide light and warmth. In *La Psychanalyse du feu*, Gaston Bachelard—one of Butor's philosophy teachers at the Sorbonne—writes of the pleasures to be had from the conscious repression of unwelcome experiences in our past, and the pleasures too of admitting to subjective errors in that past. Fire itself, it seems, can be transmuted: 'le feu qui nous brûlait, soudain nous éclaire' (*La Psychanalyse du feu*, p. 165).[26]

Bachelard, indeed, gives a fine definition of Butor's concept of the novel as sublimation, when he talks about 'une volonté constante de redressement' (ibid., p. 165).[27] This 'redressement'

[26] the fire that had been burning us, suddenly gives us light.
[27] a constant will to correction.

necessitates the preservation of the past within the present, the preservation of two dialectically divided terms, between which a movement becomes possible. Thus, whatever the subconscious pressure is which keeps us from a wholesome self-awareness in the present, it is not to be excised, as if it were a hopelessly diseased organ, but utilized, by being preserved as a reminder of the distance the psyche has travelled and the direction it has been travelling in. This is a psycho-analytical programme of growth and individuation, quite opposed to that Freudian tendency which stresses the reduction of complexes or deviations in the interests of social health and conformity. Seen as a form of sublimation Butor's novels are not denied by reality any more than they deny it; he is striving to show how the real world and its sublimated reflection in the novel can co-exist and feed off one another, in a mutually dependent relationship which he has himself referred to as the symbolism of a work of art.

'Redressement' is very much the central concern of Butor's third, most accessible, and so most generally admired novel, *La Modification*. Here the necessary opposition in the mind of the narrator is that between two cities, one of them standing for the here and now of his life, Paris, the other for his past, Rome. The narrator, Léon Delmont, travels away from Paris towards Rome, in the anticipation of leaving his wife and settling down permanently with his mistress, who lives in Rome. But the journey itself persuades him that he is making a mistake, that the present cannot be abandoned; but, and this is a crucial recognition, Rome need not be abandoned either. When Delmont is returned to the real world after his journey is over he will be able to live more rationally in the present (Paris) for having established a proper relationship between this present and the past that had been troubling him: 'le mieux, sans doute, serait de conserver à ces deux villes leurs relations géographiques réelles . . .' (p. 236).[28]

Unsurprisingly, the subtlety of the moral scheme of *La Modification* has escaped some of this novel's more forthright commentators, who have seen it as promoting the cosy values of the *bon bourgeois*, returning to the comforts of wife and children in-

[28] the best thing, no doubt, would be to preserve for these two towns their true geographical relationships . . .

stead of enjoying himself adulterously in Rome. But Delmont's journey is not a simple one through the space of Europe; it is a journey through time, his own time. What he sets out to do is to deny the primacy of the unique present so that he can live in the past; by renouncing his mistress he is actually *denying* himself the comfort he might have had. Butor's demanding lesson, therefore, is that the past belongs behind us and that our responsibility towards the future—Delmont's children—means that we must make this past intelligible, build a model of it which reveals its essential workings in us. Delmont is not the seedy business-man of a naturalist novel, but Man, at a turning-point of life, in a novel whose schema is an ethico-philosophical one. If he suffers a defeat it is the defeat that we all suffer, at the hands of time.

La Modification is the record of a journey made away from the here and now, away from an actual address in Paris, 15, Place du Panthéon—the Panthéon being itself a link with Rome—away from what is verifiable to what is not verifiable. It is moreover a journey towards the South, the direction of sunlight and clarity, and the home of a woman called Cécile, whose name is reminiscent of that of Saint Cecilia, the patroness of music and harmony, with an academy in modern Rome. The man who undertakes the journey, Léon Delmont, is nominally a lion, a king among human animals, granted a position of eminence above the surrounding landscape. In everyday life he is a typewriter salesman, making frequent trips to his company's headquarters in Rome—a journey that has of course become a habit, that is to say a menace to him, since he is no longer acting in full consciousness of what he is doing. The journey he undertakes in *La Modification* is very different; it is not on the firm's business, but his own, he travels not first-class but third, and he takes a different train from the one he usually catches. And since it is a book that will result from his experiences on this journey there is also a transposition from a mechanical to a free method of writing; Delmont the typewriter salesman is ennobled into a novelist.

Butor's structure is a superbly coherent one, both mythical and plausible at one and the same time, to an extent which neither *Passage de Milan* nor *L'Emploi du temps* can match. In *La Modification*, as Michel Leiris says: 'c'est le récit tout entier qui se situe sur le plan du mythe, sans que jamais soit faussé ce que je serais tenté de nommer son vérisme tant on y est au ras du sol'.[29]

The railway compartment in which Delmont travels is that privileged area into which we can all withdraw, the reflective consciousness; whenever he leaves the compartment the book stops.

Every time that Delmont gets up from his seat he reserves it against his subsequent return with a book—a common stratagem but a highly significant one. The book he uses is a detective story bought at the station bookstall before getting into the train—I will discuss the importance of the detective story for Michel Butor later. Delmont never at any time on his journey opens this book, which is thus rigorously established as a sign of his *absence*,

Now the dialectic between presence and absence is a vital element in Butor's philosophy of the novel. The novel is an abstraction which has to be fought for against the powers of fascination which hold us speechless. For as long, therefore, as the source of fascination is present to the eye then no work of art is possible; what is absent in this case is the work of art itself, the reproduction or representation of the source of fascination—the consciousness is wholly absorbed, without remainder, in the object. Writing in *Portrait de l'artiste en jeune singe* about the art of the great portrait painters, Butor suggests that they could paint their sitters 'd'après nature' all except for their eyes, by which he means that the eye could not be reproduced as long as it was present to the artist—for the reasons I have outlined earlier. The eye it is that lures the artist into its formless depths—a favourite phrase of Butor's is 'l'eau de ce regard'. The portrait-painter finds salvation, for Butor, from the model's inability to sustain his pose indefinitely: 'En effet, après un quart d'heure de pose, le modèle ne pouvait plus regarder l'artiste de cette façon, et c'était une fois que le regard s'était absenté qu'il s'agissait de le retrouver vivant sur la toile' (p. 18).[30]

[29] the whole of the story is situated on the mythical plane, without what I would be tempted to call its *verismo* even being falsified, so close to the ground does it remain.
[30] Indeed, after posing for a quarter of an hour, the model could not look at the artist in that way any longer, and it was once the gaze was no longer there that it had to be rediscovered alive on the canvas.

What is absent for the artist, then, has to be *invented*. The novel is like the colouring of an eye—it is the intrusion of the unverifiable into a verifiable world of facts, the intrusion of the absent into the present: 'Cette couleur, il lui fallait donc d'abord la perdre, la noyer dans son attention même, pour pouvoir la reconstituer, l'inventer comme mode de liaison nécessaire entre le noir de la pupille et toute la coloration bien vérifiable des joues, des pommettes, des sourcils, des paupières même . . .' (p. 18).[31] The artist's invention is what ultimately makes his portrait 'habitable', endows it that is to say with the same powers of fascination as the original model. The reader's responsibility, where the work of art is a novel, is thus to resist this fascination by his own capacity for abstraction—he must mimic the activity of the artist.

The book which Delmont leaves on his seat in *La Modification* is thus what fills in the gaps between the periods of his bodily presence, it is a 'mode de liaison nécessaire'. But for as long as Delmont is in his compartment he is withdrawn from the external world, and when he leaves the compartment he is returned to it. The book thus acquires authority over him as it is the object by which he can re-orientate himself in the privacy of consciousness; it fills in those gaps when he is not present to himself but instead assailed and absorbed by the outside world.

Delmont's journey to Rome is also a journey towards a book, 'ce livre futur et nécessaire' as he calls it, in which he will communicate the modification in his stance towards the world that has resulted from his prolonged examination of himself. The book will explain to Cécile, his mistress, a decision—the decision not to visit her while he is in Rome and not to propose living permanently with her—which he feels unable to communicate to her in person, presumably for fear that he may succumb again to the fascination she exerts over him. If he were present to her the book could never come into existence, but absent from her the book is a necessary act of self-justification. The harmony which Delmont

---

[31] He had first of all to lose this colour, therefore, to drown it in his very attention, so that he could reconstitute it, could invest it as a necessary mode of connection between the black of the pupil and all the easily verifiable colouring of the cheeks, the cheekbones, the eyebrows, even the eyelids . . .

had set out to find will therefore be achieved in a way quite different from the one he had foreseen.

The didactic purposes that shape Butor's novels are given their most vigorous expression in his fourth novel, *Degrés*, published in 1960, and the last text that can be classified as a novel, for all his subsequent energy in literary creation. The scene of *Degrés* is a place of instruction, a Paris *lycée*, and the novel records the manic attempt of a schoolmaster, Pierre Vernier, at what he calls, with ironic simplicity, 'la description d'une classe'. This is an ambition he has long cherished of re-creating in a book all the possible facts concerning the lives of an entire class of schoolboys and those who teach them. His intentions are openly pedagogic, since he dedicates his book to the next generation, to his nephew, Pierre Eller.

Vernier's attempt, of course, is an excessive one doomed to failure, but *Degrés* is the revealing record of this failure. It is a call for the co-operation of the whole of humanity in the vital task of bringing everything in its individual or communal past into the healing light of day. The immense range of Butor's own field of reference as a critic and essayist, not only in literature but also in painting and music, reveals a quite unusual thirst for knowledge. It is clear that what he offers us all as a means of salvation is his own personal drive for elucidation, his own refusal to be mystified or blinded by science of any sort.

The word manic seems to me a fair one to qualify Vernier's ambition in *Degrés* because of this ambition's obviously limitless implications. Yet Vernier is presented by Butor quite without humour or even irony; in fact he is more than a little Christ-like in his acceptance of the risk of complete mental disintegration once he has grasped the enormity of what he has undertaken to do. Butor comes close to hinting that Vernier is a scapegoat for the whole world's terrible sins of omission or oblivion.

The class which Vernier takes as his object and about which he proposes to record the whole truth, contains thirty-one boys. The fact that this is the number of days in an orthodox calendar month suggests that Butor has here turned time into space, to show that oblivion is oblivion whether it extends backwards in time or outwards in space. The two subjects which Vernier is responsible for teaching to these boys are, needless to say, geography and history; he operates in both modes, space and time.

One of Vernier's problems, of course, is to decide on a stable centre for his enterprise, a point of reference that will mark the centre of his investigations. The spatial aspect of this problem has only one possible solution: it must be the classroom which is the point of assembly of the chosen boys, the place where their lives intersect. Vernier's solution to the temporal aspect of the problem is more revealing—a special, extra-curricular lesson which he has decided to give on the Discovery of America. This extra-curricularity, like Delmont's travelling to Rome by a different train and in a different class from the ones he usually takes, or Revel's arrival in Bleston by a train different from the one he had been supposed to take, indicates that the blandishments of routine are already being resisted.

The Discovery of America is apt for Vernier's purpose because it is the discovery of a New World, or a multiplication of the Old World by two; the new world which Vernier is setting out to discover is the mental construct that is intended to make the old world intelligible. The idea of Discovery is constantly being stressed in *Degrés*, and the lesson which Vernier chooses is a reminder that Butor himself once told a questioner that his favourite historical character was Christopher Columbus. It is also worth emphasizing that it is the great feats of exploration, like that of Columbus, which shatter most readily and profoundly the existent categories of philosophical and social thought, and call for the construction of a new image of the world. As an admirer of Columbus, Butor appears to be welcoming the tempo of scientific discovery in the contemporary world, which makes the need for re-thinking so crucial to survival.

Vernier draws the attention of his class to the importance of what he has to say about Columbus: 'aujourd'hui je voudrais vous rappeler de quelle façon s'est produit cet événement tellement important, cette multiplication par deux soudainement des dimensions de l'univers, la découverte et la conquête de l'Amérique . . .' (p. 66).[32]

---

[32] today I would like to remind you how it was that this extremely important event came about, this sudden multiplication by two of the dimensions of the world, the discovery and conquest of America . . .

This multiplication of the Old World, which is made possible by the mind's capacity to withdraw from involvement in it and reconstitute it in comparative if fragile calm, bestows considerable privileges on those who practise it. One of Vernier's class, a boy called Régnier, is distinguished from all the others because he is a *doublant*, he is repeating a year's schooling that is to say, for having failed some of his exams the previous summer; Régnier's surname classes him with those who rule, the royalty I have already discussed in connection with *Passage de Milan* and *La Modification*. Régnier's great hobby—his favourite form of play that is—is stamp-collecting, and he has a collection that is beautifully organized, whereas the album of another boy, denied the privileges of repetition, is chaotic. Régnier is thus doing what Vernier is also doing in his spare time, organizing signs into a coherent scheme. The boy's failure in his exams had not been complete and was due to sickness. This situation precisely foreshadows Vernier's own ultimate failure in his task—he too succeeds partially and then falls ill. If one pursues the analogy to its limit, as one is fully entitled to do in view of Butor's methods, then the fact that Régnier *was examined* (passive tense) by an outside authority is an indication that Butor does not see Vernier, or those who feel called to emulate him, as free to evade the examinations set for us by the real world.

Another of Vernier's favourite historical periods, very properly and understandably, is the Renaissance, and it is notable that he never uses the word without coupling it with the Reformation; Butor, that is, is optimistic enough to believe that if the past is reanimated within us then the results can only be morally beneficial —an arguable assumption even if it is a very common one.

Unlike *La Modification*, where a book is, as it were, the unforeseen outcome of a quite un-literary ambition, *Degrés* is planned by Vernier in advance; to this extent his method is a return to that of Revel in *L'Emploi du temps*. He had originally taken the decision to write his description in Greece, during the summer holiday immediately prior to the school term when the book is actually begun. Vernier, like Butor himself, has visited Delphi and appreciated its lesson—he is ready to play the part of Apollo and bring a beneficial if oblique lesson in harmony to the world.

In the course of his holiday Vernier has met a girl called Micheline Pavin, also from Paris, with whom he re-establishes contact on his return home. This girl, who embodies for him his experience in Greece, acts as a Muse, but in a peculiarly intricate way. It is she who loosens his tongue, for instance, and grants him the necessary powers of speech: 'C'est que j'ai tellement bien su vous tirer de votre mutisme . . .' (p. 318).[33] But Micheline Pavin, like the sorcerer's apprentice, cannot control the forces she has set free; the sound of her own name (*pas-vin*?) is precautionary and is thoroughly belied by Vernier's subsequent career once his tongue has been truly loosened. Intoxication is both an *aide-mémoire* and a danger.

In his astonishing *Histoire Extraordinaire*, a sort of literary psycho-analysis of a dream of which Baudelaire has left a written account, Butor contrives to uncover all kinds of connections between the dream and the reality of Baudelaire's life, and in particular with Baudelaire's reading and translating of Edgar Allan Poe. Butor quotes one especially revealing comment of Baudelaire on Poe's method of working: 'je crois que dans beaucoup de cas, non pas certainement dans tous, l'ivrognerie de Poe était un moyen mnémonique, une méthode de travail, méthode énergique et mortelle, mais appropriée à sa nature passionée' (p. 159).[34] This applies directly to the methods of Vernier in *Degrés*.

The title of this novel can be read in at least three different ways —Butor is never slow to exploit the semantic polyvalence of a single word. In the first place it must be taken to refer to the degrees of kinship, an important element in the genesis and sub-sequent structuring of the novel that I will return to in a moment; in the second place there are 'degrés' as 'steps', reflecting the ascending movement of knowledge and, above all, of initiation; and in the third place there are 'degrees' of alcohol. The tempo of the novel is one of gathering intoxication; the sobriety of the beginning—it is over cups of tea that Micheline Pavin first dis-

[33] The fact is that I was able so easily to draw you out from your silence.
[34] I think that in many cases, but certainly not in all, Poe's drunkenness was a mnemonic device, a method of working, an energetic and fatal method, but one appropriate to his passionate nature.

cusses Vernier's literary ambitions with him—is swept away as Vernier comes to realize the truly infinite ramifications of history and geography. This movement towards delirium and ultimate collapse is neatly configured in an episode in *Degrés* where one of Vernier's class, Michel Daval (*d'aval?*), on holiday in the South— just as Vernier had been on holiday in the South (and still is, since his book is a form of play or release from work)—dares to dance for the first time in his life:

C'est ce jour-là que Michel a appris ses premiers pas, lui qui jusqu'alors s'était toujours préposé pour changer les disques. Il a été tout étonné de son succès. Il transpirait, a beaucoup bu; il y avait de l'orangeade, mais aussi du gin pour faire des mélanges; il en a bu dont le degré d'alcool augmentait à chaque verre; soudain pris d'un malaise, il s'est éclipsé, s'est effondré sur un lit, s'est endormi (p. 289).[35]

Again then, as with Régnier, a partial success is overshadowed by subsequent failure. The freedom of movement of the dance, which Butor has already adopted as a metaphor for the movement of the novel itself in *Passage de Milan*, after the cyclical and so anonymous routine of putting on gramophone records, finally destroys or silences Daval, just as Vernier will be silenced. The end of both is 'eclipse' and 'sleep', eclipse to show that it is a potential source of illumination that has been extinguished, the eye which, as Butor likes to recall, the ancients likened to the sun.

The parallel between the novel and the dance is a precise one, as I have tried to show in connection with *Passage de Milan*. The dance fulfils admirably Lévi-Strauss's definition of the game: 'le jeu produit des événements à partir d'une structure' (*La Pensée sauvage*, p. 47).[36] Without a primary structure, a principle of organization, Vernier cannot even start on his description; a wholly uncontrolled movement away from his starting-point is out of the question. Since he is concerned with the lives of thirty-one boys, together with the eleven masters who teach them, he must decide,

[35] That was the day when Michel learned his first steps, he who until then had always been in charge of changing the records. He was quite amazed by his success. He sweated, drank a lot; there was orangeade but also gin for mixing with it; he drank some whose degree of alcohol increased with each glass; suddenly feeling sick, he vanished from sight, collapsed on to a bed, fell asleep.

[36] the game produces events starting from a structure.

for example, which boy to take first. Without some necessary relationship between isolated phenomena no novel is possible. In fact, the grid with which Vernier hopefully sets out to challenge the demon oblivion is a family one, a triangular relationship between a nephew and two uncles. This is, of course, the same relationship as exists in *Passage de Milan* between the two Ralons and Louis Lécuyer, between the writer, the teacher, and the young initiate. In connection with Butor's use of this family schema Jean Roudaut observes that in the development of the conscious life as a whole it is family relationships that we use as a paradigm for all relationships, in our earliest attempts to make sense of the nonself. The application of this classification is therefore an instinctive one, as Butor makes quite clear in *Degrés*, since the existence of this particular triangle of uncles and nephew is *given* to Vernier as an opportunity. At one point in the novel he remembers having discussed his intentions with Micheline Pavin: 'Vous avez commandé du thé et c'est alors que tu lui as parlé de cette conjonction de relations familiales à l'intérieur de ta classe de seconde, de cette occasion à ne pas manquer, cette constellation dont on ne pouvait raisonnablement espérer qu'elle se reproduirait une année prochaine; c'était donc le moment où jamais d'entreprendre la description?' (p. 171).[37]

Conjunctions and constellations amount to an astrological assurance to Vernier, a horoscopical hint to put alongside the omen in *Passage de Milan*, the bird of the title which the *abbé* sees hovering in the sky above Paris before he leaves his window. Vernier may still be drinking tea, but the constellation, a pattern of light in the night sky, represents the first soliciting of the will to order which Butor always detects in disorder, it is the sign that his class, like Revel's Bleston, is demanding that he, its teacher, recognize his responsibilities and grant it the power of expressing itself through him. But despite the existence of a favourable sign, Vernier still needs an order to begin, which he in turn solicits and

---

[37] You ordered some tea and it was then that you talked to her about that conjunction of family relationships within your second form, that opportunity not to be missed, that constellation which could not reasonably be expected to recur another year; this was the moment if ever to undertake the description.

receives from his Muse, Micheline Pavin. If *Degrés* followed the pattern of Butor's other novels then Pavin could be expelled from it before the end, having served her purpose. Angèle Vertigues, in *Passage de Milan*, who has loosened the tongue of Louis Lécuyer, 'ce grand taciturne' (p. 189), is killed by him; the sisters Anne and Rose Bailey, whom Revel sees as his guides to the labyrinth of Bleston, are both married off to other men as the book proceeds; Cécile, for whom Delmont undertakes his hazardous journey, is supplanted by the book he will write. But Micheline Pavin is still present at the end of *Degrés*, bending over Vernier in his hospital bed, for all his earlier recognitions that if he is to finish his book he must give up seeing her. 'Ton oncle Pierre n'écrira plus; c'est moi qui te dirai que ce texte est pour toi, et c'est Micheline Pavin que j'en ferai dépositaire. Vous êtes tous deux penchés sur son lit. Il a les yeux ouverts, mais c'est vous qu'il regarde, il ne fait pas attention à moi. Je le salue; il murmure: "qui parle?" ' (p. 389).[38]

Many readers of *Degrés* may be prompted to echo this last anguished question, given the difficulty of determining the ownership of the apparently divergent voices that narrate the novel. There are three sections to the book, embodying three supposedly different viewpoints: those of Vernier himself, of his nephew whom he is led to ask to help him and to whom the whole endeavour is dedicated, and of this boy's other uncle, Henri Jouret, whose name, Jour-et, hints at the imminence of the night. Jouret, in this last section of *Degrés*, represents Vernier in his capacity as novelist or narrator. In the quotation from the last page of the novel Jouret is thus excluded from Vernier's gaze—'il ne fait pas attention à moi'; instead Vernier only has eyes for Micheline and for his nephew. What is on the point of ending is his period of mediation, the record of which is to be entrusted to Pavin. She, therefore, the Muse, can be identified with the phenomenal world itself and with the fascinations of reality. To this reality a text has

[38] Your uncle Pierre will write no more; it is I who will tell you that this text is for you, and I shall make Micheline Pavin the guardian of it. You are both leaning over his bed. He has his eyes open, but it is you he is looking at, he pays no attention to me. I greet him; he murmurs: 'Who is speaking?'

now been added, for the benefit of those among the generations of the future adept enough to interpret it. Vernier is once more trapped by the spectacle of the visible world, but his final question can be read as an appeal to others, to us as readers, to take up the task of recuperation.

For all the swirling waters of oblivion *Degrés* certainly does not end without hope. Vernier's elaborate construction is, as it happens, reflected by that of his nephew, Pierre Eller, who is a patrol leader in the Boy Scouts—a position of authority which offers a somewhat humourless model for Vernier's earnest and beneficient intentions; it may seem a little disappointing to be led to the conclusion that Michel Butor's motto is that of the Boy Scout movement: 'Be Prepared.' Eller has spent his holidays, or a part of them, trying to build a log cabin in the woods. The landlord of the site chosen is a Baron Storck no less, a forbidding borrowing from Anglo-Saxon folklore, in which King Stork was a monarch who ate his own subjects, just as Time must be said to. Eller's cabin is never finished: 'Aux étangs les pluies sont venues, les grandes orages qui contrariaient votre construction dans les bois' (p. 289).[39]

As *Degrés* nears its end Vernier comes to be haunted by visions of returning animality. A magazine called *Fiction*, which circulates constantly among the pupils in his class, just like his own narrative (or the travelling fair in *L'Emploi du temps*), contains a story of a were-wolf, a man, that is to say, returning from human to animal status. He loses first all sense of time and finally the powers of speech; he is both submerged and dispersed. Vernier too loses all sense of time, because the moment of past time he had chosen as the pivot of his whole enterprise, the lesson on the Discovery of the New World, has receded from him with gathering speed, until an impossible gap has opened up between the time he is writing about and the time when he is writing it. The reality that had inspired him is now remote: 'Que vous me manquez!' he writes ultimately to Micheline Pavin, 'Depuis le début je vous ai demandé de me pardonner, il faut continuer à me pardonner; j'ai l'impression que nous sommes sur les deux rives d'un fleuve qui

[39] At the Ponds the rains came, the great storms which interfered with your construction in the woods.

K

s'agrandit, qui s'est agrandi monstrueusement . . .' (p. 65).[40] The final adverb is carefully chosen, and silence cannot be long delayed. The guilt which Vernier feels in respect of Micheline, whose absence has been a condition of the coming into being of his book, is the same guilt as Revel expressed in respect of Bleston. I think it would be wrong, perhaps even absurd, to interpret this guilt as the narrator's sense of disloyalty to the real world, which he has betrayed by making it intelligible; it is presumably the guilt of his own absence from reality, since during the time that his consciousness is withdrawn that reality is changing and demands his return, as one of those qualified to make sense of these changes.

As a final and savage reminder that speech is the one weapon men possess with which to render harmless the monsters of the individual or collective subconscious, Butor has introduced into *Degrés* the sinister figure of a North African, whose presence in the text is an indication of its date of composition. At this time, in 1960, the problem of Algeria was still the most divisive force in French society. Butor's North African lurks on the boulevards of Paris, his mouth sealed with sticking-plaster; he is a wolf staring at the fleeing king, Vernier, who is about to abandon his needy subjects: 'Boulevard Saint-Germain: le grand Nord-Africain au masque de sparadrap assis sur un banc, t'a regardé passer, t'a suivi de son regard de loup' (p. 376).[41]

But if Vernier is forced to renounce his crown then Butor certainly intends that we should all be ready to take it up, and help remove the sticking-plaster from the North African's mouth. It is through us that he will find self-expression, since it is by rationalizing our own attitudes towards him that he will be integrated into our society. This is the process which Butor lays down as the essence of a writer's responsibilities. His novels represent a dialogue between repression and elucidation, or irrationality and lucidity. The problem, as I see it, is that he has chosen the Appol-

[40] How I miss you . . . Right from the start I have been asking you to forgive me, you must continue to forgive me; I feel that we are on the two banks of a river which is growing wider, which has grown monstrously wider . . .
[41] Boulevard Saint-Germain: the tall North African with the mask of sticking-plaster sitting on a bench, watched you go past, followed you with his wolflike stare.

Ionian way of teaching by riddles or puzzles and has, in most of his books, over-estimated the intelligence and patience of his readers or victims. It seems doubtful whether moral lessons, or one moral lesson, taught so deviously can ever be properly appreciated or followed. Moreover, in his more naturalistic moments, as in most of *Degrés* for example, Butor is likely to confuse or even exasperate his readers more damagingly still, since they will be lulled into the false belief that these apparently anodyne configurations of the everyday are deprived of any depth at all—whereas they are in fact the fabrications of a learned and acute mind, and the objective *gestalt* of a novelist composing in public.

II

Of the three novelists analysed in this book Michel Butor is by far the most dauntingly cerebral. In the previous chapter I have tried to interpret his novels from a single aspect, to offer a guide to only one of the possible ways of reading them. To interpret them from every aspect would be a massive undertaking and quite possibly a misguided one, since the complexity of Butor's books is clearly intended to offer different readers different views of his work. As a result each reader will understand most readily what corresponds with his own particular preoccupations, and once he has detected one recurrent pattern in the work he will be bound to use this to try and make sense of the rest of it.

Since abandoning the novel form as such, Butor has grown increasingly aware of the possibilities of creating literary structures or models of reality which no two people are likely to experience in quite the same way. In his study of Niagara Falls, for instance, *6 810 000 litres d'eau par seconde*—whose title is a majestic reminder of the destructive potentialities of water—different pathways are prescribed for the reader or, where applicable, to the radio producer of the piece, enabling them to omit certain sections of the work and concentrate on a single aspect of it. It is arguable whether this really represents an improvement in Butor's method, even if it undeniably represents a simplification of it. Butor's aim has not changed; he still wants the journey through his text to be one of self-discovery for the reader, but the imposition of a route seems to mark a return to a passivity in the reader which was previously avoided by presenting him with a text that solicited his interpretation more deviously. Similarly, in the opera he wrote with the French serialist composer Henri Pousseur, Butor offers the audience an opportunity of intervention by asking them to select a continuation for the piece at the end of each act, out of a limited number of provided alternatives. The decision here, taken in a theatre with an audience of several hundreds or more people, is intended as a lesson in democracy no doubt, since only a majority decision can be accepted.

Butor's work has an exemplary quality which a great many people will not be able to respond to with much warmth, because they are unused to, or even suspicious of, anyone who takes such an exalted view of the novel's function as a form of social hygiene: 'la notion même de roman, qui évolue très lentement mais inévitablement ... vers une espèce nouvelle de poésie à la fois épique et didactique' (*Répertoire* 2, p. 11).[42]

Butor seems to be saying that what the novel, or novels in general, must ultimately be able to offer us, is a means towards the discovery of a collective identity, a temporary set of co-ordinates that will help us to find our way about the multifarious present and to project a rational future. His preoccupation with the past is equally (and reasonably) a preoccupation with the future; recovering the past is not an end in itself but a means of achieving a necessarily limited and temporary stability in the present.

The danger to our stability comes from two directions, from the phenomenal world around us or the present, and from the unresolved complexes of our individual past. The ideal novel, therefore, is one that could include *everything*, without distortion, a sort of Book of Life, reminiscent of the novel which Gide's Edouard works on in *Les Faux-Monnayeurs*:

Comprenez-moi; je voudrais tout y faire entrer, dans ce roman. Pas de coup de ciseaux pour arrêter, ici plutôt que là, sa substance. Depuis plus d'un an que j'y travaille, il ne m'arrive rien que je n'y verse, et que je

[42] the very notion of the novel, which is evolving very slowly but inevitably ... towards a new kind of poetry at once epic and didactic.

n'y veuille faire entrer: ce que je vois, ce que je sais, tout ce que m'apprend la vie des autres et la mienne (p. 238).[43]

But Edouard is soon made aware that reality will only allow itself to be trapped by some form of stylization, hence his determination to put himself into his novel, and to make the true subject of it the struggle between the multiplicity and continuity of experience and the necessary unity and discontinuity of the novel. He maps out very accurately the path which Butor too has followed, the only path a writer can follow if he wants to show his readers how a human mind sets about coping with the universe. The peace or rationality which his heroes manage to achieve, however, has grown increasingly precarious. There is a moment in *Portrait de l'artiste en jeune singe* when the narrator, who is Butor himself as a young student staying in a German château, inadvertently switches on an alarm system, intended for the protection of the château's many treasures: books, minerals, paintings, and other objects. Just before the alarm bell shatters his calm Butor has been promising himself an 'orgie de déchiffrage' among the books in the library: the old texts largely concerned with the history of the château itself and with the alchemist's art, which he will examine in accordance with his needs of the moment. The château in fact is the privileged scene of his deciphering of the past, the equivalent of Delmont's railway compartment in *La Modification*. But the moment the alarm sounds this privilege is withdrawn; people come running into the courtyard outside and Butor's work is interrupted. But the disturbance is ended by the arrival of a *garde*, who operates a switch or 'interrupteur', which again cuts off the outside world. The memory of the din and disarray remains as a threat to the solitary decipherer:

Après cela, je savais que le silence de la cellule était comme un fragile pont bâti sur un gouffre de hurlement. Ce château tout entier était une bulle de temps passé, miraculeusement épargné par les flammes, une île dans le temps, aux rives, aux enceintes battues par les marées, les

[43] Understand; I want to put everything into this novel. No snips of the scissors so as to cut off its substance here rather than there. I've been working on it for more than a year and nothing has happened to me that I haven't poured into it, that I haven't wanted to get into it: what I see, what I find out, everything other people's lives and my own life have taught me.

laves d'aujourd'hui, une île qui avait recueilli tous ces rescapés d'une autre région du Saint-Empire, d'une autre bulle de temps passé qui, elle, avait expiré sous la fureur (p. 105).[44]

The defences of the writer, the man whose sacred and sovereign mission (as a member of the Saint-Empire) it is to give a contemporary meaning to the text of the world, are thus exposed in all their extreme fragility. His chances of comprehending the past cannot be considered good when the present is only restrained by what Butor refers to as the 'iridescent wall' of an air-bubble. Moreover, to recover the past in its entirety would mean to re-live it, would involve that is to say a repetition exact in every detail; to recover a year in full would take a year, and to take a year is to annul a year, since the act of recuperation means withdrawing from the present moment.

The novelist, therefore, has to admit that he cannot possibly bring everything back to memory, all that he can achieve is a sort of mnemonic, whose gaps or discontinuities generate a response sufficient for the mind to leap them in the way electricity can be conducted across a gap. Butor is proposing that our responsibility is to make a two-dimensional map of our past experience, so that we can consult it when the need arises and restore a three-dimensional landscape that would otherwise have been lost for ever.

What is required then is a method of projection, a conversion factor capable of transforming reality into language; not for nothing has the would-be novelist of *Degrés* been given the name of Vernier, a word defined in the *Concise Oxford Dictionary* as a 'small movable scale for obtaining fractional parts of the subdivisions on fixed scale of barometer, sextant, etc.'. This relationship between the movable and the fixed is a fundamental one for Butor, and it is reflected in the characteristically polyvalent title of a work he himself describes as being an 'étude pour une représentation' of the United States: *Mobile*.

[44] After this, I knew that the silence of the cell was like a fragile bridge built over a gulf of shouting. The whole of the château was a bubble of time past, miraculously spared by the flames, an island in time, whose shores, whose walls were battered by the tides and the lava of today, an island which had gathered in all these survivors from another region of the Saint-Empire, from another bubble of time past which had expired under the fury.

This title refers most obviously to the mobile as an art-form, a shifting, three-dimensional structure, whose configuration changes according to the position of the spectator. But more important is the implied reference to the presence concealed in the book, which is that of Butor himself, the visitor to the United States. *Mobile* reconstructs Butor's United States out of his immobile memories of the country. The position of the writer in the book is therefore, in words that Butor has himself used in a different context, that of a 'mobile parmi les immeubles'. Hence the remarkable aptness of the discovery recorded in *Portrait de l'artiste en jeune singe* that in Hungarian his own name, Butor, means much the same as the French word *mobilier*.

Like the novels that preceded it, *Mobile* is intended to reawaken certain slumbering memories of the past and so clarify the present. It is, to use the imposing term found for it by Roland Barthes from the medical world, an 'anamnesis', a guarantee that the experience of America cannot now vanish without trace for Butor, or for us. But *Mobile* is directed not only at the European mind, but also at the American mind; indeed its moral is aimed far more pertinently at the inhabitants of that country than at its visitors. It is the past of America that Butor has sought to recover in the interests of certain groups living there. An arrogant lesson some might think, but so discreetly conveyed as to appear quite inoffensive.

Butor, therefore, is trying to explain America to itself, trying to do what Revel does in *L'Emploi du temps* for the town of Bleston. Far from being satisfied with the common notion that America is a country without a past he sets out to relate its past to the present. It is not difficult to see why America should have suggested itself to Butor as a peculiarly suitable subject for him; it is huge, a reality that is bound to overflow the attention an individual can give it, and it is also the home of a sinister repression of the national culture. It lends itself to his preoccupations both in the technical and the moral spheres.

Mobile is built out of fragments both from the past and the present of the United States, from its physical reality and from its written texts; thus the book contains enumerations of motor-cars and birds, as well as quotations from Benjamin Franklin or constitutional documents. It also contains urgent evidence of the country's need for the sort of anamnesiac structure which *Mobile* offers. Butor has found subtle typographical equations for the lack of self-expression that has always threatened to rend the superficial fabric of American society in two. Thanks to the flexibility of the French word 'blanc', for example, his early references to notices saying 'Whites Only' turn later into simple blanks in the text of the book, and similarly with the word 'réservations', the isolated communities into which the country's original inhabitants have been herded. It is above all these two repressed ethnic groups, the Negroes and the American Indians, who need *Mobile* as a means of self-expression. The voice of the writer, a conventionally liberal voice, is their hope of acceptance and of their ultimate incorporation into a proper role in contemporary society. The moral of *Mobile* is the same as that of Butor's novels; connections must be established with the true past of the country. To many Americans Salem is the name of a mentholated cigarette and nothing else; to Butor, in *Mobile*, it is not only the name of a cigarette but also the scene of the witchcraft trials, from the court records of which he quotes at great length. He does so in the belief that to revive memories of intolerance and persecution is to lessen the chances of their recrudescence.

In *Mobile*, more clearly perhaps than in the novels, Michel Butor's principles of composition are exposed, principles very lucidly summarized by Roland Barthes:

Michel Butor a conçu ses romans comme une seule et même recherche structurale dont le principe pourrait être le suivant: c'est en *essayant* entre eux des fragments d'événements, que le sens naît, c'est en transformant inlassablement ces événements en fonctions que la structure s'édifie: comme le bricoleur, l'écrivain . . . ne *voit* le sens des unités inertes qu'il a devant lui qu'en les rapportant . . . (*Essais critiques*, p. 186).[45]

Butor's structuralism, here defined, is the logical outcome of his austere and exalted view of the writer's social role. True contin-

---

[45] Michel Butor has seen his novels as a single quest for a structure whose principle might be the following: it is by *trying out* fragments of events that the sense is born, it is by transforming these events tirelessly into functions that the structure is erected: like the *bricoleur* the writer . . . can only *see* the sense of the inert units he has in front of him by joining them together . . .

uity is impossible in a work of creative reproduction, and the artist must create in the full awareness of discontinuity. But an assemblage of discontinuous elements, such as notes of music, is accepted as a work of art, and just as the serialist composer now works to a method that draws the utmost attention to itself, by selecting a sequence of notes and then trying them out in different combinations, so Butor, the 'serialist' novelist, creates a meaningful work of art through enumerations, conjunctions, oppositions, and the other possible relationships that can be established between isolated elements.

It is in this respect that his technique as a critic prolongs his technique as a creator. What Butor presents, for each of the writers (or occasionally the painters) about whom he has written, is a reading of their work. The critic, like the creative writer, must select or accept a certain point of view with regard to the reality he will try to interpret, and thereafter that is what he remains, a point of view. The elements with which Butor works as a critic are quotations; he quotes at great length and with great frequency. But these quotations do not all come from the same area of a writer's or a painter's *œuvre*—their sequence is the critic's own, it is his invention. Thus the articulation of these quotations in a new order constitutes the new reading of an artist's work.

Frequently in Butor's essays this method has been employed with great conviction, and has led to what would seem to be important revaluations of the French literary past. What Butor examines is the artist's method of *composition*, which he tries to relate to that artist's known circumstances in the world and to his explicit philosophy. Thus Butor's quotations are taken both from literature (or painting) and from life or history. And by studying forms of composition the critic is studying the way in which an artist discovers or constitutes himself in the non-self or the non-present.

Theoretically, Butor would seem to be working towards a form of criticism in which the critic could hope to suppress all explicit comment of his own on the works he is criticizing and make his point simply by arranging his selected quotations in the order that reveals a certain message. The critic becomes an anthologist or lexicographer, yet remains a spokesman for himself alone—although never appearing to himself as an object in his own text he is present as the point of convergence of all that that text contains —he is deducible as a presence by his readers.

It is this particular aspect of the structuralist movement, with its promotion of the system at the expense of the individual who expresses himself through that system, which has been so uneasily taken to be a form of anti-humanism. But it could also be argued that, far from diminishing himself, the critic who refuses to appear in person in front of his readers is set on playing the role of God, that he is actually the most self-assertive critic of all. His is the absence which signifies, or at least it will be until such time as *all* critics adopt the same stance with regard to their profession.

As I have already said, this reticent, subjective presence is revealed in the novel, as practised by Butor, by its movement—it is the link, the totalization of all the heterogeneous elements which the book contains. In *Mobile* it is the traveller who originally absorbed all the multifarious information about the present and the past of the United States and who again emerges as the traveller when that information is reproduced as a work of art.

It should now be easy to see why the action of Butor's first novel, *Passage de Milan*, takes place in an *immeuble*. This building is not a social microcosm, representing the diversity of contemporary Paris, but an ontological microcosm; it does not stand for a cross-section of society but for the reflective consciousness of an individual:

Tout immeuble est un entrepôt, avec ses étages et son trafic, les meubles qu'on emménage ou qu'on emporte, ces humains qui ont là leur lieu d'attache, avec leurs parents et leurs possessions, et ceux qui ne reviendront plus.

Comme toute tête est un entrepôt, où dorment des statues de dieux et de démons de toute taille et de tout âge, dont l'inventaire n'est jamais dressé (p. 281).[46]

[46] Every *immeuble* is a warehouse, with its different floors and its commerce, the furniture that is brought in or taken out, those human beings who have their base there, with their relatives and their possessions, and those who will not return. Just as every head is a warehouse, in which sleep statues of gods and demons of every size and age, whose inventory is never complete.

The *immeuble* is thus identified with the mind of the narrator or central character of the novel, the *abbé*, and everything that happens in *Passage de Milan*, is susceptible of being linked with the *abbé*'s preoccupations. To determine these links is a harsh challenge for the reader, who is being asked to do what the *abbé* himself is doing, to pursue the inventory of his mind and, above all, to awaken the slumbering gods and demons so that they can be exorcized, and lose their power over his present and his future.

Thus for Butor the 'je' *is* this inventory, the sum of a complex network of relationships with the external world, established in the immediate past as well as the more distant past: 'chaque personnage n'existe que dans ses relations avec ce qui l'entoure: gens, objets matériels ou culturels' (*Répertoire* 2, p. 85).[47] The novelist's job is to exemplify the method whereby these relationships can be made intelligible by a patient reconstitution or reordering of the available evidence. The novelist is a taxonomist, seeking the one classification of his experience which will reveal the past self to the present self. This classification is not a public one, made in accordance with some anonymous system, but a private one, only made public by exposition in a novel. Butor describes the function of the novel, therefore, as being to penetrate into a profound and personal realm where secret connections can be established between phenomena: 'le roman au contraire oppose à la hiérarchie patente une autre secrète' (ibid, p. 77).[48]

This inward movement into the depths of the individual consciousness is necessarily figured in Butor's novels, at moments when he employs a dynamic contrast between systems of classification that signify something personal and other systems that do not. Phenomena may be related to one another neutrally or anonymously, for example, by recording their disposition in time or space; or again by reference, if the nature of the phenomena warrants it, to some system of classification such as the alphabet which, if not wholly anonymous, is as insignificant as any system

[47] each character only exists in its relations with what surrounds it: people, material or cultural objects.
[48] the novel on the other hand opposes another, secret hierarchy to the apparent one.

well could be. (Even time and space, after all, are not wholly anonymous categories, as emerges in the case of Robbe-Grillet, where it is important to distinguish between the natural view of the world and the mathematical one.)

These public hierarchies, accepted by all, are the ones with which Butor shows the novelist as setting out on his task. *Passage de Milan*, for instance, is divided into twelve sections, one for each hour of Jean Ralon's night, and when the novel begins the various inhabitants of the *immeuble* are all 'at home'—in their familiar apartments, that is. The relationship between these different apartments is spatial—the Mognes are described as living above the Ralons and so on. But this comfortable sense of a public order will not survive very far into the night, so bewildering are all the comings and goings between floors, as visits are paid from one apartment to another. There are three ways in which this commerce can be effected, the mechanical way, by lift, which is that adopted by those who come into the *immeuble* from outside, the representatives of contingency that is; and the two staircases used as a method of circulation by the inhabitants of the *immeuble*, separated, as I have described earlier, by a pane of glass into a masters' staircase and a servants' staircase. The panes of glass, of course, symbolize the separation between the mind inextricably caught up in the world and the reflective mind withdrawn behind its flimsy shield. In *Passage de Milan* the division of the narrative into hours is never threatened or disturbed, because Butor does not, unlike Robbe-Grillet, want to allow us the illusion that the novel takes place outside time altogether, But the division of the night by the clock grows increasingly conventional as the *abbé* is plunged deeper and deeper into areas of his consciousness he would have preferred not to have to re-examine.

The transition from one hierarchical scheme to the other is neatly summarized in *Passage de Milan* in the curious description of the Mogne family at table. This description, intentionally or not, is perhaps the nearest Michel Butor comes anywhere to striking a humorous note in his novels: 'Félix prend le plat des mains de Marie Merédat et le passe à Henri. Maman allait en faire autant, elle se sert. Les deux cercles retraversent parallèlement le rectangle pour aboutir l'un à Frédéric, l'autre à Jeanne, qui le passe rapidement à Vincent, d'où il arrive jusqu'à Viola, "brûlant" la station "Martine" . . .' (p. 62).[49]

This passage, which I have reduced in length, is worth detailed attention. Eating is a biological and anonymous activity, whose significance is neutral—hence the geometrical disposition of the family around the table. But the provision of refreshment—providing for the 'inner man' would be a particularly fitting cliché in this context—is also the function of the novel. Thus what Butor stresses in his description of the Mogne family is the circulation of the dish, which is the mobile element circulating among the immobile elements. To start with the trajectory it follows reveals nothing, but then something seems to go wrong—'Martine' gets left out. The classification of Martine as a station is still legitimate and is linked with the cyclical and mechanical passage of métro trains beneath the *abbé*'s *immeuble* during the earlier part of the night, but the verb 'brûler' is an indication that such a 'hiérarchie patente' will falter as the night proceeds. Butor has used the word deliberately (of course) in the same way as he uses it in *L'Emploi du temps*: the hierarchy which the novel establishes involves a death (that of Angèle Vertigues in the case of *Passage de Milan*), and this death is matched later in the novel by a fire in the artist's studio at the top of the *immeuble*, in which some of the figures on his canvas get burned. But this is the fire that purges and enlightens as well as destroys. The Mogne family supper is a very accurate and attractive *mise en abyme* of *Passage de Milan*.

The slowly growing discrepancy between fixed, impersonal values and private ones is one that can be detected in all Butor's novels. This is the discrepancy, of course, between the map of Bleston which Revel buys and the book which he writes in the hope of replacing it, where the relationship between, for example, the town's two cathedrals, has little or nothing to do with their relative positions on the map. In *La Modification* Rome and Paris are linked at the start of the book only by a railway timetable, but

---

[49] Felix takes the dish from the hands of Marie Merédat and passes it to Henri. Mother was about to do the same, she helps herself. The two circles cross the rectangle again in parallel and end, one at Frédéric, the other at Jeanne, who passes it quickly to Vincent, from where it arrives at Viola, passing through 'Martine' station without stopping . . .

by the end of it their connection is seen to be very much more intricate than that:

on pourrait imaginer ces deux villes superposées l'une à l'autre, l'une souterraine par rapport à l'autre avec des trappes de communication que certains seulement connaîtraient sans qu'aucun sans doute parvînt à les connaître toutes, de telle sorte que pour aller d'un lieu à un autre il pourrait y avoir certains raccourcis ou détours inattendus, de telle sorte que la distance d'un point à un autre, le trajet d'un point à un autre, serait modifié selon la connaissance, la familiarité que l'on aurait de cette autre ville . . . (p. 232).[50]

It is the anonymous, unauthentic man therefore, the unthinking slave of cosmic time, who knows of only one route from Paris to Rome, the direct, mechanical link figured in the mathematics of a timetable. Reference to our own experience, on the other hand, soon tells us that we can sometimes be in Rome as we walk through Paris, and vice versa. Thus the initiate, through a proper self-examination, can re-establish some of the complexity of reality and carry other cities always available within him, able to re-enter and leave them again at will. But Butor stresses above all in *La Modification* that we must not confuse our Paris with our Rome, but understand that one is the city of our present and the other that of our past. Time is not abolished but shown to have secret dimensions.

As a final example of the two sorts of order which Butor contrasts to such powerful effect there are Vernier's class lists in *Degrés*. His thirty-one pupils are introduced first of all by a roll-call, with their names listed in alphabetical order. Later on in the novel there are numerous lists of the boys' names, no longer arranged alphabetically but in orders of merit, as a result of their performance in various tests. These orders of course signify the

---

[50] one might imagine the two towns superimposed one on top of the other, one underground in relation to the other with communicating trap-doors that only certain people know about but without any one of them of course managing to know about them all, so that in order to get from one place to another there could be certain short cuts or unexpected detours, so that the distance from one point to another, the journey from one point to another, would be modified according to how well one knew, to how familiar one was with this other town . . .

present state of Vernier's mind, and a complete analysis of *Degrés*
would have to explain just why these boys appear in this order at
this particular moment.

The primal task of elaborating these secret value-systems, of
building a significant structure out of the discontinuous contents
of a single consciousness, is, as I have observed in connection with
Claude Simon, the task of the palaeontologist, who sets about
reconstructing the skeleton of extinct mammals from a few
fossilized bones. Objects, says Butor, are 'les os du temps'.[51] But
where Simon undermines the whole undertaking by stressing its
ultimate futility, Butor is more concerned with its dangers and inadequacies, when it is seen as an individual rather than a communal task.

His narrator-novelists always find their task a fearsome as well
as a limitless one. Once they have started on their journey into the
past they are no longer in full control of it, for into their consciousness will pour the forces of dispersal, threatening to overwhelm them. The grid with which they hopefully approach their
particular reality cannot ultimately capture more than a very little
of it. The names of the stations along the railway line from Paris
to Rome become less and less capable of stabilizing the mind of
Léon Delmont in the depths of the night, when he begins to
dream. This framework of stability has its reflection in the railway-
compartment itself in the heating grille in the floor, the 'tapis de
fer chauffant', on which a few relics of the past, crumbs and apple-
pips, shift about to the motion of the train, forming different
patterns in relation to the fixed pattern of the grille itself. But the
comforting anonymity of this grille ultimately begins to dissolve.
There comes a point during the night when it begins to seem to
Delmont like the gateway to Hell itself: 'vous débattant vous-
même parmi les mauvais rêves que vous entendez déjà souffler et
hurler derrière les portes de votre tête, derrière ce grillage dessiné
sur le tapis de fer qui les retient à peine . . .' (p. 159).[52]

By a simple apposition Butor equates the 'grillage' with the

---

[51] the bones of time.
[52] struggling yourself among the bad dreams which you can already hear
panting and howling behind the gates of your head, behind the pattern of
the heating grille in the floor which can hardly hold them back . . .

Gestalt of Delmont's mind and so suggests the doubtful capacity of the human reason to restrain or rationalize what threatens to unhinge it.

The *abbé* Ralon, too, is brought face to face in the night with his darkest pre-Christian dreams and does not emerge unscathed, while Revel in Bleston is deprived of the comfort of both the Bailey sisters, his Ariadne and his Phaedra, during his battle with the dark powers that dwell in the labyrinth of the town. But he, like Butor's other narrators, is aware that there is a victory to be derived from this inevitable defeat: 'C'est pourquoi je te remercie de t'être si cruellement, si évidemment vengé de moi, ville de Bleston que je vais quitter dans moins d'un mois, mais dont je demeurerai l'un des princes puisque j'ai réussi, en reconnaissant ma défaite, à exaucer ton désir secret de me voir survivre à cet engloutissement . . .' (p. 261).[53]

L'Emploi du temps, like *Degrés* or *La Modification* is a recognition of defeat, but one where the emphasis falls on the word 'recognition' and not on 'defeat'. But what is the 'désir secret' which Revel has detected in the city of Bleston? Presumably the solicitation to the human mind of chaos, which demands to be given order or expression and so demands the survival of its temporary victim. What Butor is in effect saying is that the individual consciousness is that element of the totality whose responsibility it is to set in order the other elements of that totality. Revel's consciousness does not add anything to the materiality of Bleston; on the contrary, it suppresses a great deal of it, but it imposes an order on what it is able to retain. The capacity granted to the human mind but denied to the rest of creation is that of conscious retention. We not only can but must carry our past with us—we are mobile.

Butor's travellers or narrators are moved by their experiences, that is they are forced to adopt a new stance towards the world on their return to a direct perception of it. And the discovery of a new

[53] That is why I thank you for having revenged yourself so cruelly and obviously on me, town of Bleston that I shall be leaving in less than a month, but of which I shall remain one of the princes since I have succeeded, by acknowledging my defeat, in answering your secret desire to see me survive this engulfment . . .

perspective is at the same time a reminder that the totality is constituted by a vast field of convergent individual perspectives, or what Husserl refers to as an intersubjectivity: 'The intrinsically first being, the being that precedes and bears every worldly objectivity, is transcendental intersubjectivity: the universe of monads, which effects its communion in various ways' (*Cartesian Meditations*, p. 156).

Each object is thus a point in time and space where countless perspectives can intersect, as well as being the repository of many human acts. To determine a single object in all its relations with other objects would ultimately implicate the whole world, animate and inanimate, both synchronically and diachronically.

Butor has travelled a great deal outside France and it is clear, as I have said, that each experience of another country has subjected him to the same relentless challenge with which his own narrators are confronted in their journeys into the past. The crime, so far as he is concerned, would be to return from such a journey, whether it takes place in time or space, unmoved. In *Le Génie du lieu* he gives a description of the effect which Egypt had on him as a young traveller, and of his sudden realization of how different the history of Europe must look to an Egyptian. But more significant was the modification which he had to make to his own perspective on Egypt. What he needed to correct were the myths with which, like any other European of his age and background, he had set out, the inevitable but dangerous baggage of a man ignorant of Egypt's reality. The cheap emblems of the 'mysterious East' needed to be discarded in favour of an up-to-date myth of Egypt as Butor himself experienced it, the result of his close attention to the reality of the country. This is a typically realistic description of the changed state of mind of the traveller, for whom the danger in an age of mass communications is not so much that he will impose the stereotypes of his own culture on that of another people, but that he will be prevented from investigating another culture by the distorted images of it that have been exported.

Butor describes how, shortly before leaving Egypt, he met an Egyptian chauffeur, recently returned from Paris, who showed him his snapshots of the Eiffel Tower. It is a neat conclusion, and it offers the teacher a task: that of giving people a method by

L

which they can wrench themselves, however painfully, from the tenacious grip of irrelevant myths.

Butor is anxious to impart a method of individuation; he proposes that we should investigate as fully as we are able our individual perspective on (or in) the world and then offer it to others, as a gesture towards some future recuperation of the whole of history. His ethic almost seems to derive from a neo-Marxian drive towards a 'total' literature or art, one which would reflect and redeem the entire historical process. As a critic, Butor is concerned with filling in the gaps left by previous critics of the works in question. The good critic both corrects his predecessors and supplements them. In the end the library, which is shown as offering such a fragile refuge against the clamour and confusion of reality in *Portrait de l'artiste en jeune singe*, will be not, obviously, co-extensive in every detail with that reality, but a sufficient guide to its perplexities. Some such totalization of art is, I take it, what sustains Butor in what might otherwise seem a depressingly unequal struggle. Yet even when the universal library is adequate to enable its subscribers to orientate themselves without difficulty it will still have to be kept up to date, and, if the ideologies of science continue to change at their present pace, this task in itself will be a tremendous one.

The impetus for writing a book like *L'Emploi du temps* may have been provided by Butor's experience of Manchester, but the novel is a paradigm of the human situation in a world that Butor has called 'quasi furieux', a world whose multifarious and obscure signs solicit translation into an intelligible and rational language.

For a man to stand up amidst the furore he needs, says Butor, a myth to guide him, and the novelist's job is to show him how to create one. The novel is thus a vital and extremely convenient fiction, because it shows an individual consciousness wrestling with the problems that beset all consciousnesses. Other men's problems may not be precisely ours, but their methods of solving them can be ours. In an essay called 'Le Roman et la poésie',[54] Butor defines a myth as a form of social hygiene; and if a particular society's myths are wholly forgotten or denatured then it is in danger of dissolution. What he apprehends as the gravest and

[54] In *Répertoire* 2.

most insidious danger to humanity is the growing gap between the sacred world and the profane, hence his attempt to reintroduce the myth into the midst of everyday life. Butor has undoubtedly inherited the conviction of the surrealists that art should show what men believe to be merely mundane to be also marvellous. In his novels he has often succeeded with enormous skill and intelligence in re-arranging the mundanities of common experience in accordance with the mythopaeic needs of the narrator's mind; in a book like *Degrés*, for example, the narrative remains extraordinarily plausible as Vernier sets about assembling a necessary structure out of the contingent data of life in a *lycée*; as an exercise in the transformation of the trivial this is a remarkable book. It is also one that must have involved Butor in a massive amount of careful reading, since Vernier's obsession is mirrored in a large number of real quotations from the texts his pupils are studying in class, English as well as French.

Vernier and Jacques Revel in *L'Emploi du temps* are not allowed the indulgence of a dream-life, unlike Jean Ralon or Delmont in *La Modification*, or, for that matter, Butor himself in *Portrait de l'artiste en jeune singe*. By allowing his heroes to dream Butor is able to plunge them more profoundly into their subconscious selves while remaining, as Michel Leiris notes, 'scrupulously realistic': 'puisque ceux-là même de ses éléments qui relèvent du merveilleux sont liés à la situation physique ou à l'état d'esprit du personnage . . .'[55] But the dream is also a *mise en abyme* of the novel itself, since it is an unverifiable process of the individual consciousness. In *Portrait de l'artiste en jeune Singe* Butor talks of the 'fabrication of dreams' being the novelist's task, and exemplifies this by using seven dreams to link the seven accounts of his daily life in the château. In these dreams the elements derived from his waking experience undergo certain transformations and rearrangements, in a conscious mimicking of the subconscious activity which Freud refers to as the 'dream-work'. In this way Butor defines the status of the dream, or the novel, as a 'mode de liaison nécessaire'.

But it is not only the material for the dream that is provided by

[55] since those elements of it which depend on the marvellous are linked with the physical situation or the state of mind of the character . . .

reality itself, so is the motive for dreaming. Since the reality with which Butor is concerned must be treated as a repressed past then it is logical to conclude that the urge to express or arrange it comes as an irresistible impulse to the hero of the novel. Butor has at times referred to this urge in terms of 'demons'. In *Le Génie du lieu*, for instance, it is the demons who are held to have built the pyramids of Egypt, and it is these same malevolent but creative powers whom Léon Delmont meets on his journey to the interior:

perdu parmi les lambeaux de ce projet que vous croyiez si solide, si parfaitement agencé, bien loin d'imaginer que toutes ces fissures, à l'occasion des miettes et de poussières, de tout un essaim d'événements conjugués, savamment érodant les écrous, les écrans de votre vie quotidienne et de ses contrepoids, que toutes ces déchirures irrémédiablement allaient s'y dessiner, vous livrant aux démons non de vous seulement, mais de tous ceux de votre race (p. 159).[56]

Here one can see how it happens that the everyday becomes not only marvellous but also terrifying—the sudden inrush of significance into an act or object previously accepted as trivial or habitual is almost too much for Delmont to withstand.

For Butor, the arts, originating as they do in this drive for a conscious repression to replace the fatality of a complex or 'block', are, in a sense, of collective origin; through the artist speaks a society which shares his problems. The farther Delmont penetrates into his own past the wider the scope of his examination becomes, until he finally comes face to face with an entire mythological pantheon, of the gods and emperors of Ancient Rome. He is brought to the realization that the 'fissure' in his own life, his failure to understand what the two cities of Paris and Rome really mean to him, is in communication with 'une immense fissure historique', the division between paganism and Christianity.

There are two aspects, therefore, to Butor's use of myth; not

---

[56] lost amidst the shreds of that project which you thought so solid, so perfectly articulated, very far from imagining that all these fissures, in the event crumbs and dust, of a whole swarm of conjugated events, wittingly eroding the screw-nuts the screens of your daily life and its counterpoise, that all these rents were going to appear irremediably in it, handing you over not only to your own demons but to all those of your race.

only does a myth represent a means of making sense of reality, it also points to the collective nature of the problem facing each of us as individuals. His busy narrators are not freaks but exemplary men, and their activities always include a plea for co-operation. The apparent anonymity of Butor's novels is a token of his earnestness; they are, in Lévi-Strauss's terms, a social manifestation:

Car les grandes manifestations de la vie sociale ont ceci de commun avec l'œuvre d'art qu'elles naissent au niveau de la vie inconsciente, parce qu'elles sont collectives dans le premier cas et bien qu'elles soient individuelles dans le second; mais la différence reste secondaire, elle est même seulement apparente puisque les unes sont produites *par* le public et les autres *pour* le public . . . (*Tristes tropiques*, p. 105).[57]

As his career has progressed Butor has become increasingly concerned with formal experiment in the presentation of his work, but, unlike quite a lot of *avant-garde* posturing, his inventiveness can only rightly be interpreted as a support for his didacticism. In the first place, he is obviously anxious to remove or mitigate the familiarity of the typographical message, which breeds not contempt but passivity in the reader. For all his own monumental thoroughness and particularity as a critic of other men's books, Butor has more than once written of our inability as readers to grasp more than a fragment of what we are offered, so powerful are the urges to distraction, inattention, incomprehension, and so on. His typographical gymnastics, therefore, as he practises them in a book like *Mobile*, are intended to fascinate the mind and to counter the forces that distort or obstruct a proper understanding of a printed text. Secondly, and more important, Butor has also experimented in ways of personalizing each text, of presenting a complex structure that offers the reader alternative paths in order to explore it. This is already a possibility in *Mobile*, and a necessity in some of his subsequent work. The logical end of such a presentation of a text is one fully programmed for the individual reader, offering him a constant series of choices. That this is the

[57] For the great manifestations of social life have this in common with the work of art, that they arise at the level of unconscious life, because they are collective in the first case and although they are individual in the second; but this difference is secondary, indeed it is only apparent since the first are produced *by* the public and the second *for* the public . . .

tactic adopted in teaching machines is a suggestive link between Butor's writing and the efforts of contemporary pedagogues. The possibilities of this sort of programming in literature are much richer than they are in technical education, because teaching machines deal, as yet, in right or wrong answers, whereas programmed novels might deal in moral alternatives between opposite courses of behaviour. Moreover, the polyvalent text which, in theory, enables a number of readers to enter it and emerge from it at the same points without having shared the same experiences while they were in transit, is another of Butor's reminders that it is through the summation of divergent perspectives that reality comes to be colonized by the human reason.

This point is made at some length in his first novel, *Passage de Milan*, during the fragmented and rather obscure discussion that takes place between an invited group of writers and intellectuals in the rooms of Samuel Léonard. Léonard, an Orientalist, is the man who ultimately leads the initiate, Louis Lécuyer, out of the *immeuble*—having found him cowering in the darkness of the cellar after his murder of Angèle Vertigues—and provides him with the money to leave France and set off for Egypt. Léonard's discussion group is an obvious reflection of another entertainment that is being simultaneously provided elsewhere in the *immeuble*, the Vertigues's birthday party, and is concerned explicitly with the social function of the novel. The ideas expressed turn up again later in an essay called 'La Crise de croissance de la Science-Fiction'. What Butor sees as the failure of science-fiction is its inability, so far at any rate, to create a coherent and convincing future world. The form has been exploited unsystematically, by individuals working without much reference to one another. But any individual's projection of a future world is bound to leave a great many things in that world unchanged from the way they are now, because he lacks the necessary knowledge to project their future.

What the novelist reveals, therefore, is the evidence of his own limited acquaintance with the modern world and of his own obsession, his own imagination at work on raw material that is infinitely malleable. Science-fiction, therefore, remains wholly unconvincing because it is only partly fiction. Samuel Léonard proposes to the writers he has gathered together that they create a co-operative work of fiction, one in which their interlocking subjectivities will map a whole new world; only in this way can science-fiction, or, by extension, any sort of fictional projection, measure up to its responsibilities: 'Les récits de S-F tirent leur puissance d'un grand rêve commun que nous avons, mais ils sont incapables pour l'instant de lui donner une forme unifiée. C'est une mythologie en poussière, impuissante, incapable d'orienter notre action de façon précise' (*Répertoire* 1, p. 193).[58]

The failure of Butor's narrators, therefore, to assume their own individual past in its entirety is far from being a pessimistic conclusion to their enterprise. The further they penetrate into their personal problem the closer they are brought to us, since their problems are seen to merge with ours. When he tries to establish where the limits of the town of Bleston might lie, Revel realizes that what he has to deal with is a conurbation that is literally co-extensive with the world and as old as human history. Small wonder he should demand help: 'Mais, grande ville impitoyable . . . cette lueur que tu arracheras de moi, cette lueur que tu t'arracheras par moi, restera inéluctablement faible et vaine tant que d'autres lueurs consonantes ne viendront pas les renforcer . . .' (p. 264).[59] In the same way Vernier in *Degrés* starts demanding help before the book is a third of the way through, by adopting the persona of his nephew, and, later, that of this nephew's other uncle, in order to show how the events he is struggling to record need to be situated in more perspectives than one.

Being the optimistic and dedicated missionary that he is, Butor is above all a very calculating writer, one who knows very precisely what effect he must produce. This effect can be summed up in the word 'vigilance'—such is the name given in *L'Emploi du temps* to Bleston's insurance company, visible from the window of

[58] Science-fiction stories derive their strength from a great common dream which we have, but they are for the moment incapable of giving it a unified form. It is a fragmented mythology, impotent, unable to orientate our actions in any precise way.

[59] But, great merciless town . . . this gleam that you will wrest from me, this gleam which you will wrest from yourself through me, will remain inevitably feeble and empty until such time as other consonant gleams come to reinforce it . . .

Jacques Revel's office, and the one feature of its architecture that is recorded is the lightning conductor on the roof. What Butor wants to teach the world is how to restructure the past in order to rationalize its praxis in the future. What he refuses us, above all, in his novels is the illusion of a total escape from time. In each novel there is a prolonged act of withdrawal from the external world, but there is no suggestion that this withdrawal is not itself subject to the passage of time. Quite the reverse; it is because the investigation of the past has its own time-scale that the narrator's perspective on his past cannot remain unchanged. He is forced to live the experience which Butor is anxious that we should recognize as our own, living in a state of *constant* vigilance, in which the past is in need of constant re-interpretation.

The interpenetration of past and present in Butor's novels is that of the detective story in fact, or that pure form of it which is held to have been invented by Edgar Allan Poe. Poe, according to Marshall McLuhan, 'saw that instead of directing the work to the reader, it was necessary to incorporate the reader in the work'. Poe's essay, 'The Philosophy of Composition', in which he explains the genesis of his poem, 'The Raven', is a remarkable exercise in the demonstration of the *necessity*, as opposed to the contingency, of composition. Poe knew what the effect was that he was seeking and set about determining its objective correlates, to succumb to a well-worn but valuable phrase. Such a process of induction is only implausible if one falls into the mistaken view that Poe discovered the only possible correlates; he merely discovered ones that were necessary to his purpose. In the same way Butor has to embody in each novel the process by which the mind renders its own reality intelligible and must search, amidst the infinite detail of everyday life and cultural history, for correlates that are necessary because they reflect the narrator's preoccupation. Each novel starts with the mystification of this narrator and ends with his partial illumination.

'Le nouveau roman', writes Ludovic Janvier, 'c'est le roman policier pris au sérieux,'[60] an acceptable definition but one which underestimates the conventional detective story—a form of writing that was taken seriously long before the New Novel was

[60] The New Novel . . . is the detective story taken seriously.

developed. The detective story is a form of fiction in which the relevance or necessity of the contents ought never to be in doubt; if it is rigorously constructed every presence in the book, animate or inanimate, is a clue and not a contingent intrusion for purposes of atmosphere or naturalism. The reader, like the detective himself, is challenged to interpret everything as evidence, and as the amount of evidence grows so the hypotheses accounting for it must be constantly renewed.

Many people, as is well known, do not feel inclined to pursue this process as patiently as the writer would like them to, but turn instead to the end of the book in order to foreclose on the mystery. But in Michel Butor's highly cerebral and austere versions of the detective story such a tactic is impossible, for the excellent reason that the real detective is now the reader; the narrator assembles the relevant evidence but he is denied the power to conceptualize it. The added seriousness to which Janvier refers is therefore constituted by the absence of the traditional intermediary, who guaranteed the comparative passivity of the reader. If we read a detective story properly, we need to do so in a state of constant alertness, refusing to be lulled by familiarity or banality into suppressing our suspicions. This is the same attitude which Butor prescribes for reading his own novels and, by extension, for attending to the reality around us when we have closed the book.

The crime which has been committed and which calls the novel into existence is that of forgetfulness: the murderer is Time. In his elegant analysis of the ethical scheme of the detective story in 'The Guilty Vicarage' W. H. Auden offers a reminder that 'The detective story subscribes, in fact, to the Socratic daydream: "Sin is ignorance"'. At the same time, he stresses that, as normally constructed, detective stories are escape literature and not art, because they allow us the illusion of dissociation from the murderer, thanks to the miraculous powers of the *deus ex machina* who solves the crime and restores our threatened innocence.

In Butor's novels there is no such intervention or finality: we are simply brought to the point of recognizing that we are bound to go on living in sin, as it were, since we shall never achieve total recall of the past without a permanent withdrawal from the present, and if we withdraw from the present then our past has been extended without our being properly aware of it. Where there is ignorance there is invention: we must make plans to live with our guilt.

Detective novels are introduced freely into Butor's own novels in order to typify his own intentions. Félix Mogne, a schoolboy and thus one of the class of young initiates, reads them in *Passage de Milan*, at moments when he ought to be doing his homework: the only conclusion to be drawn from this is that they represent a precious release for him from 'devoir', or necessity; the book which Delmont uses to mark his seat in the train is also a detective story and I have already tried to show how closely this book must be identified with Butor's own; detective stories are the favourite reading of the second of Vernier's two personae in *Degrés*, Henri Jouret; James Jenkins, in *L'Emploi du temps*, has a whole room full of them at his home, belonging to his dead father.

In *L'Emploi du temps* Butor exploits the structure of the detective story more directly than in any of his other novels. One of the first things that Revel does on his arrival in Bleston is to buy a book called *Le Meurtre de Bleston*. This is a murder mystery but he finds it useful in the first instance as a guide to certain aspects of the town, notably the sacred (or mythical) aspects, the Old and the New Cathedrals—which are in fact the scenes of the two crimes in the novel. When Revel buys *Le Meurtre de Bleston* he finds the name of the author given on the jacket as J.-C. Hamilton, but the space which ought to contain the author's photograph has been left blank. J.-C. Hamilton is later revealed to be the pseudonym of George William Burton, a writer living in Bleston itself, and when a subsequent edition of his novel appears, in the course of *L'Emploi du temps* (as the result of an accident that reveals Burton to be its author), both his correct name and a photograph are included in it. Thus, so far as surnames go, the road from Hamilton to Butor passes, with every plausibility, through Burton.

The ambiguity of the title of Burton's book is another indication of its true significance: does it refer to a murder that has taken place in Bleston, or to the murder of the town itself? The answer is both. Burton's fate in *L'Emploi du temps* is precisely that of Revel himself; he is run down and injured by a black car in the

street, and for a long time Burton chooses to look on this accident as an attempt at murdering him, and the suspect is James
Jenkins, who has charge of the car belonging to Matthews & Co.
The colour of the car and Jenkins's status in the novel, to which I
have already referred, indicate the nature of Burton's accident;
for it is the town of Bleston itself, or the dark processes of contingency, that have threatened his life, just as they have threatened
Revel's. Ultimately Burton is reconciled with his fate and accepts
the accident on its own terms; in the same way Revel ultimately
comes to be reconciled with Bleston, the town with which he
signs a secret pact and whose contingence cannot be finally denied,
only disguised in successive myths.

But it is the accident that reveals the author, or endows him
with his true identity. Because of the publicity he receives as a
result of being knocked down, Burton becomes known as the man
who wrote *Le Meurtre de Bleston*; the pseudonym of Hamilton can
be discarded. As it happens, Hamilton is also the name of the railway station at which Revel arrives at the start of *L'Emploi du
temps*, and to which he attempts to find his way back later. But
instead of getting back to Hamilton Station he ends up at New
Station, a mistake which is in effect a *mise en abyme* of the entire
novel; the journey which Butor's narrators undertake always
leads them in a direction they had not expected or even wanted to
take from the Old to the New. The confusion between the two
railway stations is precisely the same as Delmont's confusion
early in *La Modification* between Paris and Rome: 'les deux bâti-
ments se confondaient dans mon esprit; je n'arrivais pas à me
représenter leurs situations respectives' (p. 16).[61]

Burton, Revel, and Butor thus form a trinity, and when Burton
delivers his short sermons on his profession as a writer of detective
stories he has some revealing things to say. I call them sermons
because they are delivered on successive Sundays, not from a
pulpit, but from a seat in a Chinese restaurant, which, for Butor
(or for Robbe-Grillet) is certainly not a negligible or trivial locale.
The detective, states Burton, is the agent of truth: 'tout roman
policier est bâti donc sur deux meurtres, dont le premier, commis

---

[61] the two buildings were confused in my mind; I could not manage to
picture to myself their respective locations.

par l'assassin, n'est que l'occasion du second dans lequel il est la victime du meurtrier pur et impunissable, du détective qui le met à mort, non par un de ces moyens vils que lui-même était réduit à employer . . . mais par l'explosion de la vérité' (p. 146).[62]

In Burton's own novel the man who is murdered is a cricketer called Johnny Winn, and the murderer is his brother—this is a further parallel with the story of Cain and Abel, recorded in the *Vitrail du Meurtrier*. The first murder is that of a man dedicated to the free play of the *jeu* and corresponds to what has happened to Revel in Bleston during those dark months of winter, before he was led to recover his freedom through the use of speech. The second murder is that of the guilty brother by the detective, Burton, thinly disguised in his own book as Morton, and this of course corresponds to Revel's own attempted murder of Bleston, with the important difference that in his case the murder is not a final success, since ultimately he is forced to come to an agreement with the evil town. Butor makes it quite clear that *Le Meurtre de Bleston* is not an exact model for Revel in *L'Emploi du temps*, because the second killing in Burton's book, that of the fratricide by the detective, is too much the symmetrical image of the first. Revel criticizes Burton for trying to diminish the splendour or interest of Bleston's New Cathedral, because he is too much obsessed with the Old: 'Ah, J.-C. Hamilton ne ménage pas ses sarcasmes: "cette misérable farce", "this make-believe" (Comment traduire? Presque "cette escroquerie") ,"imitation vide d'un modèle incompris", "monument de sottise", "l'œuvre d'un singe radotant" ' (p. 121).[63]

Now what is being expressed in these contemptuous phrases is a view of the novel as a form of writing. To Burton the New Cathedral, the structure erected in order to supplement the Old,

---

[62] every detective story therefore is built on two murders, the first of which, committed by the murderer, is simply the occasion for the second, in which he is the victim of the pure and unpunishable murderer, of the detective who puts him to death, not by one of those base methods that he himself had been reduced to using . . . but by the explosion of the truth.

[63] Ah, J.-C. Hamilton is not sparing with his sarcasms: 'this miserable farce', 'this make-believe' (How is that to be translated? Almost 'this swindle'), 'an empty imitation of a misunderstood model', 'monument to folly', 'the work of an idiot monkey'.

represents not a growth or an improvement but a relapse. In his own novel, *Le Meurtre de Bleston*, the first murder is committed in the New Cathedral and the second in the Old: there is an evident movement of regression, and a denial of the primacy of the present moment. Revel, however, appreciates that the New Cathedral is a much more significant building than Burton admits, that its relationship to the Old Cathedral is a creative one; he expresses Butor's belief that a new literary invention becomes truly significant at the points where it departs from previous literary inventions, for this is the way it renews our myths. The writer is indeed a 'monkey', but not ashamed of it. In *Portrait de l'artiste en ieune singe*—a title that itself mimics those of James Joyce and Dylan Thomas—Butor has exploited his own simian status to the full, even to the point of turning himself into an especially clever monkey in the dream he uses to link the events of the separate days together. In this book he also offers a reminder that the Egyptian god of writing, Thot, was always represented as a monkey.

Thus Revel, the monkey of Bleston, understands better than Burton the relationship of the New Cathedral to the Old:

Car moi si neuf dans Bleston, j'avais bien décélé qu'il y avait tout autre chose qu'un démarquage dans cette bizarre construction, j'avais été bien obligé de sentir qu'un esprit d'une étonnante audace y dénaturait violemment les thèmes, les ornaments et les détails traditionnels, aboutissant ainsi à une œuvre certes imparfaite, je dirais presque infirme, riche pourtant d'un profond rêve irréfutable, d'un sourd pouvoir germinateur, d'un pathétique appel vers des réussites plus libres et meilleures . . . (p. 121).[64]

The definition of the novel as an 'irrefutable dream' repeats Butor's other definition quoted in my introduction, that the novel is 'le domaine phénoménologique par excellence' because it is incapable of verification.

[64] For I, so new to Bleston, had certainly discovered that there was something quite other than a plagiarism in this weird construction, I had certainly been forced to feel that in it a mind of an astonishing audacity had violently denatured the traditional themes, ornamentation, and details, thus ending up with a work that was admittedly imperfect, I would say almost infirm, yet rich with a profound and irrefutable dream, with a secret power of germination, with a pathetic appeal to freer and greater triumphs . . .

On the second occasion when he talks about his craft G. W. Burton welcomes the appearance within the best detective stories —like *L'Emploi du temps*—of what is in effect a new dimension:

nous expliquant que ce ne sont plus seulement les personnages et leurs relations qui se transforment sous les yeux du lecteur, mais ce que l'on sait de ces relations et même de leur histoire . . . de telle sorte que le récit n'est plus la simple projection plane d'une série d'événements mais la restitution de leur architecture, de leur espace, puisqu'ils se présentent différemment selon la position qu'occupe par rapport à eux le détective ou le narrateur . . . (p. 161).[65]

This new dimension is the one which encourages the full involvement of the reader in the text, because reader and narrator are in a similar situation: as time advances their perspective on the past alters and with it their degree of comprehension of past events. Any sort of final or absolute solution is thus impossible, because there is no escape from time and no way of avoiding these constant revaluations of the past—no way, that is, unless we take the common and disreputable course of ignoring the new evidence from the world which seems to contradict our laboriously formulated hypotheses.

Butor has extended his novels systematically in time, therefore, recognizing that the process of recuperation must not be disguised as a timeless one. The mind that is withdrawn into reflection cannot defend itself for long against the intrusion of sense-impressions, nor, in a world as intellectually or ideologically volatile as the contemporary one, can the mind's hypotheses survive for long without modification. This is the theme of yet another of Burton's sermons:

dans le roman policier, le récit est fait à contre-courant, ou plus exactement qu'il superpose deux séries temporelles: les jours de l'enquête qui commence au crime, et les jours du drame qui mènent à lui, ce qui est tout à fait naturel puisque, dans la réalité, ce travail de l'esprit

[65] explaining to us that it is not only the characters and their relationships which are transformed before the reader's eyes, but what we know about these relationships and even about their history . . . in such a way that the story is no longer the simple plane projection of a sequence of events but the restitution of their architecture, their space, since they appear differently according to the position which the detective or narrator occupies in relation to them . . .

tourné vers le passé s'accomplit dans le temps pendant que d'autres événements s'accumulent (p. 171).[66]

The second time-series to which Burton alludes is the model within the novel for the time-series of the reader; it is by virtue of the narrator's progress in time from ignorance to knowledge that we get the opportunity of implication in his quest. But it is also because this narrator is ineluctably trapped within cosmic time that his ambition *vis-à-vis* the past can never be more than partially realized. The elaboration of a work of art forces us to withdraw the eye from what is present to it, with the result that we are conniving at the processes of oblivion at the very moment when we set out to arrest them.

Butor explores the possibilities of this double time-series most elaborately in *L'Emploi du temps* and in *Degrés*. In the first book Revel sets out to recreate the past in a strictly linear way, by preserving a constant distance of seven months—the period of his mute hibernation in Bleston—between the time when he is writing and the time he is writing about. But already, by the second chapter of the novel, he has been forced to abandon this logical and manageable sequence, because he finds himself forced to return to episodes already recorded, these having taken on a new or fuller meaning with the subsequent progress of his researches. Ultimately, of course, he has to admit that these researches will never be complete; he quite literally does not have the time. In fact there is a somewhat skittish lacuna in Revel's timetable: at the end of *L'Emploi du temps* he explains that he has no time left to record the events of one particular day during his year in Bleston—the previous February the twenty-ninth. But it would be misleading to assume that because of this he was only foiled by a leap-year—Revel's stay in Bleston is arbitrarily limited, and if it continued he would have to return over and over again to what he had already written in order to amplify or correct it.

In the same way Vernier in *Degrés* is brought twice to what is

[66] in the detective story, the story is told against the stream, or more precisely it superposes two temporal series: the days of the investigation which starts with the crime, and the days of the drama leading up to it, which is wholly natural since, in real life, the work of the mind turned towards the past is accomplished within time as other events accumulate.

really an identical realization. When he first sets out on his description of his class he fancies that he will be able to achieve it by recording nothing but verified facts, that he will produce a documentary record that is to say; but he quickly finds that the time required for verification increases with each piece of information he has ascertained, so he has to accept the use of the imagination to fill in the gaps. But this acceptance cannot ultimately save him, for even without the time taken by verification he is defeated by the sheer burden of recording everything he imagines. His use of the present tense becomes more and more of a convention: 'mais les pages qui nous concernent . . . qui ont l'air d'avoir été écrites le jour même à cause du présent que tu y emploies, ne l'ont été en effet que bien des jours plus tard . . .' (p. 253).[67]

Vernier finally will vanish into the silence of the gap that has swallowed him up, but he has left us the record of his defeat, and the lesson it embodies. He has made a start.

In the last resort, then, Michel Butor's formidably coherent and complex structures are assembled in such a way as to make it peculiarly hard for the reader to stand back from them and treat them as a new and ingenious exploitation of naturalistic conventions. For a final and important example of the way in which Butor implicates his public is his use, for the narration of *La Modification* and *Degrés*, of the second person singular or plural. Some critics of the novelist have rather exaggerated this one stratagem at the expense of others.

This second person is more than just a direct injunction to the reader; it echoes other uses that are made of it in day-to-day life. It is common in books or films portraying court scenes, for example, where the prosecutor addresses the accused in the second person; in France it is particularly common in the projective school exercise; in all industrialized countries it is a standby of printed publicity, since advertising copywriters must appear to address their readers without intermediaries. It is, in general, a person of the verb both accusatory and hortatory, the right person to adopt

---

[67] but the pages which concern us . . . which appear to have been written on the day itself because of the present tense you use in them, were in fact only written many days later . . .

if it is your aim, as it is Butor's aim, to show the omissions of the past being rectified in the service of the future. In Butor the second person originates in psychic repression, since it indicates a gap in the self-awareness of the narrator who is, after all, addressing himself in the first instance and ourselves only in the second. Its full Brechtian significance emerges from Roland Barthes's definition: 'ce vouvoiement me paraît littéral; il est celui du créateur à la créature, nommée, constituée, créée dans tous ses actes par un juge et générateur' (*Essais critiques*, p. 103).[68]

But this judge who makes the indictment is not a divine one, he is simply a man able, like all of us, to perform acts of reflection. If we do not perform this act regularly then we come to live like animals; if we do, we live rationally. We are the judges and the generators of our own lives because we live in time, and because our lives are constituted, or can be, by a series of choices. Michel Butor is advocating that these choices should be made in the full light of self-awareness.

[68] this use of *vous* seem to me to be literal; it is that of the creator to the creature, named, constituted, created in all his acts by a judge and generator.

M

ALAIN ROBBE-GRILLET

I

AFTER the unyielding pessimism of Claude Simon and the olympian didacticism of Michel Butor, Alain Robbe-Grillet appears as a frivolous writer, content simply to make fun of the whole idea of writing novels. Yet if a somewhat facile mockery is evident in everything he writes, and if the easy-going naturalism of his attitudes is intended a little too obviously to be a reproach to the solemn pessimism of the French mages of a previous generation, his intentions are not so baldly iconoclastic as might be thought. His novels are not without their moral prescriptions, because they depend on a world-view which sees the creation of fantasy in terms of psycho-therapy.

For Robbe-Grillet, as for Butor, the reality which the novelist creates must be seen to be distinguishable from the reality in the midst of which we live. The world of transcendental objects provides us, necessarily, with the raw materials out of which we are able to construct the immanent fictional world that we need; what it cannot do is insist that we use these raw materials in one way rather than another. The public function or significance of the phenomenal world does not have to be carried over into our private worlds.

In this respect, the *nouveau roman* is exploiting the discovery of artistic freedom which painters and musicians began to exploit more than fifty years ago, and is attempting to lead the novel into what it would be tempting but misleading to think of as its period of abstraction—misleading because the freedom of the novelist in respect of language is more limited than that of the painter or composer in respect of colour, shape, and sound.

To understand Robbe-Grillet's practice of the novel it might help to borrow a distinction made by the art historian E. H. Gombrich. In his book *Art and Illusion*, in which he reinterprets the nature of aesthetic creation and experience in terms of *gestalt* psychology, Professor Gombrich uses the terms 'making' and 'matching' to point the fundamental difference between figurative and non-figurative art. Applied to the novel these terms are equally instructive, with the single proviso that, just because a writer is aiming to make and not to match, this does not mean that he is inevitably led to create a private reality into which the reader has no hope at all of penetrating. The world that is created in Robbe-Grillet's novels is not the coherent, consecutive one of the traditional novel, but it is still susceptible of an interpretation, since its topography and characterization depend, more or less overtly, on the preoccupations of a (any) novelist, while the order of scenes that constitute the whole is itself explicable, at any rate in theory, by reference to common laws of psychological association.

Robbe-Grillet once said that his favourite qualities are imagination and simplicity. While it is true that he is not especially reliable as an interviewee, since his answers are sometimes too irreverently oblique not to mislead, it is also true that his great aim as a novelist or as a film-maker has always been, right from the start, to exercise the prerogative accorded to us by the imagination. It is obvious that to exercise the imagination in the way in which Robbe-Grillet has exercised it is not to be simple at all; far from it, since it is the unexpectedness of his absolutism in this respect which has led to so much of the criticism he has had to put up with.

What has traditionally been lauded as a creative achievement in the novel is primarily a reproductive one, that is to say the simple test is applied of whether the world assembled by the novelist is plausible if measured against reality as we are quite confident we experience it. In this way we end up by assessing the quality of a novelist's discrimination as much as his imagination, and judge him as a psychologist perhaps, or as a sociologist, rather than as a true creator. Robbe-Grillet is set on displaying the novel as a truly creative achievement, by proving to us that our minds are free within the two covers of a book or, by extension, whenever we close our eyes to the contingent world in order to reassemble it without interference and without the pressure of conformity to a pre-existing aesthetic pattern.

Many of the difficulties which people have experienced in understanding or interpreting the novels of Robbe-Grillet stem simply from the fact that it is easy to forget, so conditioned are we to the view that language must represent a pre-existent and transcendent reality, that the reality of these novels is an immanent one, a subjective one in which existence precedes essence and in which the significance of any phenomenon can only be determined as the novel proceeds, by close study of the way these phenomena are deployed and transformed by consciousness.

Yet Robbe-Grillet has been very generous in providing indications of his intentions, not least in his novels themselves, where the real world is melodramatically abolished in favour of an imaginary one, this being the way, as Sartre proposes, in which we exercise our not very glorious independence of matter: 'Poser une image . . . c'est donc tenir le réel à distance, s'en affranchir, en un mot le nier' (*L'Imaginaire*, p. 352).[1]

But the world which Robbe-Grillet deploys in his fiction cannot be taken as wholly imaginary, as being totally without substance. In order to show that there is to be no final escape from the real world he must allow it to be represented within the structure of the novel; indeed the representatives of reality are what threaten the continuity of the novel and expose the fiction as a fiction. Robbe-Grillet's novels develop their characteristic tension in this way from a dialectic between the real and unreal, or between the objective and subjective modes of perception.

In his first novel, *Les Gommes,* published in 1953, Robbe-Grillet enjoys himself greatly as he dramatizes both the conditions under which a novel comes into being, or rather tries to come into being, and the relationship between the novelist and the raw material of his novel. The book starts at dawn: 'Dans la pénombre de la salle de café le patron dispose les tables et les chaises, les cendriers, les siphons d'eau gazeuse; il est six heures du matin' (p. 11).[2]

The opening of the (or any) novel coincides therefore with the

---

[1] To posit an image . . . is thus to keep the real at a distance, to free oneself from it, in a word to negate it.

[2] In the penumbra of the café the owner arranges the tables and chairs, the ash-trays, the siphons of soda water; it is six o'clock in the morning.

coming of the light, and there are many subsequent examples in Robbe-Grillet of the field of light exemplifying the field of consciousness. At this early stage of his career he seems to have missed the chance of making his message clearer by showing the source of light to be an artificial one—a mistake which has been corrected by the time we get to *Dans le labyrinthe*, for example.

The powers of the *patron* in *Les Gommes* are precisely coextensive with those of the novelist, who is able to arrange the décor of his novel but cannot, of course, create its actual substance; form is bestowed on chaos as night gives way to day. The passage I have quoted reads very deliberately like the stage directions for a play, because what is going to follow is a sequence of more or less animated scenes, played out on the screen of consciousness. Like Claude Simon, Robbe-Grillet loses no opportunity of reminding his readers that the characters of his novels are actors, not real people, but he does not exploit this theatricality for metaphysical ends, simply to stress their lack of autonomy and immediate physical presence. In *Dans le labyrinthe* there is a sly equation between the curtains across a stage and the narrator of the novel's eyelids; every time he sees the curtains his mind is projected outside into the streets of the town in which all the action of the novel takes place—yet the curtains are never drawn back.

Robbe-Grillet goes on, in *Les Gommes*, to describe the patron as 'l'unique personnage présent en scène'.[3] The novel, therefore, is a little like a play where the curtain has gone up too soon, since it reveals the author, who is also, in this post-Brechtian age, allowed to double as actor, still at work on his preparations for the performance. He has still not sloughed off all the restrictions of necessity. His first movements towards the constitution of his world are shown to be fully habitual or automatic: 'Il n'a pas besoin de voir clair, il ne sait même pas ce qu'il fait. Il dort encore. De très anciennes lois règlent le détail de ses gestes, sauvés pour une fois du flottement des intentions humaines . . .' (p. 11).[4]

Since all the *patron* has so far achieved is to have arranged the

---

[3] the only character present on stage.
[4] He has no need to see clearly, he does not even know what he is doing. He is still asleep. Very ancient laws control the detail of his movements, safe for once from the fluctuation of human intentions . . .

décor around him, the implication can only be that the 'anciennes lois' which free him from any need to be conscious of what he is doing are the fundamental ones of spatial arrangement—the laws of geometry which Robbe-Grillet, far from wanting to deny, is always very anxious to promote as the one truly rational way of setting things in order. But with the notion of 'flottement' the sign of the mind's freedom appears, and the novel's field is defined as being that of human interiority. A perceived action is a public event, a shared fact, and Robbe-Grillet is being wholly traditional when he insists that fiction should deal with motive rather than event. His novels can perhaps be seen as fighting a deliberately frivolous rearguard action against science, which may one day find out how to turn hidden feelings into public facts, through inevitable advances in neurology or bio-chemistry. Until such a time, when the novel will have lost all interest or importance as a serious study of the human mind, the function of the creative writer, as defined by Robbe-Grillet, will be to portray individual mental states directly, from inside. It is up to the reader to make what is presented to him as an immediate experience into a mediate or explicit one, or he can, if he prefers, share unquestioningly in the experience of a mind in mid-creation.

In *Les Gommes* there is a solitary event supposed to have taken place outside the time-scale of the novel, the murder of Dupont. This surname is indicative of the function in Robbe-Grillet's scheme of the murder—which destroys a bridge between a consciousness and the outside world. The novel is revealed as an attempt to account for or solve this accident which is actually self-sufficient and incapable of being explained away. The mind that investigates it is theoretically a free agent, but subjected in this case, as in all Robbe-Grillet's other novels, to a pressure it cannot resist—its tendency to impose on its contents a myth, the best-known of all literary myths, that of Oedipus.

By using such a soiled myth Robbe-Grillet is clearly taking a very different view of the value of myths in general from that taken by Michel Butor. He is thinking of myths in the way they are nowadays most often thought of, as something which is, almost by definition, irrational and illusory. All Robbe-Grillet's novels thus depend on myths, because they all represent the sub-tension of a private fantasy, distorting the real world to satisfy its own imperious needs. What happens in *Les Gommes*, therefore, can really be said to take place outside cosmic time altogether. As Olga Bernal, who sees this as the most aggressive of all anti-novels, rightly says, the bullet that kills Dupont would have taken only a fraction of a second instead of twenty-four hours, if it were not for the insistent mythomania of the imagination. Between the moment when the trigger of a gun is pressed and the moment when the bullet strikes its target, between two public and perceptible events therefore, there is a gap in the perceptions of any hypothetical observer—one which might easily be filled, if need be, by reference to the uncontroversial laws of ballistics. But with Robbe-Grillet any such minute gap in the records of the human eye is the opportunity to insert a myth, and the fact that in *Les Gommes* this gap is so truly infinitesimal that it would normally pass unnoticed is a further clue to the irony of his proceeding, since the novel itself is a substantial one.

The successive events or scenes of Robbe-Grillet's novels take place then at a tempo determined by the reader, since the time it takes to read a book stands in no determinable relationship to the time taken to write it. With the *ciné-romans*, obviously, the position changes, since the audience in the cinema cannot control the speed at which the film is run. Here Robbe-Grillet maintains a stricter control, though it is arguable whether this is to his advantage or not. Of *L'Année dernière à Marienbad* he has himself written: 'Toute l'histoire de *Marienbad* ne se passe ni en deux ans, ni en trois jours, mais exactement en une heure et demie,' (*Pour un nouveau roman*, p. 131).[5] This is another of those deceptively simple definitions, involving a more radical re-orientation of the reader's (or spectator's) habits than Robbe-Grillet apparently allows.

What he is saying is that the time-scale of the narration itself is a fixed sequence, while the time-scale of the narrative is dislocated to the point of defeating all attempts at its chronological reconstruction by the reader. But the chronological narrative is a habit that dies hard, since it is still adopted by a large majority of the

[5] The whole story of *Last Year in Marienbad* takes place not in two years, nor in three days, but in exactly one hour and a half.

world's story-tellers. Moreover, the one chronological sequence that Robbe-Grillet does permit is still a conventional one; the scenes of one of his novels or film-scripts would pass through his (or anyone's) mind far quicker than they can once they are transposed into words or even pictures. Robbe-Grillet's novels, like those of Claude Simon, purport to be instantaneous, but since the rhythm of their composition has in fact been set by the inclinations and working habits of the novelist, it is clear that a lot of room remains for artifice.

In *Les Gommes* Robbe-Grillet puts a stop to the flow of cosmic time quite unequivocally, as he already had (and in precisely the same way) in the single fragment of an earlier novel, *Un Régicide*, which has been published. The wrist-watch of Wallas, the central character and 'detective' of the novel is said to have stopped at 7.30, the time at which the supposed murder of Dupont had taken place. Once the murder has taken place again, at the end of the book, Wallas's wrist-watch is found to have started once more, disturbed by the shock of a revolver going off. The twenty-four hours of the novel's freedom are over.

This intrusion into the unalterable sequence of cosmic time is exemplified on the first page of *Les Gommes* as the *patron* continues his preparations for the fiction to get under way: 'chaque seconde marque un pur mouvement: un pas de côté, la chaise à trente centimètres, trois coups de torchon, demi-tour à droite, deux pas en avant, chaque seconde marque, parfaite, égale, sans bavure . . . Bientôt malheureusement le temps ne sera plus le maître' (p. 11).[6]

Here, for a little while longer, the *patron* is still controlled by mechanical laws in which there is no flaw ('sans bavure'). But there is also a sign that all is not well with the *patron*: his 'trois coups de torchon'. To any Frenchman reading this carefully the significance of the 'trois coups' will not be lost; it is an indication that the curtain is about to go up on a drama. But why the duster? Because the patron is reluctant, like Robbe-Grillet's subsequent mythomaniacs, to allow the drama to begin, and so he is keen to

[6] each second marks a pure movement: one step sideways, the chair thirty centimetres away, three flicks of the duster, a half-turn to the right, two paces foward, each second marks, perfect, even, without a smudge . . . Soon, alas, time will not be master any longer.

eliminate the traces of the past which are the pre-condition of its future existence, just as the narrator of *Un Régicide* is anxious to remove all trace of his own presence on the scene of the crime and the husband in *La Jalousie* will be desperate to remove the trace of the crushed millipede from the wall.

In view of the glaring implausibility of scenes like the one described, which one would have thought too stylized by far to succumb to critical attempts to naturalize them, it is surprising how many of Robbe-Grillet's exegetes, even some of the subtler ones, choose to find evidence of atmosphere in them. Yet Robbe-Grillet uses the figure of the *patron* again in *Dans le labyrinthe*, in the picture that hangs on the narrator's bedroom wall. The picture is entitled 'The Defeat at Reichenfels', yet the scene shown is a café full of a carefully assorted crowd of drinkers—an incongruity that is highly revealing. A final description of this café-scene introduces the novelist and those for whom he is writing barely disguised at all: 'Les comparses qui discutent devant lui avec tant d'animation . . .; ce ne sont que des tacticiens de cabaret qui refont l'histoire à leur guise, critiquant les ministres, corrigeant les actes des généraux, créant des épisodes imaginaires . . .' (p. 217).[7] The appearance of Robbe-Grillet's readers as the *patron*'s customers makes it clear surely that the choice of a café as a locale indicates the novelist's own assessment of the value and purpose of his books—which is to offer refreshment, a word not without ethical implications.

But to return for a moment to the passage from *Les Gommes*, in which the word 'malheureusement' is a striking intruder in the scheme of things. If we take it as expressing the apprehension felt by the *patron* himself then it indicates his reluctance to be drawn into a plot and indicates also the future tension in him between stability and instability; if it is taken more directly as expressing Robbe-Grillet's own feelings then the word is fetchingly ironic, in that the novelist is declaring his sympathy for his readers, who are about to be inflicted with a novel, and one,

---

[7] The supernumaries arguing in front of him so animatedly . . .; they are simply café tacticians remaking history as they please, criticizing the ministers, correcting the acts of the generals, creating imaginary episodes . . .

moreover, which will disturb their customary convictions about what a novel ought to be like.

This last is a thought to which Robbe-Grillet returns a little later in *Les Gommes*, with the first appearance of Wallas, who is discovered leaning against a balustrade as the town's workmen flock past in the early morning to the necessary and mechanical tasks that await them. Wallas's presence is incongruous: 'on ne va pas se promener un mardi au petit jour, d'ailleurs on ne se promène pas dans ce quartier-là. Cette indépendance vis-à-vis du lieu et de l'heure a quelque chose d'un peu choquant' (p. 45).[8]

It is hard not to read a playful humour into the last sentence, for Robbe-Grillet must have known very well at the time when he published *Les Gommes* that this was precisely one of the things that would shock his readers—his own creative independence of time and space.

Apart from the direct indication of the stopped watch in *Les Gommes* Robbe-Grillet makes the same point about the interruption which the novel represents in a mechanical sequence in other ways. Whenever, in any of his novels, a piece of machinery is introduced it is for this purpose, and to remind us inevitably of the evanescence of our instant of mental freedom, by threatening to stop the novel there and then. If this were the world of Claude Simon one could go further and say that the sound of a piece of machinery was intended as a *memento mori* to the reader, but with Robbe-Grillet this would be quite untrue, since the death of a novel represents, for him, a return to sanity, not the threat of the individual's dissolution.

In *Les Gommes* the piece of machinery most constantly kept in the reader's view is the drawbridge connecting two parts of the town, whose functioning, as it opens and shuts, reflects the motions of the novel itself and reminds one that this has been brought into existence to account for the death of another 'bridge'—Dupont. The mechanism that works the bridge is not quite perfect: 'Mais de l'autre côté de la barrière, on pouvait constater que tout n'était pas encore terminé: par suite d'une certaine élasticité de la masse, la descente du tablier n'avait pas pris fin avec l'arrêt du mécanisme: elle s'était poursuivie pendant quelques secondes, sur un centimètre peut-être, créant un léger décalage dans la continuité de la chaussée...' (p. 158).[9]

Before this tiny gap ('décalage') can be eliminated the floor of the bridge continues to oscillate up and down over increasingly minute distances: 'les oscillations, de plus en plus amorties, de moins en moins discernables—mais dont il était difficile de préciser le terme—frangeaient ainsi, par une série de prolongements et de regressions successifs de part et d'autre d'une fixité tout illusoire, un phénomène achevé, cependant, depuis un temps notable' (p. 158).[10] The oscillatory movement characteristic of all Robbe-Grillet's fictions is here, therefore, linked directly with the inability of the eye to measure an objective phenomenon with total accuracy, so that reverberations are set up which do not consort with the physical facts. The play in the mechanism is brought about by the inadequacy of our perceptual apparatus; what Robbe-Grillet is exploiting is the equivalent of the physicists' principle of indeterminacy with regard to the precise position of individual particles—the words 'élasticité de la masse' in the passage first quoted hint at this.

The same point is made very clearly in *La Jalousie*, when the husband in that novel becomes interested in the trajectories of the mosquitoes flying round his lamp. His attempts to keep track of them are, predictably, doomed: 'Du reste, qu'il s'agisse de l'amplitude, de la forme ou de la situation plus on moins excentrique, les variations sont probablement incessantes à l'intérieur de

---

[9] But from the other side of the barrier, it was possible to establish that everything was not yet finished: as a result of a certain elasticity of the mass, the apron had not finished its descent with the stopping of the machinery: it had continued for a few seconds, over a centimetre perhaps, creating a slight gap in the continuity of the roadway . . .

[10] the oscillations, which were increasingly damped down and less and less discernible—but whose conclusion it was hard to determine—thus fringed, with a series of successive prolongations and regressions either side of a completely illusory fixity, a phenomenon that had, however, come to an end an appreciable time before.

l'essaim. Il faudrait, pour les suivre, pouvoir différencier les individus. Comme c'est impossible, une certaine permanence de l'ensemble s'établit, au sein de laquelle les crises locales, les arrivées, les départs, les permutations n'entrent plus en ligne de compte' (p. 149).[11]

The creative writer's possible sphere of investigation is here delimited: the predictable behaviour of the *ensemble* is not his affair, but the scientist's; what *can* concern him are the particular movements that escape exact localization, the secret reverberations or oscillations of a mind. The fact that in the passage quoted it is mosquitoes that do duty as exemplary particles may or may not betray a deliberate mockery of human pretensions, but when Robbe-Grillet uses words like 'crises', 'arrivées', and 'départs' to describe their motions it would be silly to suppose the anthropomorphism to be simply negligence on his part. When he allows himself the dangerous luxury of such language it is necessary to ask why— here the answer is evident: it is permissible as a warning, to show that this cosy form of identification occurs when no 'ligne de compte' is possible. The field for the metaphor is whatever escapes measurement, especially, as I shall show later on, the sea, the formless element which, in Robbe-Grillet's novels as in those of Sartre or Nathalie Sarraute, is frequently used to harbour the maleficent creatures that sidle into our minds from the speechless deeps of the subconscious.

There is one final passage from *Les Gommes* which it is profitable to analyse before going on to consider how the breakdown of mechanical necessity is exemplified in Robbe-Grillet's second novel, *Le Voyeur*. This occurs towards the end of the book, when Garinati, the man who has failed to assassinate Dupont, is standing by the drawbridge and meditating on how easy it would be to disrupt its operation: 'Il suffirait d'introduire un objet dur—qui pourrait être de dimensions très réduites—dans un engrenage essentiel et tout le système s'arrêterait, avec un grincement de

[11] Moreover, whether it is a question of amplitude, form, or more or less eccentric situation, the variations are probably unceasing inside the swarm. In order to follow them, one would need to be able to differentiate the individuals. As this is impossible, a certain permanence of the whole is established, within which the local crises, arrivals, departures, permutations no longer enter into the calculation.

mécanique détraquée. Un petit objet très dur qui résisterait au broyage; la cube de lave grise . . .' (p. 222).[12]

This imagined agent of disruption is thus a characteristic Robbe-Grillet object, the geometrical lump of lava, perfectly irreducible, which is carefully described more than once during the novel but does not always remain as innocent as it should, since it comes to appear as a likely weapon with which to carry out a murder, the murder of Dupont or of the real world. The intrusion of the lava into the machinery of the bridge is thus representative of the intrusion of the novel into the machinery of time and chronological causality. The novel, like the lava, has got to resist 'broyage', that is to say the sort of structural deformation involved in the criticism that sees its contents as gratuitous references to the real world rather than the necessary sequence of a fictive one.

But Robbe-Grillet does not allow us to carry away the comforting illusion that the interruption of the working of the bridge means that we are able to achieve final victory over the processes of the external world. Garinati does not pursue his rêverie about the bridge any further, because he takes a realistic view of the outcome of any such action: 'A quoi bon? L'équipe de secours arriverait aussitôt. Demain tout marcherait comme à l'ordinaire—comme si rien ne s'était passé' (p. 223).[13]

With *Le Voyeur*, Robbe-Grillet's second novel, it becomes clearer that underlying all his books there is a dynamic conflict, analogous to that in Simon and Butor, between the forces of order and the forces of chaos. In this conflict the novel is forced to fight for its very existence. Tension develops because the hero or narrator of the novel is involved in a situation he cannot cope with. This is not particularly apparent in *Les Gommes*, even though the detective Wallas does try and get himself relieved of the responsibility of his investigation. *Le Voyeur*, on the other hand, is a

[12] It would be enough to introduce a hard object—which could be of very reduced dimensions—into an essential gear, and the whole system would stop, with the grinding sound of machinery going wrong. A small very hard object which would resist crushing; the cube of grey lava . . .

[13] What's the good? The breakdown crew would arrive in no time. Tomorrow the whole thing would be working normally—as if nothing had happened.

novel imbued with a feeling of panic. The hero, Mathias, is a watch salesman (like the Jew in Simon's *Le Tricheur*); this trade offers, as Maurice Blanchot has noted, 'un symbole facile de ce temps sans défaut' (*Le Livre à venir*, p. 200).[14] What Mathias is seeking to do, by selling people instruments that will measure out time unequivocally and without fault, is to convince them of his own innocence. If there were no 'défaut', no fault in the chronology of events, then there would be no portentous gap at the heart of *Le Voyeur*, no novel and no anguish for Mathias. But where Claude Simon's watch-salesman remained a successful guardian of the objective view, Mathias does not. His name itself is an indication of his hopes; when he first appears he is obsessed by a conflict between his violent sado-erotic tendencies and his determination to deny these expression by some very frantic *mathe*matics.

The novel opens with the sound of a ship's siren, which is in fact sounding for the *second* time, its first blast having been, therefore, like the murder of Dupont for *Les Gommes*, the event or accident that has precipitated the creation of a novel. *Le Voyeur* comes into being because of the ambiguity of the word siren in fact, innocuous as long as it signifies simply a ship's hooter, dangerous the moment it evokes the mythical creatures of the formless sea, luring men to destruction. (Robbe-Grillet also introduces a siren into *Un Régicide*, and even names her—Aimone.) By the time the novel of *Le Voyeur* actually begins the word has reverberated in the novelist's mind and its neutral meaning has been supplanted by its legendary one.

Mathias, therefore, has been tempted, and once the throb of the boat's engines ceases he will be forced to land on the island where he must be free. His attempts to order his circumnavigation of the island in accordance with a preconceived and objective time-scale will strike even the most negligent reader as preposterous, so obviously do they betray his desperation to find an alibi, and his refusal to confront the implications of his freedom.

The time of Mathias's arrival on his island and the time of his projected departure are fixed by reference to an outside agency, the steamship company (or the novelist). Because of the play that

[14] an easy symbol of this time without defect.

develops in this mechanism, Mathias in fact misses the boat he had intended to catch back to the mainland, but when he arrives he fancies that he has six and a quarter hours to account for: 'Il disposait ainsi de six heures et quinze minutes—soit trois cent soixante plus quinze, trois cent soixante-quinze minutes. Un calcul s'imposait: s'il voulait vendre ses quatre-vingt-neuf montres, combien de temps pouvait-il consacrer à chacune d'elles?' (p. 34).[15]
He is left, therefore, with something under four minutes to accomplish each sale, an absurdity which only an obsessed, or perhaps it would be better to say a guilty mind could accept. This is indeed the time-scale which Mathias applies to his trip round the island, even though it becomes increasingly incapable of fulfilment. Even when it has more or less collapsed, he remains conscious of his need for a screen of faultless mathematics to hide behind, as is shown in a desperate scene between him and Julien, the boy whom he imagines to have seen him assaulting the girl, Violette:

Mathais fut saisi de panique et passa outre, redoutant trop les explications. Il se mit à parler à une telle cadence que les objections—ou le regret de ses propres mots—devenaient tout à fait impossibles. Afin de combler les vides, il répétait souvent plusieurs fois la même phrase. Il se surprit même à réciter la table de multiplication. Pris d'une inspiration, tout à coup, il fouilla sa poche et en retira le petit bracelet-montre en métal doré . . . (p. 216).[16]

It is suggestive that here Mathias should have an alternative stratagem for the filling in of the gaps which so terrify him—repetition. The repetition of words, events, and whole scenes is an obvious feature of Robbe-Grillet's novels and one which points directly to their deliberately neurotic basis. The urge to repetition is as powerful as it is profound; in *Beyond the Pleasure Principle*

[15] He thus had six hours and fifteen minutes—or three hundred and sixty plus fifteen, three hundred and seventy-five minutes. A sum imposed itself: if he wanted to sell his eighty-nine watches, how much time could he devote to each one?
[16] Mathias was gripped by panic and pressed on, too afraid of explanations. He began to talk at such a rate that objections—or regret at his own words—became quite impossible. In order to fill in the gaps he often repeated the same sentence several times. He even surprised himself reciting the multiplication table. Seized by a sudden inspiration he searched in his pocket and brought out the little wrist-watch of gilt metal . . .

Freud writes for example: 'We cannot help but admit that there exists, in psychical life, an irresistible tendency to reproduction and repetition.'

One of the awkward features of both *Les Gommes* and *Le Voyeur*, in neither of which is there any intrusion by a first-person narrator, is that the undoubted tension that exists between the safely objective mode and the dangerous subjective one becomes disembodied—it can only be located in the mind of the novelist himself.

In *Le Voyeur* there is a further problem, with regard to the moral implications of Mathias's evasiveness: by his deperate recourse to mathematics he tries to identify himself, because of his overwhelming guilt, with the anonymous processes of mathematical law. This urge, however, must come to him from outside.

Mathias's projected timetable for his sales trip around the island is not the only mechanical system that breaks down in *Le Voyeur*; there is also the bicycle which he hires on arrival. This would seem to be every bit as guilty an act as the elaboration of the time-table or the fact that he is selling wrist-watches. To hire a 'cycle' means that he is hoping to depend on a mechanical and impersonal mode of conveyance, and it is therefore quite inevitable that the bicycle should break down, and prevent him from getting back to the harbour in time to catch his boat.

The conflict, then, in *Le Voyeur* is one between the guiltless anonymity of mathematics and the murderous promptings of Mathias's passion. The nature of his passion might lead us, helpfully, to classify him as a sexual deviant, because it forces him to deviate from the course reason would have him follow. The crime which he commits involves him leaving the path he had intended to follow round the island in order to find the place where his victim, Violette—whose name is also indicative of her rôle in the novel, as victim of a rape—is supposed to be looking after her sheep. Ludovic Janvier, perhaps remembering Sartre's dictum 'to see is to deflower', points out that Mathias's deviance is less a sexual than a metaphysical manifestation, and that the crime of rape is in fact the attempt to rip the veil of appearance from nature in order to reach the reality concealed within.[17]

---

[17] *Une Parole exigeante*, p. 138.

In Robbe-Grillet's third novel, *La Jalousie*, the same principles of construction are followed just as unambiguously. Sub-tending the entire fiction is another inescapable gap, an absence which no amount of desperate calculation will ever be able to fill in, even though the calculator, an obsessed man like Mathias, will go on trying to fill it in because he cannot resist the urges of his obsession. *La Jalousie* has met with a greater tolerance than Robbe-Grillet's other novels, perhaps because the nature of this obsession—sexual jealousy—is a more acceptable and dignified one than the melodramatic eroticism he has more often used for the same purpose.

The gap that creates *La Jalousie* is reflected over and over again in the course of the novel, but most obviously and damagingly by the trip which the narrator's wife takes with her imagined lover, Franck, to the nearby town. This absence means, of course, that they are escaping from the field of the narrator's perception, and for facts about their behaviour he will have to substitute fictions. The planning and execution of this trip plays a large part in the novel. Before they leave, the guilty pair—or rather the narrator, acting on behalf of the guilty pair—make strenuous efforts to impose the impersonal necessity of a time-table on the period of their absence from the house: 'Ils ont déjà fixé l'heure du départ ainsi que celle du retour, supputé la durée approximative des trajets, calculé le temps dont ils disposeront pour leurs affaires, compte tenu du déjeuner et du dîner.' (p. 90).[18]

Their calculations can include the time taken over meals because these, as in Butor's *Passage de Milan*, represent an essentially anonymous or mechanical activity, something without threat for the narrator of *La Jalousie*. But by the time the narrator's mind returns to this projected absence, lunch and dinner have dropped out of his calculations, as if he were beginning to lose confidence in the anonymity of the whole undertaking. The third time they recur the calculations have reached a new pitch of intensity, in accordance with the emotional graph of all Robbe-Grillet's novels, which describe a curve of growing excitement:

[18] They have already fixed their time of departure as well as the time of return, worked out the approximate duration of the journeys, calculated the time they will need for their business affairs, allowance having been made for lunch and dinner.

N

Les précisions qu'il [Franck] fournit sur son emploi du temps futur, pour cette journée en ville, seraient plus naturelles si elles venaient satisfaire quelque demande d'un interlocuteur; personne n'a pourtant manifesté le moindre intérêt aujourd'hui, concernant l'achat de son camion neuf. Et pour un peu il établirait à haute voix—à très haute voix—le détail de ses déplacements et de ses entrevues, mètre par mètre, minute par minute, en appuyant chaque fois sur la nécessité de sa conduite (p. 197).[19]

There are obvious signs here of increased guilt, since the husband no longer imagines Franck as doing his mental arithmetic in answer to a spoken question, but with a gratuitous desperation that tells an unwelcome story. When the trip takes place, of course, the wife and Franck are delayed because of a mechanical breakdown along the road, and are forced to alter their time-table and stay the night in town. This simple breakdown is the guarantee that the husband's jealousy must create a novel, because it is now freed of all restraint or alibi.

When the wife eventually returns from the town with Franck she asks her husband what he has been doing while she was away:

A... demande ce qu'il y a de nouveau, sur la plantation. Il n'y a rien de nouveau. Il n'y a toujours que les menus incidents de culture qui se reproduisent périodiquement, dans l'une ou l'autre pièce, selon le cycle des opérations. Comme les parcelles sont nombreuses ... tous les éléments du cycle ont lieu en même temps chaque jour, et les menus incidents périodiques se répètent ainsi tous à la fois, ici ou là, quotidiennement.[20]

---

[19] The details which he [Franck] provides about his future time-table, for that day in town, would be more natural if they were satisfying some demand from another speaker; however no one has shown the slightest interest today, concerning the purchase of his new lorry. And for two pins he would establish out loud—very loud—the details of his movements and his interviews, metre by metre, minute by minute, stressing each time the necessity of his conduct.

[20] A ... asks whether there is anything new on the plantation. There is nothing new. There is never anything but the trifling incidents of cultivation which are reproduced periodically, in one part or another, according to the cycle of operations. Since the plots of land are numerous ... all the elements of the cycle take place at the same time each day, and the trifling periodic incidents are thus repeated all at the same time, in one place or another, daily.

So perfectly ordered is the husband's working life—he owns a banana plantation—that every action he performs is determined by an external necessity, just as the *patron*'s were at the start of *Les Gommes*. As a planter he is simply one of the workmen whom Wallas watches cycling (the 'cycle' once again) along the road, but unfortunately for him his work cannot fill the whole of his life, and the result is *La Jalousie*. Like Mathias in *Le Voyeur* he is a reluctant novelist.

In *La Maison de rendez-vous*, a novel published in 1965, Robbe-Grillet introduces one scene which not only refers to the gap that generates a fiction, but also draws together some of the other patterns which I have tried to chart. The scene is a restaurant, anchored in Kowloon Harbour: an island surrounded by water, in fact, as well as a place offering refreshment—the novel, therefore. One of the specialities of this particular restaurant (or novelist) is human flesh; the body of a dead Japanese girl is served up:

La cuisine chinoise a l'avantage de rendre les morceaux méconnaissables. Il est évident, néanmoins, que l'origine en fut dévoilée—avec preuves à l'appui—pour quelques clients des deux sexes aux goûts dépravés, qui acceptaient de payer le prix fort pour consommer ce genre de chair; préparé avec un soin spécial, elle leur était présentée au cours de festins rituels dont la mise en scène, ainsi que les divers excès auxquels ces réunions donnaient lieu, nécessitaient un cabinet particulier situé à l'écart des salles publiques (p. 167).[21]

This good-natured disguising of the novelist's own activities as 'la cuisine chinoise' is packed with revealing equations between the preparation and consumption of a novel and that of a meal, but it is in a later description of the same restaurant that Robbe-Grillet reveals the most significant feature of all: 'Il y a peu de monde ce soir, dans la grande salle rectangulaire, trouée en son centre d'une piscine carrée où l'on aperçoit dans l'eau verte une

[21] Chinese cooking has the advantage of making the pieces unrecognizable. It is obvious, nevertheless, that their origin was disclosed—with supporting proofs—for a few customers of both sexes and of depraved tastes, who had agreed to pay the stiff price for consuming this sort of flesh; prepared with special care, it was offered to them in the course of ritual banquets whose staging, like the various excesses to which these get-togethers gave rise, necessitated a private study away from the public rooms.

multitude de gros poissons bleus, violets, rouges ou jaunes' (p. 200).[22] Here Robbe-Grillet has found a more delicate if more mysterious way of referring to the genesis of a fiction than he did, for example, in an early novel like *Le Voyeur*, where the hole in the centre is actually conveyed by blank pages in the text. It is in the improbable hole in the centre of the restaurant that the monsters of the deep dwell, and even their colours, it seems, can be connected up with the characters who inhabit *La Maison de rendez-vous*: blue because of the Villa Bleue, the scene of most of the novel's events, which are 'blue' indeed; 'violets' surely because of the homophonous 'violées'; red because of Robbe-Grillet's suggestions in this novel that the mysterious Ralph Johnson (that is, himself) is a communist agent; yellow because of the Chinese background and Eurasian girls who are the victims of the erotic experiments.

II

Robbe-Grillet's novels can be related, with more or less conviction, to a single event that has preceded them, an event that is to say in objective or cosmic time. This event is one allowed explicitly as having stopped the watch that measures cosmic time in *Les Gommes* (and similarly, in *La Maison de rendez-vous*, the alarm-clock of the murdered Manneret is said to have stopped at the moment of his death). This device for removing the events of the novel from a public time-scale, or inserting them into an interstice in that scale so tiny that it is, literally perhaps, no longer than the blinking of an eye, is a vital part of Robbe-Grillet's purpose.

He has been accused of displaying in his novels an ironic fatalism—most notably by Jean V. Alter in an excellent analysis of the novelist: *La Vision du monde d'Alain Robbe-Grillet*. Certainly, by setting his fictions outside time, so to speak, he appears to be diminishing the significance of the mind's undoubted freedom to re-order the materials it has to hand in order to make sense of the world. But if the mind proves incapable of changing anything in

[22] There are few people tonight, in the great rectangular dining-room with the hole in the middle formed by a square pool in whose green water can be seen a multitude of huge fish, blue, violet, red or yellow.

this world that is transcendent to human consciousness—'Le temps a donné la solution malgré toi'[23] says the citation to *Les Gommes*—then its activities might be deduced as futile. But Robbe-Grillet's attitudes are by no means as negative as critics like Alter often imply—the attempts which he shows the mind as making towards the imposition of a satisfying order on phenomena have a definite positive value. In order to work closer to a definition of what this value is, I shall consider Robbe-Grillet's treatment of space in his novels, having examined his treatment of time.

Here again, he makes a highly charged distinction between measurement and myth or, to be more precise, between rigorous order and the formless chaos that is a breeding-ground for the larval myths. Robbe-Grillet never minimizes the powers of darkness, even if he fails to treat them with the same solemnity as Michel Butor. The first and most obvious of the breeding-grounds where myths can flourish is, as I have already indicated, the sea, or water in general.

The town in *Les Gommes* is built on a system of canals and, at different times, both Wallas and his *dédoublement*, Garinati, are seen staring into their murky depths; these are the instants of their psychic life when the urge to measurement is weak and that to mythomania correspondingly strong. Early on in the novel there is mention of the effect which the proximity of the ocean has on the inhabitants of the town: 'Cette eau, ce mouvement aèrent les esprits. Les sirènes des cargos leur arrivent du port, par-dessus l'alignement des entrepôts et les docks, et leur apportent à l'heure de la marée l'espace, la tentation, la consolation du possible' (p. 19).[24]

The message is unequivocal and unsurprising. Robbe-Grillet might have been repeating the line of Baudelaire: 'La mer, la vaste mer, console nos labeurs,' but, unlike Baudelaire, Robbe-Grillet looks on this consolation as a threat, which is why he tries to trap it in his books, and not let it escape back into everyday life. Even

---

[23] Time has provided the solution in spite of you.
[24] This water, this movement ventilate their minds. The sirens of the cargo-ships reach them from the harbour, above the alignment of the warehouses and the docks, and bring them when the tide is in the space, the temptation, the consolation of what is possible.

in the passage quoted the sea is shown as a menace, because it has sent its message, via the ships' sirens, above the geometry of the warehouses and the docks, and the high tide is that of human passion which may easily grow too strong to be restrained.

It is in the water, and the dark, that the monsters breed: 'Au milieu de cette rue transversale coule un canal, immobile en apparence, couloir rectiligne laissé par les hommes au lac natal . . .; dernier refuge aussi, dans l'étouffement de ces terres asséchées, pour la nuit, l'eau du sommeil, sans fond, l'eau glauque remontée de la mer et pourrie de monstres invisibles' (p. 48).[25]

There is nothing particularly secretive about the way in which Robbe-Grillet injects his own philosophy into his text in *Les Gommes*. Because the canal is linked explicitly with the 'lac natal' it can obviously be identified with the dark watercourse that links the human individual with his own infancy,[26] and to the formation within him of those conflicts and complexes which may subsequently turn him, like Wallas, into the powerless creature of a myth; it is in fact at a moment when he gets a glimpse of the water at the end of a street that Wallas has his momentary conviction that the town he is visiting was the one in which he was born, the conviction that opens the way to his Oedipus complex.

Wallas, who stays at a café in the Rue des Arpenteurs and walks the town incessantly, trying to reduce it to its objective lineaments, fails in his endeavour just as Robbe-Grillet's other heroes fail, because there is a gap which he cannot account for. Wallas has been sent on his investigation by his superior Fabius, the first syllable of whose name surely reflects his tendency to mythomania; but even Fabius is no match in this respect for *his* superior, Roy-Dauzet, the Minister of the Interior, who is explicitly branded as a mythomaniac and whose name, in its extremities and its hyphen, is modelled remarkably closely on that of his creator. (Moreover, Roy-Dauzet's governmental position, Minister of

[25] In the middle of this side-street flows a canal, apparently motionless, a rectilinear corridor left by men to their native lake . . .; the last refuge too, in the airlessness of these parched lands, for the night, the bottomless water of sleep, the glaucous water mounted from the sea and rotten with invisible monsters.

[26] cf. Bachelard, *L'Eau et les Rêves*: 'Le passé de notre âme est une eau profonde.'

the Interior, indicates very clearly how limited his responsibilities are, since the Interior here is simply the individual head.) Wallas's failure as a policeman in *Les Gommes*, that is as a representative of order, is comically presented in an episode which describes him having his brain measured by Fabius and found wanting: 'Un seul centimètre—il n'a manqué que cet espace dérisoire. Il lui reste encore deux petits millimètres dont il n'a rien fait. Deux derniers petits millimètres. Deux millimètres carrés de rêve . . . Ce n'est pas beaucoup. L'eau glauque des canaux monte et déborde, franchit les quais de granit, envahit les rues, répand sur toute la ville ses monstres et sa boue . . .' (p. 262).[27]

Each element of this improbable consequence of Wallas's failure to pass the test is part of Robbe-Grillet's demonstration of the way in which myths are born. The cinematic cut from 'rêve' to 'L'eau glauque' establishes again the significance of water in the scheme of Robbe-Grillet's novels. And the dangers to the human reason of even a tiny gap in our measuring apparatus are seen to be serious, because it leads inevitably to the death of order and to the novel. It becomes more and more obvious in these circumstances that Wallas is indeed not a man who should be employed on an investigation, since he will end up by swamping reality with a myth.

In *Le Voyeur* Robbe-Grillet uses water in much the same way as in *Les Gommes*. The events of the novel actually take place on an off-shore island, as do those of *La Maison de rendez-vous*, surrounded by waters that offer threats of disorder as well as the hope of oblivion. It is the water that reveals some of the 'motives' for Mathias's crime, like the figure-of-eight mark left by an iron ring in the harbour wall, as it swings to and fro in the tide; and it is into the water that he later tries to throw the objects he fears will incriminate him. The sea, moreover, connives in his sadism with the most insistent of metaphors. At several points during the novel two waves are described as coming together with the sound of a 'slap'.

---

[27] A single centimetre—all he lacked was this derisory space. He still has two little millimetres left with which he hasn't done anything. Two last little millimetres. Two square millimetres of dream . . . It's not much. The glaucous water of the canals rises and overflows, crosses the granite jetties, invades the streets, spills its monsters and its mud over the whole town . . .

To stare into the water, as far as Robbe-Grillet is concerned—and people are described staring into the water or, worse still, trying to pull fish up out of it, in *Les Gommes*, *Le Voyeur*, *La Jalousie*, and *L'Immortelle*—is to court disaster. At one point in *Le Voyeur* there is a disarmingly disingenuous analogy between the activity of the fisherman and that of the human imagination: 'Les prunelles n'avaient pas bougé d'un millimètre; il eut pourtant l'impression—il imagina l'impression, il la tira, filet chargé de poissons, ou de trop d'algues, ou d'un peu de vase—il imagina que le regard s'arrêta sur lui' (p. 41).[28]

The subject of this passage is the guilty Mathias, and he is shown establishing an illicit communion between himself as observer and the scene he is observing; there is a transition from indifference to attention on the part of his object and a corresponding one from innocence to guilt on the part of Mathias himself—another eye is now illusorily fixed on him. This moment of transition helps to elucidate the question, inconclusively argued by critics of this novel, as to why it should be called *Le Voyeur*. Is Mathias the voyeur or is it the boy, Julien, whom he imagines as the witness of his crime? Julien is quite patently a creation of Mathias's guilty nature, which is constantly distorting reality and comes into play whenever he takes a subjective view, as here. It really does not matter, therefore, whether Mathias is taken as the voyeur or Julien, since they are both projections of a single act of the imagination, the one as killer the other as watcher. All that Robbe-Grillet is implying is that we are all voyeurs if we act like novelists and watch ourselves become embroiled in erotic situations with other embodiments of our more intimate urges. This scission within the individual consciousness, which allows us to enjoy the pleasures of being both actor and audience (not, be it noted, at precisely the same moment, but in successive moments) is one mirrored continuously by Robbe-Grillet by the introduction into the novels of voyeur or spy-figures.

In *La Maison de rendez-vous*, for example, the voyeurs have an

[28] The pupils had not moved a single millimetre; yet he had the impression—he imagined the impression, he drew it up, a net laden with fish, or with too much seaweed, or with a little mud—he imagined that the eyes fixed themselves on him.

excellent programme put on for them at the Villa Bleue, and, for good measure, the novel is permitted its spy as well, who tracks Sir Ralph Johnson, one of the novelist's more obvious representatives in the fiction, to and fro from the island of Hong Kong, but who is also presented as a double of Johnson himself, since he confronts him at one pair of symmetrical doors (of a taxi) and loses touch with him at another.

The conflict in Robbe-Grillet between the powers of order and those of disorder is necessarily weighted in favour of the latter, for if these powers were not too strong, temporarily at least, for their adversaries, then no novel would be able to come into being at all. Robbe-Grillet is characteristically ingenious or sly in showing order threatened by disorder, or form as a space cleared out of chaos. In *Le Voyeur*, for example, Mathias goes into a shop which is menacingly crowded with objects in a state of utter confusion. In the midst of this confusion of heteroclite matter two women sit working out a bill: 'Enfin les deux larges comptoirs assemblés en L, qui occupaient le reste de la place disponible, disparaissaient sous un amoncellement d'objets de toutes sortes—à l'exception toutefois d'un demimètre carré de surface libre, où s'isolait le rectangle de papier blanc couvert de chiffres sur lequel se penchaient, de part et d'autre, les deux dames' (p. 70).[29]

Here, everything seems to conspire in favour of accurate, incontestable measurement—the 'comptoirs', the 'demi-mètre carré' of freedom, the 'rectangle', and the 'chiffres'. Yet it must be with these last that doubt arises—*chiffres* can be mathematical figures and they can also be encoded messages—the way is once more open for fiction to rear its unwanted head.

In *La Jalousie*, chaos is represented, at different times, by the darkness, by water, and by the jungle. The novel takes place in a house belonging to a banana plantation, which has been cleared in the middle of a luxuriant tropical growth, a situation which resembles closely Mathias's island, or the top floor room of *Dans le*

---

[29] Finally the two wide counters laid together in an L, which occupied the remainder of the available space, disappeared beneath a pile of objects of every sort—with the exception though of half a square metre of vacant surface, in which was isolated the rectangle of white paper covered with figures over which leant, on either side, the two women.

labyrinthe, which the first person narrator cherishes as his refuge. The husband's attempts to control his emotions are exemplified in the lengthy mathematics he indulges in with regard to his banana trees. Where Wallas had walked and Mathias bicycled round their respective domains, the husband of *La Jalousie* can see his from where he stands or sits. His attempt to subject it wholly to his calculations is naturally doomed to fail, the patterns which he establishes being always incomplete by a single small detail.

The plantation represents the world of work, and the cyclical nature of this work enables the husband to remain securely anonymous; but his 'cycle', like that of Mathias, breaks down, because a missing tree in the pattern forces on him the necessity (or responsibility) of confronting the fact of his mental freedom. The world of play thus intrudes into the world of work, and the husband's mathematics can be seen as an attempt at evasion. As Olga Bernal, who has analysed this novel with particular delicacy and precision, writes: 'Ce comptage a donc un double sens; il est masque et fuite pour la conscience; il est aussi l'image précise, géométrique d'un manque' (*Le Roman de l'absence*, p. 224).[30]

A missing banana tree is therefore a reflection of what Robbe-Grillet once called 'le vide qui envahit, qui remplit tout', like the absence of the wife and Franck. Robbe-Grillet's novels in fact pose a direct contradiction to the old proverb—'Out of sight, out of mind.'

In another scene in *La Jalousie* he stresses the absolute indifference of what takes place outside the field of the novel as it were, the indifference that is to say of external phenomena in their raw state, before the imagination has got to work on them. From out of the night comes the sound of the animals—the monsters—that lurk in the jungle:

Cependant tous les cris se ressemblent; non qu'ils aient un caractère commun facile à préciser, il s'agirait plutôt d'un commun manque de caractère: ils n'ont pas l'air d'être des cris effarouchés, ou de douleur, ou menaçants, ou bien d'amour. Ce sont comme des cris machinaux, poussés sans raison décelable, n'exprimant rien, ne signalant que

---

[30] This counting therefore has a double meaning; it is a mask and an escape for consciousness; it is also the precise, geometrical image of a lack.

l'existence, la position et les déplacements respectifs de chaque animal . . . (p. 31).[31]

As a moment in the development of the jealous husband's fantasies, this can only represent an interlude of stability, an awareness of the contingency and irreducibility of all external phenomena. But it is this contingency which will be immediately abandoned the moment his passion grips him again, and since it is wild animals which he has managed to deprive of their anthropomorphic significance this must be taken as an effort of heroic lucidity; the darkness in which Robbe-Grillet deals is not, after all, only that epistemological darkness that lies beyond the rim of the perceptive field but also the subconscious darkness that eludes the probe of introspection.

This is a pertinent moment, perhaps, to raise the important question as to whether Robbe-Grillet always manages, in his novels, to maintain intact his polemic purity as the man who denies human life any consoling shades of tragedy. He refuses to predicate anything at all of human existence, and yet he seems to be proposing that the novel, embodying as it does the free play of the imagination, represents a flaw in what would otherwise have been a perfect design, 'a flaw in the diamond of the world', as Merleau-Ponty once wrote apropos of the ontological pessimism of Jean-Paul Sartre.

Certainly, there are many moments in his fiction when Robbe-Grillet seems to be mocking the freedom of the human mind, and to be showing the individual in futile conflict with the universe; at the same time, this rupture is exploited not for tragic ends but for mediocre or burlesque ones. It is unfortunate that the question can only be framed meaningfully by using words which carry their own moral implications, words like 'flaw', 'crack', and 'imperfection', when what is wanted is a vocabulary that is at least neutral.

[31] However, all the cries are alike; not that they have a common character that it would be easy to specify, it being a question rather of a (common) lack of character: they do not seem to be cries of fright, or of pain, or menacing, or even ones of love. They are like mechanical cries, uttered without detectable reason, expressing nothing, signifying only the respective existence, position and movements of each animal . . .

But what critics of Robbe-Grillet have found it hard to keep hold of is the vital truth that he is not denying that the human mind is free, he is simply asking what sort of use it ought to make of its freedom. It is wrong to see the numerous flaws and fissures in his novels as objective manifestations, with obvious meta-physical overtones. They are not imposed *on* the narrator but *by* him, they are the result of his mind's lingering on a single image. 'Prolonged inspection of any specific visual object', writes the *Gestalt* psychologist Wolfgang Köhler, 'tends to change its organization.' This consideration makes it easier to reinstate the apparent divergence between the subjective and objective modes in Robbe-Grillet within a single consciousness—the very intensity of his narrators' objectivity is itself a guarantee of an enantio-dromiatic move towards its opposite.

In *Les Gommes*, for instance, there is a lengthy description of a sectioned tomato which has more than once been used by critics hostile to Robbe-Grillet's purpose as an extreme example of his sterile and anti-humanist *chosisme*, or preoccupation with material objects for their own sake:

Un quartier de tomate en vérité sans défaut, découpé à la machine dans un fruit d'une symétrie parfaite. La chair périphérique, compacte et homogène, d'un beau rouge de chimie . . ., les pépins, jaunes, bien calibrés, maintenus en place par une mince couche de gelée verdâtre le long d'un renflement du cœur. Celui-ci . . . débute . . . par un faisceau de veines blanches, dont l'une se prolonge jusque vers les pépins... d'une façon peut-être un peu incertaine. Tout en haut, un accident à peine visible s'est produit: un coin de pelure, décollé de la chair sur un millimètre ou deux, se soulève imperceptiblement (p. 161).[32]

Any reader of *Les Gommes* would surely be reminded by this description of the weird *trompe l'œil* intensity of certain surrealist paintings; the tomato is real-er than real. There is, in fact, a frenzy

___

[32] A quarter of tomato in actual fact without defect, cut by a machine out of a perfectly symmetrical fruit. The peripheral flesh, compact and homo-geneous, of a lovely chemical red . . . the pips, yellow, well calibrated, held in place by a thin layer of greenish jelly along a swelling in the heart. The latter . . . starts as a bunch of white veins, one of which extends almost to the pips—in a perhaps rather uncertain way. Right at the top, a barely visible accident has occurred: a corner of skin, which has come away from the flesh over one or two millimetres, is imperceptibly raised.

in the observer's (Wallas) quest for geometrical perfection because of the danger to him of any flaw that is revealed. Wallas's fixation with this tomato is an indication of a mind disturbed by the oedipal pressures it cannot subjugate, and the tomato, associated as it is with the biological anonymity, stressed by Husserl himself, of the act of eating, is a perfect point of rest. In point of *fact* ('en vérité') there is nothing wrong with the fruit, it is the flawless product of a mechanical process. Yet as Wallas's mind lingers on it a tiny fault appears, 'un accident à peine visible'. It is inevitable that the first sign of uncertainty that undermines the whole description is connected with the heart of the tomato—an anthropomorphic metaphor not, it appears, as dead as most of us would have thought—and that this heart should be described as swollen—a reminder that the word Oedipus itself means 'swollen feet'.

To read this sort of description as a predetermined whole instead of the successive moments of a man's mind as it dwells on a single image is almost certain to lead to a radical misinterpretation. Understood as a *process* such a description becomes truly revealing and draws attention, above all, to the way in which language leads the mind rather than the other way about.

Another novel richly endowed with flawed surfaces is *Dans le labyrinthe*. The most notable of them is the crack which the narrator, safe in the shelter of his bedroom at the beginning of the book, later starts to notice in his ceiling: 'A droite du grand cercle lumineux dont elle suit avec régularité le pourtour, il y a dans l'angle du plafond, une petite ligne noire, très fine, longue d'une dizaine de centimètres, à peine perceptible: une fissure dans le plâtre . . .' (p. 126).[33]

The only point of the room from which this imperfection in the ceiling is visible is the bed, indicating, therefore, that the narrator of the novel is in bed and that his fantasies are, presumably, intended to be interpreted erotically, even though they are much less openly tumescent than those of Robbe-Grillet's other novels or *ciné-romans*. As the emotional temperature rises in *Dans le*

[33] To the right of the big luminous circle whose circumference it follows with regularity, there is in the corner of the ceiling, a little black line, very fine, about ten centimetres long, barely perceptible: a crack in the plaster . . .

labyrinthe and the sense of delirium builds up, so the flaw in his
ceiling come to obsess the narrator's attention, and he finds in it a
pattern that looks more and more like the bewildering pattern of
the narrative we are reading (it would be interesting to know
whether Robbe-Grillet was aware of the similar games played by
Sterne in *Tristram Shandy*, where the narrative line is portrayed in
all its irregularity by a comic series of squiggles): 'la fissure... dont
la forme, elle aussi, a quelque chose d'à la fois précis et compliqué,
qu'il serait nécessaire de suivre avec application de coude en
coude, avec ses courbes, tremblements, incertitudes, changements
de direction subits, infléchissements, reprises, légers retours en
arrière, mais il faudrait encore du temps, un peu de temps, quelques minutes, quelques secondes, et il est déjà, maintenant, trop
tard' (p. 211).[34]

This last desperate *glissade* into the present moment, as the mind
loses its hold over the course of its recent travels—a defeat foreshadowed by the use of the conditional tense in 'serait'—precedes
a startling change of perspective in *Dans le labyrinthe*, with the
announcement that the hero, the unnamed soldier who trudges
through its pages on a hopeless mission, is dead.

Subsequently, in *La Maison de rendez-vous*, Robbe-Grillet has
introduced a very suggestive variation on this basic theme of the
flaw in the design, by linking it slyly with the erotic inspiration of
the novel. The most obtrusive of the flaws in this novel is in a
cushion covered in moleskin which is on the passenger's seat of a
Hong Kong rickshaw. At its first appearance in the novel the
cushion is in fact concealed by the raised hood of the vehicle, with
the result that the description of it is turned explicitly into an
imaginative one. This description is predictably detailed and draws
attention to the point where the moleskin has split, allowing the
stuffing to escape. The split is a triangular one, and the significance of this particular shape in *La Maison de rendez-vous* becomes
increasingly sexual.

[34] the crack ... whose shape also has something both precise and complicated about it, which it would be necessary to follow attentively from
bend to bend, with its curves, tremors, uncertainties, sudden changes of
direction, inflections, repetitions, slight turnings back, but it would
need more time, a little time, a few minutes, a few seconds and it is already,
now, too late.

The first triangle that is mentioned is the leather toe-piece of a girl's sandal; the girl is bending forward to tie the sandal up and, as she does so, she exposes the nape of her neck to be a focus for the erotic fantasies that subsequently constitute the novel. The second triangle is a fragment of silk in a scene of wild sadism in which a dog strips a girl of her clothing with its teeth: 'Le chien, qui a pour cela subi un dressage spécial, doit déshabiller entièrement la prisonnière . . . jusqu'au dernier triangle de soie, il déchire avec ses crocs les vêtements . . . Les accidents, lorsqu'il y en a, sont toujours superficiels et sans gravité; ils ne nuisent pas à l'intérêt du numéro, bien au contraire' (p. 43).[35]

No one reading this passage, I imagine, would fail to locate the last triangle referred to as covering the girl's sexual organs— traditionally concealed by triangles of material in erotic performances of this sort. The last sentence quoted contains the pleasant assurance that the interests of the 'number' are not ultimately harmed by any 'superficial accidents'. Since these superficial accidents are those imperfections found in the surfaces of things by Robbe-Grillet's fixated narrators, he is re-stating his case—that measurement will always win over myth, however ferocious the hounds of the subconscious may appear to be. He perhaps does more than just re-state his case in the words 'au contraire', be- cause the implication here is that the philosophy of measurement is made especially vital because of the existence of such powerful urges to deny it.

The erotic connotations of the triangle as a shape in *La Maison de rendez-vous* become very apparent once the narrator is allowed to sit in the rickshaw and feel the defect in its cushion: 'Ma main, posée sur le coussin de molesquine rendu collant par la chaleur humide, rencontre à nouveau la déchirure triangulaire, par où s'échappe une touffe de crins moites. Un lambeau de phrase tout à coup, sans raison, m'est venu à l'esprit, quelque chose comme

---

[35] The dog, which has undergone special training for this, has to undress the prisoner entirely . . . down to the last triangle of silk, it tears the clothes with its fangs . . . The accidents, when there are any, are always super- ficial and not serious; they do not harm the interest of the number—quite the reverse.

"... dans la splendeur des catacombes, un crime aux ornaments inutiles, baroques ..." ' (p. 51).[36]

The triangle undergoes one more highly significant metamorphosis before *La Maison de rendez-vous* ends, in one of the many episodes in the novel where a glass is broken, an accident which I will allude to later. On this particular occasion the bowl of a champagne glass is almost completely shattered, only the stem being left intact, together with a 'triangle de cristal recourbé, pointu comme un poignard...' (p. 171).[37] This sudden murderous comparison is no longer unexpected in connection with the shape of the triangle.

This brief analysis of a single set of *déchirures* from one novel certainly suggests that Robbe-Grillet has tried in *La Maison de rendez-vous* to make it clear (to those interested or patient enough to puzzle out his meaning) that it is the sexual drives that are man's most ready source of invention. On the other hand, where he has departed from previous practice, and dangerously so perhaps, is in identifying this source of invention with an objective feature of the female body. It is true that the women who can be taken as the raw materials of the female characters in this particular novel are dummies in a shop window and so, presumably, anatomically incomplete, but this is a refinement which may well escape the analyst, and lead to further charges of fatalism.

But what is really at stake in Robbe-Grillet's novels is not the existence of the mind's freedom *vis-à-vis* the external world, which is never denied, but, as I have said, the use that is made of it. The fact that each of his narrators or heroes makes a dangerous or exaggerated use of it does not make Robbe-Grillet himself a tragic humanist. The dialectical tension within each fiction, between the opposite poles of rest and unrest for the mind involved, is itself evidence of the possibility of salvation. Once it is able to steady itself in its objective or mathematical stance, the mind has an inkling of health and security. But this does not

[36] My hand, placed on the moleskin cushion made sticky by the damp heat, again comes into contact with the triangular rent, from which escapes a tuft of moist horsehair. A fragment of a sentence suddenly comes into my mind, for no reason, something like '... in the splendour of the catacombs, a crime of useless, baroque ornamentation ...'

[37] triangle of curved glass, pointed like a dagger ...

mean that it is deprived at this moment of its freedom—on the contrary. The mistake which several of Robbe-Grillet's critics seem to have made is to have confused objectivity with a sort of epistemological servitude to the object.

But the objective or mathematical stance itself is a freely chosen one, however great the pressure which the scientific culture of the present exerts on intelligent men to adopt it. 'The arithmetical world', writes Husserl, 'is there for me only when and so long as I occupy the arithmetical standpoint. But the natural world, the world in the ordinary sense of the word, is constantly there for me . . .'

In order to grasp what Robbe-Grillet's purpose is, and in order to resolve any possible contradictions between what he has preached in his theoretical essays and practised in his fiction, it is imperative to see the objective and subjective modes of perception as virtualities of one mind. The structure of some of his earlier novels is such as to lead to criticisms of the author's intrusion, at those moments of stability represented by a mathematical or geometrical description. But Robbe-Grillet does not need to intrude in this way, his novels are all intrusion in that they consist of the successive images of a single mind in the throes of creation. He has taken to turning up in the text of his novels in disguises that are less and less difficult to penetrate—in his splendid analysis of *La Maison de rendez-vous*, for example, Jean V. Alter shows how directly all the male characters of that novel are projections of the novelist himself. Thus there is no difficulty in accepting that the anonymous first-person narrator of that novel, or the first-person narrator of *Dans le labyrinthe*, is Robbe-Grillet, but Robbe-Grillet *qua* novelist, not *qua* autobiographer. His fictions, like those of Michel Butor, have their exemplary aspects; they are the product of *this* novelist, but also of *any* novelist, and *any* novelist includes all those able to use their imagination.

III

In his essay (one of comparatively few that he has written on an individual writer) on the surrealist poet Joë Bousquet, whose spine was shattered by a bullet in the First World War, but who

o

lived on for more than thirty years almost wholly paralysed and confined to his bedroom in Carcassonne, Robbe-Grillet makes the point that Bousquet's situation was a cruel model of that of any truly imaginative writer—who should write without the possibility of verifying the 'truth' of the scenes or characters he is describing. Elsewhere, he has said that during the writing of *Le Voyeur* he felt a temptation to check his own image of a seagull against the reality, a temptation which he bravely resisted!

Robbe-Grillet, therefore, shows the novelist to be a creator who must rely, when he sits down to write, on the lumber of his own mind and not dash out in order to supplement this with a little direct observation. There are several scenes in his novels similar to the one I have drawn attention to at the start of Michel Butor's first novel, *Passage de Milan*, in which the hero is discovered surrounded by debris of one sort or another. Because of the erratic progress of his novels, and the constant threats posed to their structure, Robbe-Grillet does not need to place these scenes at the beginning—set into the middle of the text they represent another moment of disintegration. In *La Maison de rendez-vous*, for example, there is an especially blatant one, placed immediately after the breaking of a champagne glass: 'la cour est encombrée par une quantité d'objets au rebut: un pousse-pousse hors d'usage, de vieux balais en paille de riz, des tréteaux démontés, plusieurs statues en plâtre, de nombreuses caisses non fermées où sont rassemblées pêle-mêle des débris, de vaisselle ou des verres cassés . . .' (p. 133).[38]

The artificial nature of the events of the novel, momentarily suspended, is clearly exposed. The word 'cour' connects nicely with the idea of the novelist as King, an idea already explored in Michel Butor and to which I shall return in respect of Robbe-Grillet: this courtyard can only be the writer's head. The rickshaw and the brooms are both representatives of movement in *La Maison de rendez-vous*, while the trestles are ambiguous, supporting as they do both the refreshments provided by the buffet (the novel)

---

[38] the courtyard is cluttered with a quantity of discarded objects: a disused rickshaw, old rice-straw brooms, dismantled trestles, several plaster statues, numerous boxes not closed in which are assembled higgledy-piggledy fragments, of broken china or glasses . . .

and the stage performances at the Villa Bleue; the crates full of broken glass—since glass represents the flimsy barrier that circumscribes and protects a world projected only in the imagination or reflective consciousness—are *open*, an indication that now the fiction is in pieces the real world is able to intrude once more. This debris, out of which successive fictions will be erected, consists, then, of immobile elements. At the same time this immobility is a token of the powers of the human mind which, by transforming the continuity of experience into the discontinuity of memory, is able to offer the illusion of having arrested the advance of time. In *Les Gommes* Robbe-Grillet shows directly how the immobility of a scene—he has introduced a number of *scènes figées* into his film-scripts with great effect—is linked to the distortions practised on reality by the deranged mind of a novelist. Jean Bonaventure, the head of the organization that has dispatched Garinati to assassinate Dupont and, as his name indicates, a would-be foreteller of the future, sits staring in an almost empty room and through glass at the town outside, which has undergone a profound transformation, its proportions having been completely altered: 'Les distances en sont tellement affectées qu'elles en deviennent à peu près méconnaissables, sans que l'on puisse dire exactement dans quel sens elles se sont transformées: étirées, ou bien réduites—ou les deux à la fois—à moins qu'elles n'aient acquis une qualité nouvelle ne relevant plus de la géométrie . . .' (p. 101).[39]

The town is likened to those that have been petrified in some natural cataclysm, withdrawn in fact from time, since no change is now possible for them. Bonaventure concludes that 'il vient de frapper la ville de stupeur'.[40] Since it is he who has brought about what the inhabitants of the town believe to be the murder of Dupont it is clear that this assassination and his performance at the window are one and the same event—the destruction of the mind's link with the external world, that is, the institution of its freedom.

[39] The distances have been so affected that they have become almost unrecognizable, without it being possible exactly to say in what direction they have been transformed: extended, or else reduced—or both at once—unless they have acquired a new quality no longer dependent on geometry . . .

[40] he has just stupefied the town.

Apart from its original immobility, the other characteristic of the image in Robbe-Grillet is its susceptibility to change, to a transformation which proves the capacity of the human mind to deny the integrity of the physical world. This transformation is, as Sartre shows, closely connected with the fear of the imagination:

ces objets-fantômes sont ambigus, fuyants, à la fois eux-mêmes et autre chose qu'eux-mêmes, ils se font le support de qualités contradictoires . . . Cette ambiguïté essentielle de l'objet irréel nous paraît être un des principaux facteurs de la peur d'imagination. . . . Nous dirions volontiers que cette ambiguïté constitue la seule profondeur de l'objet en image. Elle représente en lui comme un semblant d'opacité (*L'Imaginaire*, pp. 254–5).[41]

By emphasizing the fear of the imagination at the expense of its attraction Sartre is naturally led to find a corresponding reassurance for the mind in direct perception, the same dynamic extremism which is to be found throughout Robbe-Grillet. But a direct perception of reality is not possible in a novel, which deals exclusively with a reflected world. Every time, therefore, that the errant consciousness of the narrator in a Robbe-Grillet novel is halted, every time it comes up against what Roland Barthes calls the object as 'an optical resistance',[42] the novelist might be accused of practising a deception on his readers, and allowing himself a moment or two of special pleading. For as long as the narrator finds peace and stability in geometry or measurement he becomes an exemplary figure, the prototype of the New Man whom Robbe-Grillet has not hesitated to say that the novel can help to create. At other times, in succumbing to the promptings of the imagination, he is poor, benighted, traditional man, trying to impose his own emotional needs on an indifferent image.

Yet, because of what it implies for their peace of mind, the narrators of Robbe-Grillet's fictions are led to attend to the configuration of a single image with such intensity that it is self-

[41] these phantom-objects are ambiguous, fleeting, at once themselves and something other than themselves, they become the support of contradictory qualities . . . This essential ambiguity of the unreal object seems to us to be one of the principal factors in the fear of imagination . . . We are ready to say that this ambiguity constitutes the one depth of the object as image. It represents in it as it were an appearance of opacity.
[42] *Essais critiques*, p. 30.

destroying—with the result that the mind is provoked to continue on its travels and to effect ever more fervid metamorphoses of its stock of images.

According to his fellow-novelist Claude Ollier, Robbe-Grillet started writing *La Jalousie* simply by describing a woman combing her hair, and that the emotion of jealousy emerged from the description, thus giving rise to a novel. The emotion, in fact, is the inevitable outcome of the mind's fixation, while the mind's fixation is itself the inevitable outcome of the writer's own situation, since in order to describe a woman combing her hair he will be forced to concentrate his attention on a single scene over a considerable period of time. Ollier's explanation of the genesis of *La Jalousie* is one that deserves to be taken seriously, even if it is not entirely satisfactory. The description of the hair is, after all, one undertaken by Robbe-Grillet with a particular preconception of what a description must be—that is, an accurate and complete record of the visual field. The descriptions of the wife combing her hair in *La Jalousie* are characterized, predictably, by the inability of the eye to follow each individual hair that constitutes the fibrous mass.

Once an emotion has been stimulated in this way, whether or not the novelist is truly being taken by surprise, then a movement becomes possible or, rather, inevitable, together with the pattern of anguished repetition, fragmentation and transformation which marks Robbe-Grillet's work. This pattern is produced because there is a resistance in things, which both disturbs and fascinates the troubled mind, as Merleau-Ponty defines it in *Phéno-ménologie de la perception*: 'Être ému, c'est se trouver engagé dans une situation à laquelle on ne réussit pas à faire face et qu'on ne veut pourtant pas quitter. Plutôt que d'accepter l'échec ou de revenir sur ses pas, le sujet, dans cette impasse existentielle, fait voler en éclats le monde objectif . . .' (p. 101).[43]

Thus if the mind of the hero were not in some way deranged the world of representation which he subtends would match the

---

[43] To be moved, is to find oneself involved in a situation which one cannot manage to face up to and yet which one does not want to leave alone. Rather than accept failure or retrace its steps, the subject, in this existential impasse, causes the objective world to burst in fragments . . .

real one of everyday reference, it would have none of the laby-
rinthine qualities of the world which the narrator tries to erect
around him in, for example, *Dans le labyrinthe*.

In each of Robbe-Grillet's novels we have the record of a
frantic imagination at work, playing with images as if they were
chessmen. It is noticeable in *Les Gommes* that when Garinati,
the incompetent killer, shifts the ornaments about on his mantle-
piece this is described as an 'ouvrage', a word no doubt intended to
turn our minds towards the novel we are reading: 'Il contemple
son ouvrage. Quelque chose encore choque le regard. Le pot à
tabac, l'aveugle, le bougeoir. . . . Il échange l'un pour l'autre les
deux derniers objets' (p. 220).[44]

The emotionally disturbed mind is one 'shocked', therefore, by
any substantial disposition that does not match its needs; and the
mental work on that world in which it finds itself involved will
simply map out for us the nature of a particular obsession.

There is a generalized description of the meaningful distortion
which the reflective consciousness practises on reality in one of
the *Visions réfléchies*, in Robbe-Grillet's collection of short
pieces, *Instantanés*. A schoolboy is asked to give a summary of
a passage from a history book which his class has been reading:
'Malgré de fréquentes hésitations et reprises, il le faisait de façon à
peu près cohérente. Cependant il donnait beaucoup trop d'importance à des faits secondaires et, au contraire, mentionnait à peine, ou
même pas du tout, certains événements de premier plan' (p. 20).[45]

What the boy creates is well on the way to being a Robbe-
Grillet novel, with its 'reprises' and its 'hesitations'. This passage,
moreover, makes an interesting comparison with a very similar
sequence in Michel Butor's *Degrés* concerned with another schoolboy, Régnier, the *doublant* in Vernier's class. With Butor the
proper use of the reflective powers of the human mind confers a
privilege of sovereignty and an ultimate guarantee of temporary

---

[44] He contemplates his handiwork. Something still offends the eye. The
tobacco jar, the blind man, the candle-holder. . . . He exchanges one of
these two latter objects for the other.

[45] In spite of frequent hesitations and repetitions, he did it in a more or less
coherent fashion. However, he gave too much importance to secondary
facts and, conversely, barely mentioned, or did not mention at all, certain
events in the foreground.

stability, but with Robbe-Grillet the situation is quite different. His schoolboy has the text which he is trying to repeat by heart still in front of him on his desk, with the result that his oral version can and will be compared with another version whose form he must accept as objective. Butor's Régnier is repeating not a text but a year's schooling, a temporal interval that has vanished into the dangerous waters of oblivion; in his case any representation is better than none. Robbe-Grillet, therefore, is not a relativist in the sense in which Butor is, because he insists on referring all our private versions of reality to what he sees as the one objective one, that provided for us by science.

The novel of Robbe-Grillet's which shows most openly how a powerful emotion involves a deviation from or a distortion of the mind's true function is *La Jalousie*. The title of this novel is a gift from the French language to the novelist, so neatly ambiguous is it. The Venetian blind to which it refers, like the emotion of jealousy itself, has the effect of destroying the coherence of the field of consciousness: 'lorsque les jalousies sont ouvertes au maximum, les lames sont presque horizontales et montrent leur tranchant. Le versant opposé du vallon apparaît alors en bandes successives, superposées, séparées par des blancs un peu plus étroits' (p. 180).[46]

What is fragmented here by the pattern of the blind is the hillside on which the husband's banana trees are planted; the interruptions mirror those brought about by the missing tree to the anonymous cycle of work. Each slat of the blind is an interstice in the continuum of the visual field, and thus a compulsive invitation to the imagination to supplement an incomplete reality. But the bands of reality are wider than those of the imagination, which leaves no doubt as to which contestant Robbe-Grillet is promising ultimate victory.

Elsewhere in *La Jalousie* there is a scene displaying something more than the mere breaking up of reality; in the double window that overlooks the piece of vacant ground in front of the house

---

[46] when the Venetian blinds are as far open as they will go, the slats are almost horizontal and show their thin edge. The opposite slope of the valley then appears in successive bands one above the other, separated by slightly narrower blank spaces.

there are imperfections in the glass: 'Les vitres sont d'une pro-
preté parfaite et, dans le panneau de droite, la disposition des
lignes n'est qu'à peine altérée par les défauts du verre. . . . Mais
dans le panneau de gauche . . . l'image réfléchie est franchement
distordue . . .' (p. 73).[47]

Passages like these must represent moments of self-awareness to
the narrator, since they form part of the reality he is projecting
about himself as well as reflecting the distortions his mind is
practising on the other 'real' reality. This is as near as Robbe-
Grillet ever comes to a traditional and explicit auto-analysis, in
which the victim of fantasy can comment on his own problems.

For Robbe-Grillet the irruption into consciousness of strong
emotion is portrayed formally, in terms of the contiguity, repetition, and intensity of images. Once the chosen emotion has pos-
sessed the mind then the sequence of images which follows can
be held to be necessary. The one element of true gratuity or contingency that Robbe-Grillet, however much he might like to, can
never avoid, is the choice of the object or objects that motivate
the narrator's imagination in the very first instance. The imagination can transform the contingency of the external world into a
temporary necessity, by imposing (or trying to impose) a structure
on it, but it is unable to create the object that has provoked it into
doing so.

There is certainly no clear indication within Robbe-Grillet's
novels as to what the one original datum from which they have
sprung is, or whether, indeed, a single datum is sufficient to
account for the entire fiction. Some critics have assumed that the
novelist starts out from a number of neutral objects; Roland
Barthes, for example, in the case of Le Voyeur, talks of 'quelques
objets surgis peu à peu de l'espace et du temps sans aucune con-
tiguité causale avouée: une petite fille . . . une cordelette, un pieu,
un pilier, des bonbons' (Essais critiques, p. 65).[48]

But for all the lack of avowed causal contiguity these objects are

---

[47] The panes are perfectly clean and, in the right-hand panel, the layout of
the lines is only slightly altered by the faults in the glass. . . . But in the
left-hand panel . . . the reflected image is frankly distorted . . .

[48] a few objects which have gradually come into view out of space and time
without any avowed causal contiguity: a little girl . . . a bit of string, a
stake, a pillar, some sweets.

surely not as innocent as they might be, they seem to hint only too closely at the sadistic fantasies that follow in *Le Voyeur*. It is sensible to assume that they form a chain of associated nouns, and not an arbitrary assemblage. If they were simply objects scattered in Mathias's path by a supposedly indifferent universe then Robbe-Grillet would be guilty of the crime he has indeed been accused of before now—of implicating the external world in Mathias's crime; without the piece of string, or the loops of iron in the harbour-wall, so the argument goes, Mathias's sadism could not have been aroused. But if his sadism precedes the appearance of these objects, as it does, if the order of events in the novel is taken as the order of events in the novelist's mind, then the argument of a tragic connivance, similar to that introduced into *L'Étranger* by Camus, collapses, and we are left with the reasonable conclusion that *Le Voyeur*, like Robbe-Grillet's other novels, is the product of a single image (but which one?) too long pondered.

It has been a common mistake among those who have written about Robbe-Grillet to insist that the products of an obsessed mind are in actual fact its motives, an apparently trivial reversal of values which allows a metaphysic to be derived from Robbe-Grillet's technique. What underlies the novels is what Sartre characterizes as man's 'projet fondamental': 'c'est donc plutôt par une *comparaison* des diverses tendances empiriques d'un sujet que nous tenterons de découvrir et de dégager le projet fondamental qui leur est commun à toutes . . .' (*L'Être et le néant*, p. 651).[49]

In *La Maison de rendez-vous* the gathering momentum of composition is enacted unequivocally in the opening pages of the novel. The first image present to the narrator's mind is one of female flesh, generalized yet infinitely suggestive: 'La chair des femmes a toujours occupé, sans doute, une grande place dans mes rêves.'[50] The mock ignorance of 'sans doute' is a delicate gesture. Immediately, a focus for the narrator's sadism comes into view,

---

[49] it is thus rather by a *comparison* of the various empirical tendencies of a subject that we shall try to discover and to isolate the fundamental project which is common to all of them . . .

[50] Women's flesh has always occupied, no doubt, a great place in my dreams.

the inviting and compliant nape of a girl's neck as she bends forward to do up her shoe, and the narrator's inability to restrain his imagination is admitted: 'je la vois aussitôt soumise à quelque complaisance, tout de suite excessive'.[51] From here it is a simple transition to Hong Kong, where girls wear skirts that are slit as far as the thigh and invite the mind to erotic speculation; there follows a heady enumeration of some of the paraphernalia of sexual obsession: 'Le fouet de cuir, dans la vitrine d'un sellier parisien, les seins exposés des mannequins de cire, une affiche de spectacle, la réclame pour des jarretelles ou pour un parfum, deux lèvres humides, disjointes, un bracelet de fer, un collier à chien, dressent autour de moi leur décor insistant, provocateur' (pp. 11–12).[52]

Nobody could mistake this for a haphazard collection of objects, presumably, even if, at least until the introduction of the dog collar, they are all objects that might be seen along a shopping street of any town—Robbe-Grillet asks for no privileges, but insists that the décor of urban man's everyday life is quite sufficient to bring a novel into his mind. Although the objects enumerated here are still static it will clearly not be long before the narrator's intensity of emotion is sufficient to endow them with movement, and the fiction will be under way.

There is of course a danger that when the narrator sets out on his journey in *La Maison de rendez-vous*, and finds that it leads him, not to the anonymous plantation of *La Jalousie* or the schematic island of *Le Voyeur*, but to a real place that can be found on actual maps, Hong Kong, Robbe-Grillet will have difficulty in preserving the imaginary status of his landscape. He defends himself against any charges that may be levelled at him in a very playful foreword to this novel: 'Si quelque lecteur, habitué des escales d'Extrême-Orient, venait à penser que les lieux décrits ici ne sont pas conformes à la réalité, l'auteur, qui y a lui-même passé la plus grande partie de sa vie, lui conseillerait d'y revenir voir et de

---

[51] I immediately see her subjected to some compliance, suddenly excessive.
[52] The leather whip, in the window of a Parisian saddler, the exposed breasts of the wax dummies, a theatre poster, the advertisment for suspenders or for a perfume, two moist, parted lips, an iron bracelet, a dog collar, erect around me their insistent, provocative décor.

regarder mieux: les choses changent vite sous ces climats' (p. 9).[53]

The Hong Kong to which we are introduced is, of course, one of the mind, a mythical one, betrayed by the fact that it is *too* like what we imagine Hong Kong to be like, with its rickshaws, its dope pedlars, its British policemen in shorts, and so on. These are images whose possible documentary interest has been amortized by their frequent use in films, books, and magazines, so that they can be introduced into the novel as fragments of existing myths, and confront the reader with the problem of working out why these fragments have been chosen and not others.

Robbe-Grillet had already relied on the same technique in his *ciné-roman*, *L'Immortelle*, though here his position was made more awkward by the presence, in the film, of the visual images of a real town, Istanbul. In *La Maison de rendez-vous* Robbe-Grillet keeps on repeating, throughout the novel, as an insurance against being misunderstood, the words 'tout le monde connaît Hong Kong',[54] having already proclaimed fiercely in his foreword to the book: 'L'auteur tient à préciser que ce roman ne peut, en aucune manière, être considéré comme un document sur la vie dans le territoire anglais de Hong Kong.'[55]

This ability to introduce real locations into his fictions, while depriving them of all documentary value, is another gift to Robbe-Grillet from Raymond Roussel. Roussel was a very rich man and a prodigious traveller, but he is reputed to have gone right round the world without ever leaving the cabin of his ship, convinced, as he claimed to be, that the landscapes of his mind—which were the distillation of some very uninspired secondary sources— deserved to retain their priority over the real thing. In the same way, as I have said, Robbe-Grillet refused to go out and look

---

[53] If any reader, used to ports of call in the Far East, should think that the places described here are not in accordance with the reality, the author, who has himself spent the greater part of his life there, would advise him to go back and see and to look more closely: things change quickly in those climes.

[54] everyone knows Hong Kong.

[55] The author is anxious to make clear that this novel cannot, in any way, be considered as a document on life in the English territory of Hong Kong.

at a real sea-gull at a time when he was about to introduce one into *Le Voyeur*. The sea-gulls in that novel have the generalized rigidity of emblems and none of the specific variations that might make them life-like.

Like the Africa which Roussel presents in *Impressions d'Afrique*, therefore, Robbe-Grillet's Istanbul in *L'Immortelle* is a picture-postcard town, the Istanbul anyone might evoke by reference to a few inferior novels and trivial films. N., the narrator, learns of the quality of his imagination when he first encounters L., the girl of the story, who is herself the unlikely product of the exotic towns-cape: 'Vous venez d'arriver dans une Turquie de légende. . . . Les mosquées, les châteaux forts, les jardins secrets, les harems . . .' (p. 32).[56]

It is possible to say, therefore, that in a film like *L'Immortelle*, or a novel like *La Maison de rendez-vous*, Robbe-Grillet sets out boldly not to recreate the real scenes of Istanbul or Hong Kong but to abolish them. Because of the risks he is taking of being misunderstood—and people have even found likenesses to a real town in the prodigiously formalized streets and houses of *Dans le labyrinthe*—he makes his point about the function of the imagination more powerfully than ever before.

His task is to make sure that the events he introduces and their settings should be as exotic as possible. In *L'Immortelle*, for example, there are multiple images depicting the subjection of women, the jealousy of Moslem husbands, and so on. Yet there is, as it happens, nothing specifically Oriental about this exoticism, since it has the same qualities as the excesses of *Le Voyeur* or *La Jalousie*.

It is this excess which ought to be, for Robbe-Grillet's readers, a warning as to the total inauthenticity of what they are reading. The immobile representations of the mind have a *trompe l'œil* quality of being too real to be true, like the dog that is seen in a shop-window display in *La Maison de rendez-vous*: 'Et si ce n'était son immobilité totale, sa raideur un peu trop accentuée, ses yeux de verre trop brillants sans doute, et trop fixes, l'intérieur peut-être trop rose de sa gueule entrouverte, ses dents trop blanches,

---

[56] You have just arrived in a legendary Turkey. . . . The mosques, the fortified castles, the secret gardens, the harems . . .

on croirait qu'il va terminer le mouvement interrompu . . .' (p. 14).[57]

After this lingering, sensual description, whose intensity is at complete variance with the reminders of the dog's unreality, it is hardly surprising when the dog *does* complete the movement that seemed to have been interrupted and, before very long, appears no longer in the shop-window but in the street.

A Robbe-Grillet novel or film is, therefore, a waking dream; and melodrama, as the theatre writer Eric Bentley observes, 'is the naturalism of the dream-life'. Yet because they are dream-like it does not at all follow that Robbe-Grillet's writings are inaccessible in the way that a great deal of Surrealist writing is inaccessible. Right from the start, when he used the Oedipus myth in *Les Gommes*, Robbe-Grillet has chosen to deal in the most recognizable myths of contemporary man. The dynamic principle which forces the narrator to undertake his journey through the fiction is never hard to grasp, except, possibly, in *Dans le labyrinthe*; the sado-eroticism of *Le Voyeur*, *L'Année dernière à Marienbad*, or *L'Immortelle*, the sexual jealousy of *La Jalousie*, are hardly concealed, and Robbe-Grillet need not have been wholly disingenuous when he wrote: 'j'étais persuadé d'écrire pour le grand public, je souffrais d'être considéré comme un auteur "difficile"' (*Pour un nouveau roman*. p. 8).[58] The fact that he has, in recent years, become more and more of a film-maker and less and less of a writer, is indicative, no doubt, of his determination to situate himself more readily as being on the side of ordinary men and not a darling only of the intellectuals.

What is interesting or revealing in Robbe-Grillet is certainly not the *quality* of the imagination involved, but its methods, which are intended as exemplary, as being those of the imagination in general. Robbe-Grillet shows the imagination at work, creating or trying to create a coherent and consoling structure out of bits and

[57] And if it were not for its total immobility, its slightly over-accentuated stiffness, its over-shiny and over-fixed glass eyes no doubt, the perhaps over-pink interior of its half-open mouth, its over-white teeth, one might think that it is about to finish the movement that had been interrupted . . .
[58] I was convinced I was writing for the public at large, it hurt me to be thought of as a 'difficult' writer.

pieces of the real world, a structure that will answer to the psyche's desperate needs of the moment. But we are in no danger of confusing these mental worlds with the real world, because they do not obey the same laws; the relationship between one image and the next is a dynamic and affective one, the relationship between one object and the next in the everyday world is a spatial or a temporal one. The private pattern which one of Robbe-Grillet's narrators imposes on his stock of images cannot be one that will survive a confrontation with the world of common reference. There is no danger that the values which the millipede mark comes to hold for the husband in *La Jalousie* will become permanent ones, because they have been established to be wholly private.

This is the nub of Robbe-Grillet's over-publicized quarrel with anthropomorphic metaphors, which he attacks lucidly and uncompromisingly in his essay, 'Nature, humanisme, tragédie'. The importance of this quarrel has often been exaggerated, for in the last resort it becomes a matter of which preposition we choose, as to whether we project human emotion *on* to objects or *in*to them. The essence of Robbe-Grillet's perfectly rational position is that a certain object can and must have associations for the individual who observes it, but that these associations are neither permanent nor universal. We must not, once again, confuse the image with the reality, for the first is immanent and the other transcendant; an image is something that we have borrowed from the real world, and we cannot therefore make statements about its essence, which must always escape us. There can surely be no argument that the language, and the way of thinking, to which Robbe-Grillet takes objection, have often been guilty of mistaking a relative situation for an absolute one, and if this mistake is made repeatedly it is likely to result in the birth of an unwholesome cliché, whereby a certain portion of the phenomenal world is definitively appropriated for human use and for our metaphysical comfort.

The weakness of Robbe-Grillet's position is that he treats the standpoint of science as if *it* were an absolute one, and, consequently, a source of comfort. He needs to go to considerable lengths, for example, to defend his own neutrality: 'il n'y a pas du tout dans le mot "objet" une notion de froideur, mais simplement une notion d'extériorité.'[59]

Here he fails to acknowledge that his own attitude is only significant because of the existence of other possible attitudes, and to those large numbers of people who are still accustomed to enjoying a warmly anthropomorphic relationship with nature his proposals must appear very chilling indeed. At the end of 'Nature, humanisme, tragédie', on the other hand, Robbe-Grillet does seem to recognize that his own stance is not an absolute one, and that it enjoys a dialectical relationship with other possible stances: 'Cette lutte, me dira-t-on, est justement l'illusion tragique par excellence: vouloir combattre l'idée de tragédie, c'est déjà y succomber . . .' (*Pour un nouveau roman*, p. 67).[60]

Of themselves, for as long as they remain 'out there', objects have no significance, but once they are absorbed into the memory —and even measurement is a form of appropriation of the external world, whatever Robbe-Grillet may say—then they will become loaded with association. An isolated memory-image, emerging into consciousness, solicits us simply by its presence: it has a message that may be elicited through a series of free associations. Images, indeed, may secrete an autobiography, as Robbe-Grillet notes, quoting from the surrealist poet, Joë Bousquet: 'Le rêve est plus réel que la vie éveillée parce que l'objet n'est plus négligeable: le revolver, l'aiguille et la pendule y résument des événements qui, sans eux, ne seraient pas. L'événement et l'objet y sont rigoureusement interchangeables' (ibid., p. 87).[61]

But what appeals to Robbe-Grillet, as one would expect, about the dream-life, is that its 'objects' have the precedence: it is they that support the anecdote and not the other way round. And one object might equally well support a thousand different aneccdotes; it is real, and they are merely virtual: 'Et l'on s'aperçoit vite que le

[59] there is absolutely no idea of coldness in the word 'object', but simply an idea of externality.
[60] This struggle, I shall be told, is simply the tragic illusion *par excellence*: to seek to combat the idea of tragedy is in fact to succumb to it . . .
[61] The dream is more real than waking life because the object can no longer be ignored: in it the revolver, the needle, and the clock epitomize events which, but for them, would not be. The event and the object are strictly interchangeable.

sens utilitaire de ces mots, comme la signification anecdotique de ces objets criminels, n'ont au fond aucun intérêt. Ce ne sont que des sous-produits possibles des choses elles-mêmes, qui restent seules nécessaires, irremplaçables' (ibid., p. 87).[62]

What happens when we dream then is, for Robbe-Grillet, the best example we have of the vital distinction between irreducible facts and private fictions. One of the effects of his novels, which all register the defeat of a too vigorous imagination, unable finally to overcome the contingent presence of the external world, is to restore to this world—or the irreducible images that represent it in the novel—an integrity it had been in serious danger of forfeiting.

Because Robbe-Grillet's fictions have to start from an image that is neutral, one that is the common possession of the world at large, they also start in a world that is inexpressive, deprived of essential significance. The imposition, or attempted imposition, of significance takes place as the novel proceeds, and is revealed as the imperious necessity of an excited mind. Robbe-Grillet's heroes or narrators are always strangers to the world they find themselves in—with the single exception of the husband in *La Jalousie*, but even he surveys the rooms of his house as if he had never been in them before. Moreover, as well as being strangers they are also visitors, a status that foreshadows their ultimate release from a landscape whose presence is not altogether welcome to them.

Wallas's tireless pedestrian survey of the town in which he finds himself in *Les Gommes* is described in the novel as a search for self-recognition: 'il va profiter de ce répit dont il dispose avant de se rendre aux bureaux de police, où le service normal ne commence qu'à huit heures, pour tâcher de se reconnaître à travers l'enchevêtrement des rues' (p. 47).[63]

What betrays the illicit nature of Wallas's ambition is that he is

---

[62] And one quickly notices that the utilitarian meaning of these words, like the anecdotal significance of the criminal objects, have at bottom no interest. They are only possible by-products of the things themselves, which alone remain necessary and irreplaceable.

[63] he will make use of this breathing-space he has got before going to the police station, where normal service only starts at eight o'clock, to try and find his bearings through the tangle of streets.

seeking *re*cognition and not simply cognition; the fallacy of philosophical essentialism leads him to suppose that there is a meaning in things (as a whole) which pre-existed his own present confrontation with them. Thus, both Wallas and Mathias in *Le Voyeur* are said to be returning to a childhood scene, one, that is to say, which they feel the urge to recognize and which may be able, if they do recognize it, to set their troubled minds at ease.

Once his journey is under way, it is the hero or narrator himself who is constituted by the successive dispositions of images that are themselves immobile. But, whatever the metamorphoses that these images may undergo, their integrity is only threatened, it is never finally destroyed. Their original immobility is a guarantee that they are never going to be conjured wholly away, by being absorbed into a definitive causal sequence: 'Wallas revient sans cesse à la vision du petit homme en manteau vert arrêté au milieu du trottoir, comme si cette présence avait quelque chose d'irréductible, dont aucune explication—si plausible soit-elle—ne puisse venir à bout' (p. 193).[64]

If the mind is forced to return over and over again like this to the same mental image, then it must eventually become apparent that this image is of a different epistemological order from the explanations provided for it. Robbe-Grillet's heroes keep on having to return to facts, which will come to transmit a more and more potent emotional charge as the novel proceeds. Thus the successive appearances of a particular object or image constitute a barometer, a consultation of which allows the reader to measure off the intensity of the imaginative efforts which the narrator is making to finalize his fiction to his own satisfaction.

In Robbe-Grillet's more recent work the most blatant of the archetypes he has introduced are the girls who will become the victim of the sado-erotic urges of the hero. Their archetypal status is underlined by the fact that they have almost all been given names that start with the letter L. (or 'elle'); in the course of *L'Immortelle* and *La Maison de rendez-vous* each L. is allowed a

---

[64] Wallas comes back unceasingly to the sight of the little man in a green overcoat stopped in the middle of the pavement, as if this presence had something irreducible about it, which cannot be got rid of by any explanation—however plausible it may be.

P

series of alternative Christian names, the one constant feature of which is the initial letter—this letter is therefore the irreducible 'fact' from which there is to be no escape. The characteristic which all these L.'s share is their compliance towards the hero or story-teller. Frequently the master-slave relationship is made explicit, both in words and gestures. This relationship is in fact the paradigm for all relationships between a novelist and the characters he meets with in his mind—the playthings of his fantasy.

Once an L. has made her appearance in the novel the derangement of the narrator's mind cannot be long delayed. As his methods have grown more brutal and assured, Robbe-Grillet has accelerated, or exaggerated, the tempo of the mind's disturbance. In *La Maison de rendez-vous*, for example, visual expressions are permitted to change at a hysterical speed: 'elle offre soudain vers lui son visage lisse au regard démésuré, consentant, révolté, soumis, vide, sans expression'; or: 'lui suivant un peu en arrière et la surveillant du regard, un regard indifférent, passionné, glacial . . .' (p. 47).[65]

These facial images are essentially reflective ones, therefore, they register the state of the narrator's emotions, not those of any possible interlocutor. Already, in *L'Immortelle*, Robbe-Grillet had used the face of L. to tell a great deal of the story. When L. is first introduced into the film it is as an expressionless image, a face awaiting an imprint: 'Elle est immobile, tournée de trois quarts mais regardant vers la caméra, de ses grands yeux très ouverts, au regard vide' (p. 14).[66]

But a few seconds later, this impassivity has begun to be contaminated, and faint signs of mobility, of the reflection of a motive, are apparent: 'Les traits du visage sont parfaitement immobiles et n'expriment rien, si ce n'est un lointain sourire, un peu tendre, un peu dangereux' (p. 15).[67] The next time the girl's

---

[65] she suddenly offers him her smooth face, with its excessive, compliant, rebellious, submissive, empty, expressionless stare [or] following slightly behind her and keeping his eyes on her, eyes that are indifferent, passionate, icy . . .

[66] She is motionless, in quarter profile but looking towards the camera, her big eyes opened wide, her stare empty.

[67] The features of her face are perfectly motionless and express nothing, unless it is a distant smile, slightly tender, slightly dangerous.

face is seen it is partially concealed by a Venetian blind, a *jalousie*, whose presence and function are precisely the same as in the novel of that name; a 'plot' is therefore beginning to take shape in the mind of the narrator. L. begins to materialize with more conviction and, consequently, more menace: she adds to her alluring face a body, clothes, and a silver chain wound around her neck 'à deux tours'. This last word in its ambiguity increases the risk the narrator is now running, and his next image has L. on top of a turret (*tourelle*) in a fort. Subsequently she appears on the deck of a local steamer, leaning against the rail, which is supplied with a lifebelt; the French word for a ship's rail, and for other similar sorts of balustrade, is *garde-fou*, so that this image may be read as a pleasant reminder that all is not yet lost for N., that there is still a chance of salvation from the madness that threatens him: from the water, in fact.

But the next shot of the film, alas, puts L. into the midst of a Moslem cemetery, where she leans against a strikingly phallic monument. The sadistic nature of N.'s imagination grows much more apparent: L's body is now 'légèrement tordu',[68] her arms are 'ramenés en arrière',[69] the chain around her neck has been drawn tighter. Soon she appears in the narrator's own room, still enigmatic but already prompting the sound of baying dogs.

It is only once he has managed to suppress, temporarily, this ugly sound, that N. proves capable of removing L. from his mind. But by the time she returns things have got worse: a third party, M., has appeared, to form a troublesome triangle with L. and N. This M. is introduced talking to a fisherman on the harbourside, to a man trying, that is, to haul up monsters from the water—the novelist. M.'s function is clear, therefore: he is a threat to a continuation of the novel, he is the character who will try and deprive N. of the consoling but dangerous presence of L. It is M. who owns the dogs already heard baying and who keeps them firmly on the leash, and M. whose eyes, the moment they are turned on N., cause a rush of guilt and a sudden cut in the sequence of the film. Thus the triangular relationship between these three initials is a simple Freudian one, incarnating that dynamic trinity of ego, id, and superego. From this point of view

[68] slightly twisted.　　　　[69] pulled behind her.

L'Immortelle is perhaps the most schematic of all Robbe-Grillet's fictions, although the same triangular relationship is also established in *L'Année dernière à Marienbad*. (In *La Maison de rendez-vous* it has been partially submerged again into a more complex intrigue, though the three apices are still operative: the storyteller in his multiple avatars, the compliant girls, and the police who are always threatening to disrupt the 'entertainment' at the house of Lada Ava.)

Carefully interpreted, the end of *L'Immortelle* is as instructive as the beginning. A few shots before the conclusion of the film there comes the accident to the narrator, N., an accident which, of course, represents the intrusion of reality or contingency into the fictive sequence he will not be able to sustain any longer. N.'s functions are over, and Robbe-Grillet's prolonged and playful projection of himself is almost ended. L., significantly, survives N., even though he had apparently managed earlier on in the film to suppress her, by making her the victim of a road accident like the one to which he eventually succumbs himself. L. is shown in the penultimate shot of the film, dissolving in a process exactly symmetrical to that whereby she had originally materialized on the screen. Immediately after her features have finally faded into nothing, however, there is a loud concert of boats' sirens and L.'s face returns to the screen. She is dressed with great decorum by now, and it is twilight; after a brief, 'silent' laugh, her face becomes serious and is immobilized, to the sound of a melancholy Turkish chant already heard earlier in *L'Immortelle*.

There are ambiguities in this conclusion, but the synchronization of the static image of the girl's face with the mournful music suggests the novelist's or mythomaniac's regret at being separated from his erotic reveries, as well as a promise that these can easily be renewed at some subsequent date, since woman remains as an inescapable and encouraging guarantee of the mobility of man's imagination.

IV

Many people have been disconcerted by the complete lack of finality in Robbe-Grillet's novels; they are worried because they do not find themselves being carried confidently along from point A in time and space to point B. To judge Robbe-Grillet fairly we need to grasp that each of his fictions consists of a sequence of shorter fictions, the successive attempts of a disturbed mind to create a myth. These attempts describe a parabola of increasing emotional intensity, one which aspires to a moment of extreme violence and then subsides, suggesting that the novel has some therapeutic value for the mind that struggles through it.

In view of the overt eroticism of the fantasies in which Robbe-Grillet has chosen to deal, the pattern of each fiction might be taken to be one of a growing tumescence, followed by a sexual climax, and a relief of tension. Oddly enough, *Dans le labyrinthe*, which is, on the face of things, by far the *least* erotic of Robbe-Grillet's novels, actually contains the most direct indication of their genesis in sexual reverie. The first-person narrator of this novel gives a meticulous description of the refuge in which he is working: a room at the top of a house—a traditional trope from the baroque period, where the human body is envisaged as a house (as it is in dreams) and, consequently, the head becomes a room at the top of that house. (Another contemporary French writer, and a considerable influence on the New Novel, Raymond Queneau, uses precisely the same device at the start of a typically cunning and entertaining novel, *Les Fleurs bleues*.) But the position of the narrator in his room in *Dans le labyrinthe* is what matters and, as I have earlier shown, it is clear that he is in bed, since it is only from the bed that the flaw in his ceiling becomes visible. This being so, the often sombre and Kafkaesque interpretations that have been put on this particular novel are in obvious need of revaluation.

Certainly, Robbe-Grillet has always tried, often very wittily, to show that the mind that seeks to write a novel is one temporarily out of balance. But he has never suggested—it would be ludicrous to do so—that men can live their lives without these moments of imbalance; all he has done is to preach the conviction, which he shares with Michel Butor, that we must not pretend to ourselves that the hypotheses our minds are capable of formulating about the meaning of the external world are definitive ones, valid for all times and all places.

There is lighthearted evidence within Robbe-Grillet's novels that, as a novelist, he is prepared to admit that he too is mad. I have already mentioned his own appearance as a character in *Les Gommes*, in the furtive and easily penetrable disguise of Roy-Dauzet, referred to at one point as an old madman: 'Une pareille histoire de complot est bien digne de l'imagination funambulesque de ce vieux fou. Le voilà en train de lancer à travers le pays toute sa clique d'agents secrets et de détectives . . .' (p. 78).[70]

It seems that the imagination works at night, therefore, that its movements are those of a sleep-walker, which reinforces the link between fiction and eroticism. At the same time, it is at night that we are freed from the necessities of the day: the word 'funambulesque' enjoys a double determination. Roy-Dauzet is not only a madman, he is also, in the first syllable of his name, a King— Robbe-Grillet here is echoing Butor in establishing the novelist as the King of the reflective consciousness, or of the Realm of Meaning.

He has returned to this equation of sovereignty with insanity in *La Maison de rendez-vous*, where tell-tale (the word is peculiarly suitable in this context) stains appear on the ceiling of Lady Ava's bedroom, highly reminiscent of those that flawed the surface of the ceiling in *Dans le labyrinthe*: 'En levant la tête, j'aperçois à mon tour les taches rougeâtres aux découpures compliquées et précises: des îles, des fleuves, des continents, des poissons exotiques. C'est le fou qui habite audessus qui, un jour de crise, a fait couler on ne sait quoi sur son plancher' (p. 187).[71]

This old madman, whose 'crise' has produced such revealingly insular and aquatic patterns on an otherwise unblemished surface, is later identified as King Boris. Before the novel ends an aural dimension is added to his activity upstairs; the verb 'taper' is used to describe the sounds he is making, an indication that *La Maison de rendez-vous* was written, presumably, on a type-writer and not by hand, and later King Boris is heard stamping up and down: 'Elle

[70] Such talk of a plot is certainly worthy of the funambulistic imagination of that old madman. There he is, busy launching his whole gang of secret agents and detectives across the country . . .
[71] Lifting my head, I can see in my turn the reddish stains whose indentations are both complicated and precise: islands, rivers, continents, exotic fish. It's the madman who lives above who had an attack one day and upset who knows what on his floor.

entend des bruits de canne. Elle dit qu'il faudrait monter là-haut pour voir ce qui se passe. Il y a sans doute quelqu'un de malade, ou de blessé, qui appelle à l'aide. Mais aussitôt elle change d'avis: "C'est le vieux roi Boris, dit-elle, qui se balance sur son ferryboat"' (p. 209).[72]

The name Boris, no doubt because of its fragile phonetic links with his own, has always appealed to Robbe-Grillet, since in the fragment of 'Un régicide' he also introduces a King Boris—as the designated victim of the narrator, who is waiting to assassinate him. This narrator is, in fact, proposing to annihilate himself in his function as narrator, like the sleuth in the detective story. This is the Oedipal role I have mentioned in connection with Michel Butor's *L'Emploi du temps*, and makes it easy to see why Robbe-Grillet's first published fiction should have been *Les Gommes*.

Boris's ferry-boat in *La Maison de rendez-vous* itself points to the motion that creates a fiction, according to Robbe-Grillet, the constant movement between irreducible fact and monstrous fantasy, or creation and destruction. There is nothing remotely revolutionary about Robbe-Grillet as far as this goes: novels have always been part observation and part invention. He is an innovator only in so far as he displays, within the novel itself, where one begins and the other leaves off. The illusion fostered by the traditional novel was that the imagination can achieve ultimate victory over reality: Robbe-Grillet insists that its constructs are only temporary. The last words of the colourful impresario of the Villa Bleue in *La Maison de rendez-vous* might stand as a legend beneath his whole *œuvre*: 'Les choses ne sont jamais définitivement en ordre' (p. 209).[73]

The blatant contradictions which Robbe-Grillet inserts into his novels are therefore an omen of the ultimate victory of the phenomenal world over the individual imagination. By returning over and over again to the same image or scene the imagination presages its defeat and final relapse into silence. But the dubious

---

[72] She can hear the sounds of a stick. She says they will have to go up and see what's going on. No doubt there is someone sick or injured, calling for help. But she at once changes her mind: 'It's old king Boris,' she says, 'rocking on his ferry-boat.'

[73] Things are never finally in order.

structures which it manages to erect meanwhile are also menaced with collapse—thus the true end of the novel is preceded by a varying number of false ends.

In his time Robbe-Grillet has used several different methods of undermining the stability of his fictions from within, by introducing representatives of the destructive process itself. (It would perhaps be better to think of these particular objects not so much as agents of destruction as obstacles, since the fiction does in fact survive them.)

In two of his novels, *Dans le labyrinthe* and *La Maison de rendez-vous*, the continuation of the fictional scheme is threatened by a doctor. In the first-named novel, a doctor is introduced without any previous warning at a point near the end, to announce, and in the first-person, that the soldier who has hitherto been the focus of the narrative, in the third person, has died, and that he did not need the third injection which the doctor had called in to give him. Since the soldier has indeed suffered two wounds on his way through the novel, one in the heel of his boot and one in the side, the doctor's third injection is clearly of the same category as these. The doctor's function, in fact, is identical with that of the accident or contingent event in Robbe-Grillet's novels; rather like in Molière's plays or in Voltaire's *contes*, the doctor turns out to be the man who kills his patients instead of saving them!

In *La Maison de rendez-vous*, Ralph Johnson recognizes the threat of the fiction's extinction at a moment when he himself is posing as a doctor: 'Johnson se dit aussi que le vrai docteur ne va pas tarder à interrompre la comédie' (p. 191).[74] Again, the divided consciousness of the novelist is embodied in two opposed characters: in the story-teller, Johnson (who is reputed to grow Indian hemp on his estate), and the watchful spy, policeman or, in this case, doctor, who finally has the last word. Since the creative aspect of the novelist's art is a measure of his insanity, it is only fitting that it should be a doctor who arrives to put an end to it.

Of the objects that are introduced with the same responsibilities to discharge as the doctors the one that has attracted most attention is the india-rubber, because of its role in *Les Gommes*. Wallas's

[74] Johnson also tells himself that it will not be long before the real doctor interrupts the play.

search in the stationers' shops in that novel for a particular brand of eraser mirrors his other search, for the murderer of Dupont; if he is successful in his detective work then he abolishes the need for his own presence in the town—he abolishes the novel, that is to say. But he never finds the eraser he is looking for any more than he finds the murderer; if he did he would have enjoyed the triumph of distorting reality in the interests of the imagination, he would have founded a lasting myth. A simple point about *Les Gommes*, which it is easy to forget in the dazzling light cast on the structure of the novel by Professor Morrissette's analysis of its Oedipal elements,[75] is that Wallas is not a successful Oedipus but a failed one. He is only able to remember two of the six letters in the name of the eraser he wants, and he is no more successful in re-enacting the life of his mythical model—he does not, for instance, commit incest with the woman who may be his mother, even if, as Morrissette shows, his encounters with her carry a considerable erotic charge.

India-rubbers turn up elsewhere in Robbe-Grillet's novels too. In *La Jalousie*, for example, the husband uses one to try and erase the persistent mark of the crushed millipede from the wall; in *L'Immortelle*, a whole collection of them is revealed in a drawer, immediately after the most torrid shot in the whole film, which shows the Narrator's hand beginning to squeeze the nape of L.'s neck with murderous intent. This same gesture is then reproduced in the shot of the drawer, even though it is not revealed what the object is round which N.'s hand is closing. Both shots, however, are directly linked with the accident which occurs in the film, the apparent death of L., in a car smash. Such accidents, of course, like the smashing of the champagne glass—the receptacle of the pleasure-giving drug, alcohol—in *L'Année dernière à Marienbad* or *La Maison de rendez-vous* are the least equivocal of all Robbe-Grillet's interpolated reminders of the contingent world.

In *La Maison de rendez-vous* he has also, as it happens, found a very plausible substitute for the india-rubbers of the earlier books. These are the road-sweepers who make a number of appearances in the novel. The to-and-fro motion of their brooms echoes the to-and-fro motion of the eraser when it is used. The function of

[75] See *Les Romans de Robbe-Grillet*.

the roadsweepers is to dispatch the debris that litters the streets of Hong Kong into the drains. But this debris, as I have said, is the raw material out of which the novelist builds, so that there is no difficulty in grasping the significance of the men who sweep it away. They are the representatives of time or necessity, dressed in fact in 'bleus de mécanicien'. In the last resort the roadsweepers are one more avatar of the novelist himself, this time in his more socially responsible role as the hygienic destroyer of anthropomorphic myths. There is one attractive moment in *La Maison de rendez-vous* where Robbe-Grillet exemplifies the virtues of keeping one's eye on one's work, instead of letting it be distracted by the provocatively divided skirts of the local Eurasian girls:

un balai de riz, qui effleure les pavés à l'aveuglette, hors du regard perdu d'un employé municipal en bleu de chauffe, dont l'œil ensommeillé abandonne bientôt les brèves apparitions périodiques de la jambe entre les pans de la robe fendue, pour se reporter un instant sur son travail: le faisceau de paille de riz dont l'extrémité recourbée par l'usage ramène vers le caniveau une image bariolée: la couverture d'un illustré chinois (p. 35).[76]

A further point worth making about this passage is that it can also serve as a reflection of the novelist's own situation: once he diverts his attention from the behaviour of his characters and instead considers himself at work, then the fiction comes to a halt. This scene, and the many others structurally identical with it in Robbe-Grillet, may also be an intentional reminder that the novelist does not write a whole novel in one sitting (unless he is William Faulkner), but is forced to create it 'periodically'.

Robbe-Grillet, then, is a master of disillusion, so much so that he prompts the question what precisely he has left behind him by the time he reaches the last page of a novel. But before answering that question, I must point to something that he has, so to speak, left ahead of him—the guilty organ of creation itself, the imagina-

---

[76] a rice broom, which brushes blindly across the surface of the road, out of the lost stare of the municipal workman in blue dungarees, whose sleepy eye soon abandons the brief periodic appearances of the leg between the folds of the slit dress, to return for a moment to his work: the bundle of rice straw whose end curled up by use returns a gaudy picture towards the gutter: the cover of a Chinese picture-paper.

tion. The imagination that has fought in vain to maintain its fictions is not abolished once and for all by Robbe-Grillet, it is merely returned to the everyday world. This everyday or contingent world appears to it a chaos, because it does not display the order the imagination would like it to display. Robbe-Grillet never, therefore, leaves us in any doubt that it will not be long before the imagination sets out on another of its vain quests. The final appearance of the *patron* in *Les Gommes*, for example, shows him still to be at the centre of a circle of protean spectres or of objects found floating in the sea:

Autour de lui les spectres familiers dansent la valse, comme des phalènes qui se cognent en rond contre un abat-jour, comme de la poussière dans le soleil, comme les petits bateaux perdus sur la mer, qui bercent au gré de la houle leur cargaison fragile, les vieux tonneaux, les poissons morts, les poulies et les cordages, les bouées, le pain rassis, les couteaux et les hommes (p. 266).[77]

Since these objects are what cannot ultimately be denied, they alone are to be recognized as necessary by the fact of their presence. Robbe-Grillet denies our right to try and abolish any part of our real environment, be it human or not, by over-familiarity, by seeing it, that is to say, as simply one element of some permanent myth. He is proposing an orthodox existentialist view, by which a man is judged, objectively, as the sum of his acts, and not as the sum of his possible motives or abortive acts as well. Confronted with the words, gestures or bodily movements of another human being the human observer will inevitably arrange these into a causal chain and deduce, as he or she thinks, their necessary motive. But this observer ought really to admit, if challenged, that what has been deduced are not facts but fictions—they are projections of the observer's own motives for acting in analogous ways to those he has observed. The ethical benefits of this austere epistemological distinction between facts and fictions are self-evident, since what it would lead to, if rigorously accepted, would

[77] Around him the familiar spectres dance the waltz, like moths knocking in a circle against a lamp-shade, like dust in the sunlight, like the little ships lost on the sea, which rock at the mercy of the waves their fragile cargo, the old barrels, the dead fish, the pulleys and the ropes, the buoys, the stale bread, the knives and the men.

be an infinitely greater tolerance of other people's behaviour, and an acceptance of uncertainty which ought, in theory, to be a barrier against aggression. When we are led, as we are every day, to cement the gaps between facts with the projections of our imagination then we add nothing substantial to these facts themselves, we simply reveal something of the temporary or perhaps even the permanent state of our own psyche. I am not suggesting that we are always wrong when we attribute motives to the actions of others, but only that we should recognize the possibility that we are wrong.

And now as to the question of what is left *behind* at the end of a Robbe-Grillet novel; the answer is the novel itself, the record of the imagination's lively struggle with reality. Another real and irreducible object has been added to the common stock, ready to suffer numerous distortions as readers and critics try and force it into harmony with their preconceived notions and particular obsessions. It is this fact—that by the time the novel ends something new is in existence in the phenomenal world—which constitutes the one true transformation effected by the narrator's journey from the first page to the last. It would be misleading for this reason to over-emphasize the circularity of Robbe-Grillet's novels and assume from this that the narrator's journey is a futile one, in the course of which he makes no useful self-discoveries. This narrator is a projection of the novelist, and Robbe-Grillet is certainly not interested in using the novel to psychoanalyse himself—he is interested in laying bare the creative process in the hope that his readers may learn something about themselves, not so much during the reading of the novel as afterwards.

In his essay on Raymond Roussel, published in 1963, Robbe-Grillet quite rightly stresses that this freak ancestor of the *nouveau roman* saw a fiction as marking a progress from a situation, A, to the same situation very slightly modified, A_1. These slight modifications are figured in the phonic distortions which Roussel made into the motive for his fictional journeys. Robbe-Grillet stresses that these journeys of Roussel's are not quite circular: 'Car il faut insister sur l'importance que Roussel attache à cette très légère *modification* de son séparant les deux phrases-clefs . . . le texte "se mord la queue", mais avec une petite irrégularité, une petite entorse . . . et qui change tout.' (*Pour un nouveau roman*, p. 75).[78]

It was quite natural that Roussel should attach great importance to his modifications of the original sound, because without them there would have been no fiction at all. The modifications exemplify in fact the freedom of the mind to depart from the world of given facts, and Roussel's books can therefore be read, just like Robbe-Grillet's own, as a record of that freedom and, above all, of the limits that the given world imposes on it. Roussel is a sterile writer, in the sense that ultimately he subjects the imagination to one or more linguistic accidents—those phonic distortions which also entail a semantic transformation of the original words; it is as if he wanted to prove the imagination's freedom and deny it all in one movement, and here he displays the same sort of fear which is also to be found among Robbe-Grillet's narrators. But although they may be afraid, and with good cause, of the freedom which their minds allow them, these narrators go far enough to reveal themselves, they are impelled by an obsession we can quickly recognize as human, for all its exaggeration. The mere fact that these minds are obsessed, that their powers of distortion are exaggerated by Robbe-Grillet in an essentially humorous way, should put us on our guard against becoming too concerned with the actual nature of their obsessions, which are those that have been most freely exploited by merchants of cheap fantasy in books and films of the last twenty years or so. What Robbe-Grillet has really done by presenting such crudely inflated imaginations is to make us more readily aware of the function of fantasy in our mental lives, in the same way that an anatomist might demand a vastly enlarged diagram of a bodily organ in order to explain its functioning adequately to his students.

What is no doubt inconsistent is that imaginations of this degree of potency should ever be defeated at all by the undramatic forces of reality; they should surely be able to subtend a fictive world both satisfying and wholly illusory without fear of interruption.

---

[78] For we must insist on the importance which Roussel attaches to this very slight *modification* of sound separating the two key-phrases . . . the text 'bites its own tail', but with a tiny irregularity, a tiny wrench . . . which alters everything.

The fact that Robbe-Grillet undermines the process of creation so frequently is, to my mind, a token of his didactic intentions; he is not prepared to allow anything even approaching a coherent fantasy to develop, which would be equivalent to a new metaphysic, an established myth by which to interpret subsequent events in the phenomenal world. By showing a mind obsessed yet fearful of its obsession, Robbe-Grillet shows a mind condemned to shuttle between its own world and ours. The difference between a normal mind and that, say, of Mathias in *Le Voyeur*, is only one of degree and not one of kind.

The graph which the shuttling mind leaves behind it, after its frustrating passage through the novel, can be likened to that baroque artefact which Robbe-Grillet might adopt as a blazon, the labyrinth. But those who set out to penetrate to the heart of an actual labyrinth are kept going by the knowledge that there *is* a correct path, if only they can find it. The hero of a Robbe-Grillet novel shares the same ambition, but what in real life is knowledge is in his case illusion, for if there were a path to the centre of the labyrinth then he would be able to impose a final order on his troubled world. As far as Robbe-Grillet is concerned, to do this in our own day and age is a preposterous ambition, and it is therefore one that he must show to be doomed even as it takes shape. To the cameraman in *L'Année dernière* for example he gives explicit directions: 'Le chemin qu'on parcourt ainsi doit être extrêmement chargé en passages divers tels que colonnes, portiques, vestibules, chicanes, petits escaliers, carrefours de couloirs, etc. En outre l'effet de labyrinthe est augmenté par la présence de glaces monumentales, qui renvoient d'autres perspectives de passages compliqués' (p. 98).[79]

Whenever Robbe-Grillet introduces roads, corridors, staircases and so on, he always does so in this fragmented and deliberately bewildering way. The progress of the narrator who tries to follow them and link them together into a coherent townscape or piece of

---

[79] The path which we thus follow must be extremely well provided with various passages such as pillars, porticos, vestibules, chicanes, little staircases, intersecting corridors, etc. Moreover, the effect of a labyrinth is magnified by the presence of monumental mirrors, which reflect other perspectives of complicated passages.

architecture represents the will to find comfort in a definitive order of things. But the motion which Robbe-Grillet permits is only brief and fragmentary, each section of street, corridor, or the like, being simply the evidence of the mind's frustration.

Yet if the narrator is doomed to fail to draw up his map, the same does not apply to the reader of Robbe-Grillet's novels. Once the novel has come into being, or as it comes into being, its objects, that is to say the discontinuous units out of which it has been constructed, confront the reader with the same sort of problems as the narrator has been confronted with by the objects of his own world. It is we who are challenged to apprehend them. Like Michel Butor, Robbe-Grillet is very insistent on the need for the full co-operation of the reader: 'Car, loin de le négliger, l'auteur aujourd'hui proclame l'absolu besoin qu'il a se son concours, un concours actif, conscient, créateur. Ce qu'il lui demande, ce n'est plus de recevoir tout fait un monde achevé, plein, clos sur lui-même, c'est au contraire de participer à une création, d'inventer à son tour l'œuvre' (*Pour un nouveau roman*, p. 134).[80]

There is more than a trace here of Sartre's painstaking justifications of the creative writer in *Qu'est-ce que la littérature?* For example: 'C'est l'effort conjugué de l'auteur et du lecteur qui fera surgir cet objet concret et imaginaire qu'est l'œuvre de l'esprit. Il n'y a d'art que pour et par autrui.'[81]

Sartre may have been over-anxious at this stage of his life to defend the practical virtues of the writer, who changes the world by changing people's attitudes towards it; he rather implies that the work of art which is brought into existence by the joint efforts of writer and reader is an essential complex of stimuli and reactions, whereas there are as many different works of art as there are readers of a book. But Robbe-Grillet is asking us to work on his novels in order to understand them, and to treat them as

[80] For, far from ignoring him, today's author proclaims his absolute need of his co-operation, a co-operation that is active, conscious, and creative. What he asks of him is no longer to receive ready-made a world that is finished, full, and closed in on itself, but, on the contrary, to take part in a creation, to invent the work in his turn.

[81] It is the joint effort of writer and reader which will cause this concrete and imaginary object that is the work of the mind to appear. There is art only for and through others.

phenomenological objects, unverifiable but open to our investigations, and sure to reflect our own myths back at us if we fail to
extract their true measurements.

There are two somewhat contradictory ways in which one
might set to work on a Robbe-Grillet novel. First, by trying to rearrange the contents in order to form them into a traditional
chronological narrative. Professor Morrissette has done this with
great skill and perverse ambition in *Les Romans de Robbe-Grillet*,
though even he admits defeat confronted by the fragmentation of
Dans le labyrinthe. The assumption behind such an attempted re-
arrangement is that a 'text' exists from which Robbe-Grillet's own
version represents a departure—that the imagination expresses in
fact rather than creates. But the hypothetical 'text' for Robbe-
Grillet is only a reference, never a reality; he shows the imagination at work creating fictive sequences out of discontinuous
materials, not trying to create the one true, mathematical sequence.

The second approach to Robbe-Grillet is really the precise
opposite of the first, since it depends on studying the events of
the novel rigorously in the order in which they are narrated, since
this offers the real hope of making sense of them. What Robbe-
Grillet writes down in a novel is, as it were, the electro-encephalo-
graph of a highly active brain, and it is absurd to treat the sequence
of waves as if it were an arbitrary one. On the contrary, it is a
necessary sequence, 'un voyage lointain, et non pas gratuit . . .
mais nécessaire',[82] as *La Maison de rendez-vous* declares in a characteristic moment of self-summary.

A careful study of the moments when one scene is replaced by
another is indispensable for understanding what the significance
of each element is for the imagination that exploits it. The
structure of *Dans le labyrinthe* becomes clearer right at the start,
for example, when it is appreciated that each time the eye of the
narrator falls on the red curtains masking one of the four walls of
his bedroom (I would interpret these curtains as the narrator's
closed eyelids), his mind is projected out into the town which he
then struggles to explore and to rationalize in the persona of the
soldier.

Sequence, then, reveals the affective mechanism of the imagina-

[82] a distant voyage, and not gratuitous . . . but necessary.

tion in Robbe-Grillet's confected dreams. So does the configuration of individual scenes—the manipulation of elements within a single scene as well as the transformations these elements undergo between their appearance and their reappearance. It is a daunting thought for the reader, and above all for the would-be exegete of these novels, that *nothing* which they contain is gratuitous, but that every last scene is susceptible of an interpretation relating it in minute detail to the preoccupations of a mythomaniac mind. Such a total exegesis remains as a challenge; what I have myself done, I hope, is to indicate a method of achieving it.

Above all, one must, when reading Robbe-Grillet, respect the integrity of the novels, and limit any interpretation to the events actually described, not attempt to warp these permanently into some private pattern of our own. There is one point in *La Jalousie* where the wife and her supposed lover, Franck, during one of the many conversations they have about a certain novel that they have been reading, start inventing alternative episodes, then further alternatives, depending on the first ones, and so on. They have discovered the heady pleasures of the critical imagination:

'Mais, par malheur, il est justement rentré plus tôt ce jour-là, ce que personne ne pouvait prévoir.' Franck balaya ainsi d'un seul coup les fictions qu'ils viennent d'échafauder ensemble. Rien ne sert de faire des suppositions contraires, puisque les choses sont ce qu'elles sont: on ne change rien à la réalité (p. 83).[83]

This passage, in which, once again, fiction is shown as succumbing to the clock, contains two lessons, one for literary critics and one for metaphysicians. For the critic, or the attentive reader, a novel constitutes a reality, and any interpretation of it which contradicts or is contradicted by a single fact in that reality is invalid. Anything, moreover, which is added to these facts, by way of exegesis, will be a fiction of our own invention.

The metaphysical lesson is similar, but it is by no means as gloomy or as fatalistic as it may sound. All that Robbe-Grillet is

[83] 'But, unfortunately, that was the very day he came home early, which no one could have foreseen.' Franck thus swept away at a single blow the fictions they have just erected together. There is no point in making contrary suppositions, since things are what they are: you cannot change anything in reality.

Q

asking is that we should not preserve our fictions beyond the moment of time when facts have contradicted them. Like the scientist altering his hypothesis to accord with fresh experimental data, so must we all constantly recognize that our imaginative constructs are only temporary.

It was a surprisingly long time before anyone took the apparently obvious step of treating Robbe-Grillet's novels as if they were psycho-analytical confessions, in which, as we know, contiguity of apparently disparate images or words and massive distortions play a role of paramount importance. The reader of Robbe-Grillet is indeed offered the part of the analyst, and since the novelist has limited himself to the more colourful and blatant of contemporary psychoses this is far from being an impossible part for the reader to play successfully. Each novel is a plea for help, therefore, since it has something to hide and does nothing but draw attention to the fact that it has something to hide. The device, as the English critic Christine Brooke-Rose has shown, in connection with *Dans le labyrinthe*, is an old one known to the rhetoricians and named by them *occupatio*.

Nowadays, *occupatio* is a stratagem which I imagine most of us would associate with a lack of serious commitment in a writer or speaker who used it to excess, and to treat Robbe-Grillet's fiction as serious psychoanalytical material would be a preposterous mistake. The global answer to the problems posed psychologically by a novel like *Le Voyeur* is an extremely easy one; Mathias is not a very devious sado-eroticist, he is everyone's idea of a sado-eroticist—the analyst's final diagnosis of his complaint need not take long. Robbe-Grillet has himself disclaimed vigorously the traditional psychological ambitions of the novelist, and nothing is to be gained in reading *Le Voyeur* as if it were a solemn and instructive case history. It is a novel which acknowledges the existence of and indicates in no uncertain way the dangers of the freedom that the mind enjoys in its commerce with the external world—of the play in the machine.

It is customary to treat the function of play in our lives as a therapeutic or restorative one, as a means of adjustment for our more serious activities. Robbe-Grillet is proposing that the function of the novel be recognized as precisely this. His fictions are the artful dreams of a waking man, but dreams too, even before they are analysed, may have a therapeutic effect on the troubled mind. Freud quotes approvingly the nineteenth-century view that dreams are 'the guardians of sleep, not its disturbers', an attitude that seems lately to have become much more widespread among schools of psychiatric medicine. While the traditional virtue of the dream that has been properly interpreted to the dreamer is to enlighten him to the way things are in his waking life.

For Robbe-Grillet a fiction is a fabricated dream; it is not real but neither is it useless. The aim of what he writes is to define the true priority of fact over fiction and to show that the more excessive flights of the imagination are best confined to bed and to books. When we wake up, or put down the book, we can return to the real world not only purged in some measure but also aware that there *is* a gap between our minds and our environment, to measure which is both a personal and a responsible task. It is a gap we can only hope to bridge temporarily and relatively, not finally and absolutely.

SELECT BIBLIOGRAPHY

Philosophical Background

Husserl, E., *Ideas, General Introduction to Pure Phenomenology*, tr. W. Boyce Gibson, London, George Allen & Unwin, 1958.
Cartesian Meditations, An Introduction to Phenomenology, tr. D. Cairns, The Hague, Martinus Nijhoff, 1960.
Merleau-Ponty, M., *Phénoménologie de la Perception*, Paris, Gallimard, 1945.
Sartre, J.-P., *L'Être et le néant*, Paris, Gallimard, 1943.
L'Imaginaire, Psychologie phénoménologique de l'imagination, Paris, Gallimard Collection 'Idées', 1966.

Literary Background

Albérès, R-M., *Histoire du roman moderne*, Paris, Albin Michel, 1962.
Métamorphoses du roman, Paris, Albin Michel, 1966.
Barthes, R., *Essais critiques*, Paris, Éditions du Seuil, 1964.
Le Degré zéro de la littérature, Paris, Éditions Gonthier, 1965.
Blanchot, M., *Le Livre à venir*, Paris, Gallimard, 1959.
Faye, J.-P., *Le Récit hunique*, Paris, Éditions du Seuil, 1967.
Haedans, K., *Paradoxe sur le roman*, Paris, Grasset, 1964.
Jean, R., *La Littérature et le réel*, Paris, Albin Michel, 1965.
Lukács, G., *La Théorie du roman*, Paris, Éditions Gonthier, 1963.
Sarraute, N., *L'Ère du soupçon*, Paris, Gallimard Collection 'Idées', 1964.

Full-length Studies of the New Novel

Barrère, J-B., *La Cure d'amaigrissement du roman*, Paris, Albin Michel, 1964.
Bloch-Michel, J., *Le Présent de l'indicatif*, Paris, Gallimard, 1963.
Janvier, L., *Une Parole exigeante*, Paris, Éditions de Minuit, 1964.
Ricardou, J., *Problèmes du nouveau roman*, Paris, Éditions du Seuil, 1967.

Special Numbers of Periodicals

Arguments, Feb. 1958, 'Le Roman d'aujourd'hui'.
Esprit, July/August 1958, 'Le Nouveau roman'.
Revue des Lettres Modernes, Nos. 94/9, 1964(1), 'Un Nouveau roman?'
Yale French Studies, No. 24, Summer 1959, 'Midnight Novelists'.

Claude Simon

Novels

Le Tricheur, Paris, Éditions du Sagittaire, 1946.
Gulliver, Paris, Calmann-Lévy, 1952.
Le Sacre du printemps, Paris, Calmann-Lévy, 1954.
Le Vent, Paris, Éditions de Minuit, 1957.
L'Herbe, Paris, Éditions de Minuit, 1958.
La Route des Flandres, Paris, Éditions de Minuit, 1960. (Reprinted 1963, in 10/18 series, Paris, Union Générale d'Éditions.)
Le Palace, Paris, Éditions de Minuit, 1962.
Histoire, Paris, Éditions de Minuit, 1967.

Plays

La Séparation. This play was produced at the Théâtre de Lutèce in Paris in the Spring of 1963, but no text has as yet been published.

Essays

La Corde raide, Paris, Éditions du Sagittaire, 1947.

Articles

Berger, Y., 'L'Enfer, le temps', *NNRF*, Jan. 1961, pp. 95–109.
Déguy, M., 'Claude Simon et la représentation', *Critique*, Dec. 1962, pp. 1009–32.
Howlett, J., 'La Route des Flandres', *Les Lettres Nouvelles*, Dec. 1960, pp. 178–81.
Merleau-Ponty, M., 'Cinq notes sur Claude Simon', *Médiations*, Winter 1961/2, pp. 5–9.
Ollier, C., 'L'Herbe', *NNRF*, Jan. 1959, pp. 136–7.
Pingaud, B., 'La Route des Flandres', *Les Temps modernes*, No. 178, 1961, pp. 1026–37.

Michel Butor

Novels

Passage de Milan, Paris, Éditions de Minuit, 1954.
L'Emploi du temps, Paris, Éditions de Minuit, 1957. (Reprinted in 10/18 series, Paris, Union Générale d'Éditions, 1966.)

238 THE FRENCH NEW NOVEL

La Modification, Paris, Éditions de Minuit, 1957. (Reprinted in 10/18 series, Paris, Union Générale d'Éditions, 1962.)
Degrés, Paris, Gallimard, 1960.

Other Fiction

Mobile, Paris, Gallimard, 1962.
Réseau aérien (pièce radiophonique), Paris, Gallimard, 1962.
Description de San Marco, Paris, Gallimard, 1964.
Illustrations, Paris, Gallimard, 1964.
6 810 000 litres d'eau par seconde (étude stéréophonique), Paris, Gallimard, 1965.
Portrait de l'artiste en jeune singe, Paris, Gallimard, 1967.

Essays, Criticism, etc.

Le Génie du lieu, Paris, Grasset, 1958.
Histoire extraordinaire: Essai sur un rêve de Baudelaire, Paris, Gallimard, 1960.
Répertoire 1, Paris, Éditions de Minuit, 1960.
Répertoire 2, Paris, Éditions de Minuit, 1963.
Essais sur les modernes (contains material reprinted from *Répertoire 1* and *2*), Paris, Gallimard Collection 'Idées', 1964.
Répertoire 3, Paris, Éditions de Minuit, 1968.
Essais sur les essais, Paris, Gallimard, 1968.

Studies

Albérès, R-M., *Michel Butor,* Paris, Éditions Universitaires, Classiques du vingtième siècle, 1964.
Charbonnier, G., *Entretiens avec Michel Butor,* Paris, Gallimard, 1967.
Raillard, G., *Michel Butor,* Paris, Gallimard, Bibliothèque Idéale, 1968.
Roudaut, J., *Michel Butor ou le livre futur,* Paris, Gallimard, 1964.
Roudiez, L., *Michel Butor,* New York, Columbia University Essays on Modern Writers, No. 9, 1965.

Articles

Albérès, R-M., 'Michel Butor ou le roman transcendental', *La Revue de Paris,* March 1961, pp. 61–71.
Leiris, M., 'Le Réalisme mythologique de M. Butor', *Critique,* Feb. 1958, pp. 99–118. (Reprinted in *La Modification,* 10/18 ed. q.v.)
Morrissette, B., 'Narrative "you" in Contemporary Literature', *Comparative Literature Studies,* Vol. 2, No. 1, 1965, pp. 1–24.

Pouillon, J., 'A Propos de "La Modification"', *Les Temps modernes*, Dec. 1957, pp. 1099–1105.

Raillard, G., 'De quelques éléments baroques dans "L'Emploi du Temps"', *Cahiers de l'Association Internationale des Études Françaises*, Vol. 14, 1962, pp. 179–94.

Ricardou, J., 'Michel Butor', *NNRF*, June 1960, pp. 1157–61.

Spitzer, L., 'Quelques aspects de la technique des romans de Michel Butor', *Archivum Linguisticum*, Vol. 13, No. 2, 1961, pp. 171–95; Vol. 14, No. 1, 1962, pp. 49–76.

Alain Robbe-Grillet

Novels, etc.

Les Gommes, Paris, Éditions de Minuit, 1953. (Reprinted in 10/18 series, Paris, Union Générale d'Éditions, 1962.)

Le Voyeur, Paris, Éditions de Minuit, 1955.

La Jalousie, Paris, Éditions de Minuit, 1957.

Dans le labyrinthe, Paris, Éditions de Minuit, 1959. (Reprinted in 10/18 series, Paris, Union Générale d'Éditions, 1964.)

Instantanés, Paris, Éditions de Minuit, 1962.

La Maison de rendez-vous, Paris, Éditions de Minuit, 1965.

Ciné-romans

L'Année dernière à Marienbad, Paris, Éditions de Minuit, 1961.

L'Immortelle, Paris, Éditions de Minuit, 1963.

Criticism, etc.

Pour un nouveau roman, Paris, Éditions de Minuit, 1963. (Reprinted in Gallimard Collection 'Idées', 1964.)

Studies

Alter, J. V., *La Vision du monde d'Alain Robbe-Grillet*, Geneva, Librairie Droz, 1966.

Bernal, O., *Alain Robbe-Grillet: le roman de l'absence*, Paris, Gallimard, 1964.

Miesch, J., *Robbe-Grillet*, Paris, Éditions Universitaires, Classiques du vingtième siècle, 1965.

Morrissette, B., *Les Romans de Robbe-Grillet*, Paris, Éditions de Minuit, 1963.

Morrissette, B., *Alain Robbe-Grillet*, New York, Columbia University
  Essays on Modern Writers, No. 11, 1965.
Stoltzfus, B., *Alain Robbe-Grillet and the New French Novel*, Southern
  Illinois University Press, 1964.

Articles

Anzieu, D., 'Le Discours de l'obsessionnel dans les romans de Robbe-
  Grillet', *Les Temps Modernes*, Oct. 1965, pp. 608–37.
Barnes, H., 'The Ins and Outs of Alain Robbe-Grillet', *Chicago Review*,
  Vol. 15, No. 3, Winter 1962, pp. 21–43.
Genette, G., 'Vertige Fixé', in *Dans le labyrinthe*, 10/18 ed. q. v. pp.
  273-306.
Goldmann, L., 'Les Deux avant-gardes', *Médiations*, No. 4, Winter
  1961/2, pp. 63–83.
  'Nouveau roman et réalité', *Revue de L'Institut de Sociologie* (Brussels),
  1963, No. 2, pp. 449–67.
Hahn, B., 'Plan du labyrinthe de Robbe-Grillet', *Les Temps Modernes*,
  July 1960, pp. 150–68.
Janvier, L., 'Robbe-Grillet, Hong Kong, Alice', *Critique*, Dec. 1965,
  pp. 1044–51.
Morrissette, B., 'Une voie pour le nouveau cinéma', *Critique*, March
  1964, pp. 411–33.
Ollier, C., 'Ce soir à Marienbad', *NNRF*, Oct. 1961, pp. 711–19; Nov.
  1961, pp. 906–12.
Pingaud, B., 'L'Oeuvre et l'analyse', *Les Temps Modernes*, Oct. 1965,
  pp. 637–46.
Sollers, P., 'Sept propositions sur Robbe-Grillet', *Tel Quel*, Summer
  1960, pp. 49–53.
  'Le Rêve en plein jour', *NNRF*, May 1963, pp. 904–11.
Weightman, J., 'Robbe-Grillet', *Encounter*, March 1962, pp. 30–9.
  (Reprinted in Cruickshank, J. (ed): *The Novelist as Philosopher*,
  Oxford University Press, 1962.)

INDEX

absurd, philosophy of the, 73
Albérès, R.-M., 24
Alter, Jean V., 188, 189, 201
Année dernière à Marienbad, L', 41,
   175, 213, 220, 225, 230
anti-novel, 5 ff., 10, 86
archetypes, *see* myth
Artaud, Antonin, 15
Auden, W. H., 161
Auerbach, Erich, 5
Austen, Jane, 6

Bachelard, Gaston, 125, 190 n.
Balzac, Honoré de, 9, 30, 38, 92
Baroque style, 51 ff., 60
Barthes, Roland, 3, 34, 113, 143, 144,
   169, 204, 208
Baudelaire, Charles, 23, 133, 189
Beckett, Samuel, 3, 5
Bentley, Eric, 213
Bernal, Olga, 194
Blanchot, Maurice, 98, 182
Bogart, Humphrey, 18
Bousquet, Joë, 201–2, 215
Brecht, Bertold, 15, 169
Brentano, Franz, 27
Brooke-Rose, Christine, 234
Burroughs, William, 98

Camus, Albert, 70, 209
Capote, Truman, 17–18
Carroll, Lewis, 86
Cervantes, Miguel de, 6
Cézanne, Paul, 45 ff., 74
chosisme, 2, 26, 53, 196
cinema, 30, 58, 61, 65, 175, 213
ciné-romans, 175, 197, 211
Clézio, J. M. G. le, 20
Corde raide, La, 45, 50, 53, 60–1, 70,
   73 ff., 81, 85, 92

'Crise de croissance de la Science-
   Fiction, La', 158
'Critique et invention', 12

Dans le labyrinthe, 34, 172, 177,
   193–4, 197–8, 201, 206, 212,
   213, 221, 222, 224, 230, 232,
   234
death, 50–1, 54, 57, 68, 74 ff.
Declaration of the 121 on Algeria,
   39
Degrés, 105, 114, 130–9, 142, 150 ff.,
   155, 159, 162, 167, 168, 206
Descartes, René, 27
Description de San Marco, 109–10
detective stories, 160 ff.
Dostoevsky, Feodor, 92
dramatic irony, 59
Drame, 37
dreams, 34, 58, 133, 155–6, 165, 233,
   235
Dujardin, Edouard, 20, 21
Duras, Marguerite, 3

école de Minuit, l', 2
école du regard, l', 2
Éditions de Minuit, 2, 43
Einstein, Albert, 14
Emploi du temps, L', 35, 105, 116–25,
   127, 132, 143, 149, 152, 154, 155,
   159, 162–7, 223
epochè, 25, 30, 102
eroticism, 217, 221, 222, 234
Esprit, 2, 39
existentialism, 31, 52, 84, 227

Faulkner, William, 5, 101, 226
Faye, Jean-Pierre, 6, 36
Fielding, Henry, 6
Flaubert, Gustave, 6, 34

Freud, Sigmund, 22, 34, 94, 116, 126, 155, 184, 219, 235
Fuentes, Carlos, 38

Génie du lieu, Le, 118, 119, 122, 153, 156
Gide, André, 4–5, 14, 140
Gombrich, E. H., 170–1
Gommes, Les, 2, 4, 172–81, 182, 184, 187 ff., 203, 206, 213, 216, 222 ff.
Guicharnaud, Jacques, 99
Gulliver, 51, 57, 70, 73, 77, 79 ff., 95

Hegel, F. W. G., 8, 11, 52, 88
Heidegger, M., 24
Herbe, L', 45, 54–5, 60, 62, 63, 68, 75, 77, 87, 90, 92, 93, 96
heredity, 67 ff.
Hermeticism, 110, 125
Histoire, 50, 54, 55, 57–8, 62, 63, 77, 79, 82, 83, 89 ff., 96, 97, 99
Histoire Extraordinaire, 133
Hugo, Victor, 108
Husserl, Edmund, 24, 25, 27, 28, 38, 56, 102, 104, 153, 201

imagination, 19, 23, 215, 226–8
Immortelle, L', 192, 211 ff., 218–20, 225
individuation, 126, 154
insanity, 183, 221, 224
instability of matter, *see* transience
Instantanés, 206
intentionality, 28, 56

Jalousie, La, 28, 177, 179, 185–7, 192 ff., 205, 207–8, 210, 212 ff., 225, 233
James, Henry, 30, 60
Janvier, Ludovic, 69, 110, 119, 160, 161, 184
Joyce, James, 5, 12, 20, 165

Kafka, Franz, 5, 12, 221
Köhler, Wolfgang, 196

language, 22, 37, 87–8;
  Simon's use of participles, 101–3
Leiris, Michel, 107, 127, 155
Leningrad conference, 1963, 38
Lévi-Strauss, Claude, 124, 134
Lhote, André, 51
Lindon, Jérôme, 2
'Livre comme objet, Le', 106
Lucretius, 74
Lukács, Georg, 5

McLuhan, Marshall, 160
Maison de rendez-vous, La, 187–8, 191, 192, 198 ff., 209 ff., 218, 220, 222 ff., 232
marxist criticism, 5, 6, 11, 28, 38, 44, 154
Mauriac, Claude, 30
Mauriac, François, 14
memory, 54, 56 ff., 89
Merleau-Ponty, M., 24, 30, 46, 47, 52, 57, 86, 195, 205
mise en abyme, 54, 57, 93, 109, 120, 149, 155, 163
Mobile, 107, 110, 142–4, 146, 157
Modification, La, 34, 105, 111, 126–9, 132, 141, 149–50, 152, 155, 163, 168
Molière, 224
Montaigne, Michel de, 105
Morrissette, B., 225, 232
myth, 154–7, 191, 217, 221, 227, 233
  Oedipus, 123, 174, 190, 197, 213, 223, 225

Nabokov, Vladimir, 7
'Nature, humanisme, tragédie', 214, 215
necessity, mechanical, 57, 70–1, 73
neuroticism, *see* insanity
nouveau nouveau roman, 36, 37
nouveau roman, 1–4 *et al.*

occupatio, 234
Oedipus, *see* myth
'Oeuvres d'art imaginaires chez Marcel Proust', 108

Ollier, Claude, 4, 30, 62, 205
opera, 105, 140

painting, 45, 51, 91, 106, 108, 170,
    196
Palace, Le, 49, 53, 55, 57, 61, 66, 74,
    79, 83, 92, 93, 96, 97, 99, 102
Parnassianism, 28, 38
parole, 22, 23, 37
Passage de Milan, 2, 105, 110–16, 127,
    132, 134 ff., 146 ff., 158, 162,
    185, 202
perception, act of, 56 ff., 61 ff., 201
phenomenology, 24 ff., 30, 33, 38,
    46, 61, 104
Pingaud, Bernard, 39
Pinget, Robert, 3
Plato, 19
Poe, Edgar Allan, 133, 160
poetry, concrete, 109
Portrait de l'artiste en jeune singe, 118,
    119, 123, 125, 128, 141, 143, 154,
    155, 165
Pour un nouveau roman, 175, 213, 214,
    231
Pousseur, Henri, 140
Proust, Marcel, 4, 5, 10 ff., 40, 88,
    108, 109, 121
psycho-analysis, 31, 34, 58, 116, 125–
    6, 234
psychologism, 28
psychology, 30, 56, 174, 184
psycho-therapy, 170

Queneau, Raymond, 125, 221

radio productions, 105
realism, 26, 32, 33
Régicide, Un, 176, 177, 182, 223
relativism, 14, 40, 52, 65, 84, 119
Réseau aérien, 105
Répertoire, 106, 140, 147, 154, 159
Ricardou, Jean, 4, 36, 56
Richardson, Samuel, 6
'Roman et la poésie, Le', 154
Roudaut, Jean, 123, 135
Roussel, Raymond, 5, 211, 212,
    228–9

Route des Flandres, La, 47 ff., 59 ff.,
    67, 74, 76, 78, 80, 81, 83, 84, 87,
    92, 96, 99, 100

Sacre du printemps, Le, 43, 71–2, 77,
    81, 83, 85, 87, 90, 93, 103
Sarraute, Nathalie, 2 ff., 7, 12, 17, 39,
    43, 180
Sartre, Jean-Paul, 7, 12, 14, 21, 24,
    27, 28, 31, 44, 58, 64, 120, 172,
    180, 184, 195, 204, 209, 231
science-fiction, 158–9
sex, act of, 55, 76–8
Sollers, Philippe, 36, 37
Sorel, Charles, 5 ff.
Spanish Civil War, 53, 66, 71, 85, 90, 92
Stendhal, 9, 10
Sterne, Laurence, 198
Structural symbols:
    Butor: dance, 134; eye, 119, 128–
        9; glass, 148; hair, 123; hand-
        kerchief, 120–1; *immeuble,* 146 ff.,
        158; journey, 127 ff.; junkyard,
        111–12; labels, 112; light, 117–
        18; separation, 148; water, 108,
        114
    Robbe-Grillet: drawbridge, 178,
        179; doctor, 224; flaws, 195 ff.;
        india-rubber, 224–5; light, 173;
        roads, 230–1; roadsweepers,
        225–6; triangle, 198 ff.; watch,
        176, 178; water, 190 ff.
    Simon: car-rides, 57; cigar-box,
        53, 54, 79; clock, 54–5; com-
        merce, 80 ff.; dust, 74; lighting,
        57; pigeons, 49–50, 74; rain, 47,
        74; ring, 72; screens, 49, 52,
        62 ff., 89, 90, 98; train, 71;
        wind, 49, 71 ff.; Wise Old Man,
        54, 83, 93
structuralist movement, 145 ff.
subjectivism, *see* phenomenology,
    psycho-analysis, psychology
surrealism, 35, 125, 155, 196, 213
Swift, Jonathan, 1

Tel Quel, 36
Thibaudeau, Jean, 36, 37

transience, 44, 46, 47, 52, 54–5, 59, 62, 65, 66, 70, 74, 79 ff., 84

Tricheur, Le, 2, 43, 58, 69, 70, 79, 80, 95, 182

Tristes tropiques, 157

Trotsky, Leo, 40

Valéry, Paul, 53

Vent, Le, 43, 49, 52, 60, 68, 72–3, 76, 80, 94, 95–6

Vienna conference, 1967, 40

'Victor Hugo romancier', 108

Visions réfléchies, 206

Voltaire, 224

Votre Faust, 105, 140

Voyeur, Le, 180, 181–4, 187, 188, 191 ff., 202, 208 ff., 212, 213, 217, 230, 234

Waugh, Evelyn, 7

Wilde, Oscar, 74

Wittgenstein, L., 29

Wölfflin, Heinrich, 52

Yale French Studies, 3

Yates, Frances, 110

Zeitgeist, 11

6 810 000 litres d'eau par seconde, 105, 107, 139

Printed in Great Britain by
Richard Clay (The Chaucer Press), Ltd.,
Bungay, Suffolk